As Though It Were Actually True

As Though It Were Actually True

A Christian Apologetics Primer

MATTHEW E. COCHRAN

RESOURCE *Publications* • Eugene, Oregon

AS THOUGH IT WERE ACTUALLY TRUE
A Christian Apologetics Primer

Copyright © 2010 Matthew E. Cochran. All rights reserved. Except for brief quotations in critical publications or reviews, no part of this book may be reproduced in any manner without prior written permission from the publisher. Write: Permissions, Wipf and Stock Publishers, 199 W. 8th Ave., Suite 3, Eugene, OR 97401.

Resource Publications
An Imprint of Wipf and Stock Publishers
199 W. 8th Ave., Suite 3
Eugene, OR 97401

www.wipfandstock.com

ISBN: 978-1-60608-820-3

Manufactured in the U.S.A.

All scripture quotations, unless otherwise indicated, are taken from the Holy Bible, New International Version®, NIV®. Copyright ©1973, 1978, 1984 by Biblica, Inc.™ Used by permission of Zondervan. All rights reserved worldwide.

Mere Christianity by C.S. Lewis copyright © C.S. Lewis Pte. Ltd. 1942, 1943, 1944, 1952.
Extract reprinted by permission.

Extract from *The Everlasting Man* by G.K. Chesterton reprinted by permission of A. P. Watt Ltd on behalf of The Royal Literary Fund.

Contents

Introduction ix

I PHILOSOPHY: CAN CHRISTIANITY BE TRUE?

    1 Faith and Reason: Everything in its Place 3

    2 What is Truth? 12

    3 Sin and Natural Law 25

    4 The Existence of God 40

II HISTORY: IS CHRISTIANITY TRUE?

    5 The New Testament as History 65

    6 Who Does Jesus Say That He Is? 85

    7 The Bible: Jesus' Inerrant Teaching 103

    8 The Genuine Gospel 121

III LIFE: IF CHRISTIANITY IS TRUE

    9 Science vs. Christianity: The Root of the Problem 142

    10 Abortion and Other Life Issues 172

    11 Biblical Sexuality: Not So Strange 187

    12 Christianity and Feminism 202

    13 The Nature of Tolerance 226

Bibliography 239

To Rachel,
a joy in the better,
a comfort in the worse.

Introduction

An Apology

EXACTLY HOW "TRUE" CAN a religion be? In some eras, this question would not have made much sense. Most people would have said that a given religion is either true or false. Jesus either died and rose or He did not. Muhammad was either God's prophet or he was not. God either exists or He does not. In America today, it is often the either/or that seems odd. To many, the question of whether Jesus actually rose from the dead is irrelevant. The more pertinent question is "why" or "what's the point?" Why bother labeling oneself a Christian? Why bother attending church? Why bother having an opinion on religion at all? Many believe that religion is great if it helps people somehow but also believe that it is able to help regardless of whether it is true or not. This belief goes hand in hand with the ideas that the particulars of religion do not really matter and that all religions are basically the same.

Christians frequently embrace this development. The consensus of the so-called Enlightenment (at least among academics and other elites) was that Christianity was false and therefore to be abandoned. Jesus did not rise from the dead, God does not reveal Himself to humans, and the Bible is merely a book of myths and moral advice that was questionable even in its own time (let alone in enlightened modern times.) Many Christians therefore embrace the emergence of postmodernism over the past few decades and its new focus on personal experience and feelings—often at the expense of objective truth. Those embarrassing factual questions are eagerly swept under the rug. Many Christians find questions of "why" easier to deal with because it is hard to give a wrong answer. Our church has good music and refreshments. God has helped me to live the best life that I can. Christianity has made me a better person. Someone can deny that any of these are true for him but cannot really deny that they are true for the Christians telling him about themselves. Who cares if the facts of Christianity are true for everyone in the same sense as the fact that I am breathing? The new focus is that Christianity has helped people before and it can help people now—maybe even non-believers, if they would just give it a chance.

The purpose of this book is not to reject this question of why. The popular question is a legitimate one which the Church must answer. However, Christians often forget that when it comes to their particular religion, the question of why finds its fullest answer in the question of truth—in the either/or. What if the question of whether I am guilty of doing terrible things has an answer as objective as the question of whether I am breathing—either I am or I am not? What if the question of whether I am forgiven for those deeds because of Jesus Christ also has an objective answer? If so, then these facts surely have bearing on the questions of why one should bother being a Christian, going to church, or having an opinion on religion. The important benefits of Christianity—the forgiveness of sins and eternal life in heaven—are meaningful only if Christianity is actually true. The purpose of this book is therefore to teach Christians how to examine these questions and find objective answers—to practice *apologetics*.

WHAT IS APOLOGETICS?

Apologetics is simply the rational defense of the truth of Christianity—the examination of questions such as whether God exists or whether Jesus rose from the dead in order to find reasonable answers. Unfortunately, this is often considered a distasteful proposition. In a society where many—both inside and outside the Church—have long separated religion from rational thought, the prospect of rejoining them can itself require a defense. What purpose could such intellectual musings serve in contemporary America where religion and real life occur at different times and in different places?

Perhaps the most common misconception among Christians is that the purpose of apologetics is to convince unbelievers to believe in Christ—to present an argument so persuasive that they will subsequently decide to convert. As those in my own denomination[1] so often and rightly point

---

1. The Lutheran Church—Missouri Synod.

out, the Bible makes it clear that conversion is the work of the Holy Spirit through means of His choosing. As Luther wrote in his Small Catechism, "I believe that I cannot by my own reason or strength believe in Jesus Christ, my Lord, or come to Him."[2] This book does not suggest that given good enough reasons and arguments, a person will consequently make a decision to follow Christ. Even in ages when people were inclined to alter their beliefs according to the results of rational discourse, human beings are in rebellion against God. That conflict can only be resolved by an act of divine grace. Many Christians abandon apologetics at this point. Why bother with learning about arguments and reason if they are useless in the church's evangelistic mission? Why not simply find ways to bring people in the door where they can hear God's word? The answer is that arguments and reason are not useless; they just do not have the uses that some people want them to have. Nevertheless, the Bible clearly gives a place to apologetics—something that any Christian should seriously consider. Whatever activities a church may engage in, apologetics ought to be among them.

The classic command for apologetics can be found in Peter's first epistle:

> Always be prepared to give an answer to everyone who asks you to give the reason for the hope that you have. But do this with gentleness and respect, keeping a clear conscience, so that those who speak maliciously against your good behavior in Christ may be ashamed of their slander.[3]

This passage provides the first purpose for studying apologetics: the presentation of the Gospel. Simply informing a person that "Jesus died for your sins" may come off as gibberish to someone who believes that Jesus was just another holy man, sees no connection between sin and death, and casually dismisses their own sin with a "nobody's perfect" and a shrug. When Peter instructs us to "always be prepared," he probably did not intend that his reader keep a copy of the Gospel of John handy just in case somebody asks for it. After the Resurrection, Jesus told His disciples how all of Scripture pointed to Him.[4] He did not just read the Old Testament and expect His disciples to understand. Jesus actually

---

2. Luther, *Small Catechism*, 144.
3. 1 Pet 3:15–16. All Scripture quotations in this book are from the NIV.
4. Luke 24:25–27.

explained its content. Learning to understand what Christians believe and why we believe it provides us with the tools needed to put together a comprehensible exposition of the Gospel and prepares us in constructing the answers that Peter instructs us to give.[5]

The command given in 1 Peter does not stand alone in Scripture. The Apostle Paul also wrote:

> The weapons we fight with are not the weapons of the world. On the contrary, they have divine power to demolish strongholds. We demolish arguments and every pretension that sets itself up against the knowledge of God, and we take captive every thought to make it obedient to Christ.[6]

These verses reveal a second purpose for apologetics. Beyond being ready to explain the Gospel, Christians are called to actively demolish any philosophies that get in the way. Faith comes from hearing the Word of God, but why would anyone tolerate hearing this Word if they think the Bible is a book of fairy tales, that God is a cosmic daddy figure born out of wishful thinking, or even that half the New Testament was written by a misogynist? Paul does not instruct Christians to cluck their tongues and complain about how God needs to be put back into the public schools. Paul tells us to be ready to enter the fray ourselves. The Bible calls worldly philosophies foolishness, but when we ground our thinking in Scripture under the leading of the Holy Spirit, our minds can use the divine weapons that Paul describes.

The final purpose of apologetics that concerns this book is the edification of Christian believers—to build us up in the faith we have been given. Too often, Christians deal with doubt in an improper way. When confronted with doubt, we often tell ourselves or even others "you just need to have faith" as though faith were something that we work towards rather than something God gives us. Too often, we deal with these confrontations by trying to suppress feelings of doubt without ever dealing with the fact of doubt. It is true enough that a Christian should not doubt

---

5. Many Christians argue that the approach taken by the evangelist is entirely irrelevant because it is the Holy Spirit who works conversion through the preaching of the Gospel. I cannot help but observe that although many of these people can read the New Testament in the original Greek, they still preach from an English translation. If the Holy Spirit has chosen linguistic communication as a means, then it seems that the comprehensibility of the communication is an inseparable part of that means.

6. 2 Cor 10:4–5.

God, but simply advising her to "stop it" does not cure doubt anymore than it does sin. Humans have a God-given need for truth and understanding. Ignoring those needs by suppressing doubt makes about as much sense as ignoring hunger or thirst in hopes that it will simply go away.

This book is therefore intended to help Christians begin to critically examine some of the most common apologetic issues in contemporary America. It does not provide lists of facts or famous arguments for memorization and regurgitation. There are good resources out there for such lists, and I highly recommend their use for study. Nevertheless, merely repeating an argument one does not understand is a poor apologetic. Likewise, this book is not purposed for teaching how to talk to a particular "type" of person (the atheist, the agnostic, etc.) or even to people in general. It touches on such things, but they are not its end. Its end is to be a means to "Prepare our minds for action"[7] in order to engage the unbelieving world. It seeks to establish a common-sense philosophical framework in which the arguments and facts surrounding a variety of issues can be evaluated. Its function is to prepare Christians' minds by providing a firm and relevant foundation in a variety of popular topics related to Christianity in modern America.

The book is divided into three different sections. The first deals with some of the basic philosophical questions that are necessary for but not specific to Christianity. It deals with questions of whether Christianity can possibly be true. Before one even begins demolishing reasoned arguments against the faith, one needs to examine how reason and faith are related. Before a Christian can lay out the truth of the Gospel, she needs to understand what truth is. Before a Christian deals with the evidence, he needs to understand the framework in which he interprets evidence.

The second section of this book deals with the essential historical facts of Christianity. Is the Gospel actually true? The idea that God became man and died to pay for our sins is a proposition that hinges on history. Did Jesus Christ actually exist? What kind of man was He? Did He actually rise from the dead? Do we need to distinguish between the historical Jesus and what the Christian Church has traditionally taught about Him? The historical evidence makes it possible to examine what this uniquely influential man taught, what He did, who He is, and ultimately, what He has done for humankind.

7. 1 Pet 1:13.

This book's final section considers the implications of Christianity. If Christianity is true, how could it contradict all the other things we understand about life? There are many teachings in the Bible that are extremely offensive to people today, and for better or for worse, the Church has placed itself in the middle of many controversial issues. Topics such as abortion or sexual morality may have little to do with Christ's atoning death, but to defend the Bible as being worth reading (let alone inerrant), one must be able to explain and defend the positions it takes on controversial issues in ways that are comprehensible to people today. If the Bible is the means by which God speaks to humans, it ought not be dismissed out of hand for reasons that are tangential to its purpose.

My hope is that individual Christians become well-versed enough in these topics to converse in their own ways as required in each unique situation. This book is intended as a small step towards that end. It is not the final word on any of the topics it addresses, but I hope that it demystifies the issues and serves as a beginning to understanding their substance.

I

PHILOSOPHY

Can Christianity be True?

1

Faith and Reason

Everything in its Place

INTRODUCTION

MANY OF THE MODERN difficulties in reconciling faith and reason stem from two common attitudes. Faith often has a bad reputation in secular circles, and reason sometimes has a bad reputation in Christian ones. In both contexts, each is perceived not simply as different from the other or more dangerous than the other but as contradictory with the other—that one cannot have faith and be reasonable at the same time. Nevertheless, as the introduction argued, the Bible instructs Christians to do both; we cannot become comfortable with contradictions without ignoring part of what the Bible tells us. In order to both have faith and practice reason in any real sense, it is necessary to remove the apparent contradiction between them. To begin unraveling the paradox, this chapter will briefly characterize both reason and faith. It will then conclude with an examination of the relationship between the two.

A BRIEF ANALYSIS OF REASON

All people are familiar with reason because everyone uses it to some extent. Whenever one person argues with another, each believes that the other ought to agree with him. If such agreement does not come about, each typically believes the other is being unreasonable. A person may argue poorly or absentmindedly, but all people still have some sense of what reason is and how it works. However, to minimize poor or absentminded reasoning, it is necessary to examine reason a little closer.

Reason is often classified according to three different categories: deductive, inductive, and abductive.[1] A deductive argument takes premises, applies a logical argument, and then arrives at a conclusion. This type of reasoning is the only kind that can provide *proofs* of an idea (as opposed to merely evidence or a theory). To quickly demonstrate this in an abstract way, we will begin with one example of a logical argument: *modus ponens*.[2] One begins with two premises: "If A then B" and "A" (where A and B are symbols representing propositions). If each of these premises is true, then one must conclude that B is also true.[3] If B were false, one would wind up with a contradiction: "If A then B" and "A but not B." Acknowledging both of these two opposite statements would violate the law of non-contradiction—that a proposition and its opposite cannot both be true in the same sense at the same time. So then, *if* the premises are true, then the conclusion is *proven* to be true—there is no possibility that it is false. Moving from the abstract to the concrete, one could consider these two premises: "He that believes and is baptized shall be saved" and "he believes and is baptized." If both of these premises are true, then he must conclude that he is, in fact, saved. "He believes and is baptized but is not saved" would contradict the first premise. One of the two must be false.

This is one example of a form of deductive argument, but there is a long list of logical arguments such as *modus ponens*. Further study of the subject is certainly edifying, but there is little point in reproducing such a list in this book merely so that one can memorize a bunch of Latin names that will soon be forgotten. There are already plenty of resources for formally studying the topic. Nevertheless, one can still practice reason without knowing everything on such a list because each human being is already equipped with the ability to reason (although he may not know the Latin). The human mind is designed in such a way that it naturally follows logic, and it still does, albeit imperfectly. The fallen human mind

---

1. Some might add other categories such as statistical, probabilistic, or defeasible reasoning to this list, but these go well beyond the scope of this book.

2. Latin for "mode that affirms."

3. For example, "A" could represent "today is Sunday" and "B" could represent "I will go to church." The argument would then run, "If today is Sunday, then I will go to church. Today is Sunday. Therefore, I will go to church."

may reason badly, but it does intuitively understand reason even if its practice of it is frequently muddled.

A deductive argument is *valid* as long as the conclusion logically follows from the premises, and *sound* if it is valid and the premises are true. Consider the following argument:

> All Christians hate women;
>
> Bob is a Christian;
>
> therefore, Bob hates women.

This is a valid argument because the conclusion logically follows from the premises. However, it is unsound because the premise "all Christians hate women" is untrue.[4] In contrast, the following argument is not valid:

> All Christians have faith in Jesus;
>
> Bob has faith in Jesus;
>
> therefore, Bob is a Christian.

The argument is not valid even though the premises (and possibly the conclusion) are true. The conclusion does not *necessarily* follow from the premises. It contains the same fallacy as this argument:

> All dogs have four legs;
>
> Whiskers has four legs;
>
> therefore, Whiskers is a dog.

The conclusion does not necessarily follow because Whiskers could just as easily be a cat or one of any number of other four-legged animals. To make the previous argument valid, one would need another premise: "Having faith in Jesus is what makes someone a Christian." Normally, people are not so formal, and because most Christians understand that they are saved by faith, such a premise seldom needs to be mentioned when making an argument. This is referred to as a *hidden premise*.[5] However, when arguing for the truth of Christianity, it is important to remember that not everybody has the same presuppositions that Christians do. Even two Christians often do not share the same presuppositions. Different people

---

4. An examination of why the premise is false can be found in chapter 12.
5. An unmentioned assumption made by all parties in a discussion.

can look at the world in very different ways. When arguing over religion, people often end up talking in circles with one another because one has a hidden premise that the other is not aware of.

In contrast to deductive reasoning, inductive and abductive reasoning do not offer certainty, only probability. This lack of certainty, however, does not reduce their utility. They are, in fact, extremely useful. However, this does imply that deductive reasoning trumps the other two when there is a conflict between them. As Sherlock Holmes maintained, "If you eliminate the impossible, whatever remains, however improbable, must be the truth."

Inductive reasoning offers premises that support, but do not ensure a conclusion. For example, one could argue that "District A has always voted Republican in previous elections, therefore the Republican candidate will win in district A." The premise supports the conclusion but does not ensure it; it is a generalization. Maybe a huge Republican fund raiser will serve tainted food, and most of the attendees will stay home sick on election day. Maybe the Republican candidate has become so ideologically dissimilar to other Republicans that his usual supporters will vote for a third party. There are any number of scenarios where the Republican candidate might not win, even if it is probable that he will. Nevertheless, while the campaign strategist cannot predict the future with certainty, generalizations can be quite useful in allocating resources and making the best predictions possible.

Abductive reasoning—closely related to inductive—is the process of finding the best explanation for the set of facts that one has been given. For example, a woman knows that her husband is usually home by five but also that it is now five thirty and he has not yet arrived. It is Tuesday, and she knows that he often has meetings towards the end of the day on Tuesdays. She decides, then, that he got stuck in a meeting that ran long. As the definition implies, the "best" explanation may not be the only possible explanation or even the correct one. He might be stuck in traffic, have gotten in an accident, be having an affair, or any other scenario that does not contradict the given facts. The late meeting scenario, however, fits them best because it does not require a large number of unknowns to be true. Based only on the information given, a late meeting is more likely than any of the other explanations.

A BRIEF ANALYSIS OF FAITH

Most people have little objection to reason understood in this way, and everyone practices it even if they do have objections. Nevertheless, it is common for many critics of Christianity (particularly those adhering to atheism or agnosticism) to believe that faith and reason are diametrically opposed—that faith is inherently irrational. One cannot entirely blame such skeptics for holding this belief about Christian faith, because many Christians unfortunately believe the same thing. The consequence is that the skeptic rejects faith so that he can embrace reason. Charges of irrationality imply that faith necessarily either embraces a contradiction (if it is incompatible with deductive reasoning), ignores evidence (incompatible with inductive), or draws wild conclusions (incompatible with abductive). As was previously mentioned, the latter two forms of reasoning do not offer certainty, merely evidence. They will therefore be dealt with in later chapters in which the evidence for Christianity is discussed. This chapter will examine the first charge: that faith means embracing a contradiction.

These sorts of charges are the reason for the common condescension that believers are—whether willfully or not—ignorant, backwards, and unable to think correctly. Christians are often tempted to dismiss such charges with the complaint that "atheists say mean things and insult Christians because they are not Godly people like we are." However, the sad fact is that the argument is valid. If the premise that faith and reason are contradictory is true, then it follows that those with faith reject reason. Furthermore, if one does not follow reason, then one is indeed ignorant of the way it works, misunderstands its purpose, and therefore does not think clearly. It is also true, sadly, that there are many Christians who *do* accept this premise as true. In the interests of charity, Christians need to be careful before we start throwing stones at those who disparage us.

In *The God Who is There*, Francis Schaeffer lays the practical beginning of the modern conception that faith and reason are opposed at the feet of Søren Kierkegaard, describing him as the first man below what he called "the line of despair," the line past which absolute truth is abandoned. In his writings, Kierkegaard investigated supposed contradictions in Christianity (most notably the incarnation—that Jesus was 100 percent God and 100 percent Man—but also Abraham's imminent sacrifice of Issac at God's command). He declared that such things are an offense to reason, but rather than therefore dismissing them as many philosophers would, he embraced the contradictions as true in what is now termed a "leap of faith."[6] Since our minds (partially bound to the rules of logic) do not allow us to truly practice contradictions in our lives (at least not indefinitely), the ultimate consequence of this leap is the disconnection of religion from reality. This means that what one believes religiously does not impact his day-to-day life, and the real world does not impact his religion. When one encounters notions such as "faith does not belong in politics" or "all religions are true even though they are contradictory," she finds that they are built on this notion of disconnection. In this way, Kierkegaard probably deserves his common appellation, "the father of modern thought." Schaeffer notes that Kierkegaard probably never intended nor supported this ultimate consequence; nevertheless, it was the logical conclusion to his ideas.[7] Kierkegaard may not have embraced that conclusion, but those following after him certainly did. One can see the logical progression of this idea over the centuries.

By embracing contradiction as truth in this way, Kierkegaard truly did in a sense abandon reason. He saw reason as a necessary stepping stone but not something that humans ought to remain in forever. Is it truly necessary to abandon reason in order to accept doctrines such as the incarnation? Answering such a question necessitates a basic understanding of the nature of faith.

Kierkegaard probably did not come to his conclusion because he could not stand the thought of abandoning Christianity but, rather, because of what he believed about faith. Kierkegaard claimed that faith relied on objective uncertainty—on doubt.[8] One cannot, for example, have faith in the existence of a desk because one can see and feel it. The experience leaves no room for doubt. Reason plays the role of causing one to realize a contradiction. The contradiction then provides the doubt of the premises. Finally, faith allows one to believe the contradiction in spite of rationality. Thus, faith turns out to be a suppression of reason in favor

---

6. Schaeffer, *The God Who is There*, 34–37.
7. Schaeffer, 36.
8. Kierkegaard, *Unscientific Postscript*, 204.

of something higher. Rationality, while an extremely important stepping stone, eventually needs to be left behind—at least some of the time. When one considers faith in this light, one can begin to see why the skeptic holds doubt in such high esteem—particularly doubt of Christianity. To him, doubt is the final result of rationality. He rightly sees that rationality should not be abandoned and therefore doubts the contradictions his reason presents him with.

Is this truly an accurate picture of the Christian concept of faith? One of the premises given above needs to be reconsidered: that faith necessitates doubt.[9] Because it is the Christian concept of faith on the table, it makes sense to allow the Bible to provide us with a definition. The author of the book of Hebrews describes faith this way: "Now faith is being sure of what we hope for and certain of what we do not see."[10]

This can be simplified to say that faith is the certainty of things unseen and hoped for. "Things unseen" is often equated with "things doubted," which probably led to the idea of doubt being a necessity of faith. However, the passage from Hebrews clearly declares that the essence of faith is "certainty." Can one really claim that the opposite of doubt requires doubt in order to exist? On the contrary, by this definition, faith is the antithesis of doubt.

So what is one to make of the modifying clause, "things unseen"? Thankfully, the author provides plenty of examples to elaborate his definition. In 11:7, he writes:

> By faith Noah, when warned about things not yet seen, in holy fear
> built an ark to save his family. By his faith he condemned the world
> and became heir of the righteousness that comes by faith.

The "unseen" in this instance is clearly the impending flood. Noah almost certainly would not have understood how it could rain enough to submerge the entire world. He had never seen such a thing before. Nevertheless, he had it on good authority (God's) that it would occur whether or not he was able to understand it. Knowing God's power over the world, Noah would not have found any contradiction in the notion of a flood at a specific time for a specific purpose. He would only have seen a mystery. In 11:11, the author writes:

---

9. Without this premise, the idea that faith requires contradictions that engender doubt also falls away.

10. Heb 11:1.

> By faith Abraham, even though he was past age—and Sarah herself was barren—was enabled to become a father because he considered him faithful who had made the promise.

This verse illustrates the same situation: the promise of an unseen and improbable thing—a child born from an old barren couple. Once again, in light of God's power, such a promise never entailed a contradiction; it merely depended on the trustworthiness of the messenger.

Thus, it becomes clear that while Biblical faith is *non*-rational (it is not arrived at by reason), it is not *ir*rational (it does not contradict reason). The irrational sort of faith that Kierkegaard proposed is usually called blind faith, but not all faith is inherently blind. This, however, does not prove that faith is good and necessary. It merely demonstrates that it cannot be rejected for the reason the skeptic gives. Even if it does not contradict reason, faith must have some legitimate place in order to be considered worthwhile.

THE FAITH IN REASON

Let us return to the skeptic. Having rejected faith, he now holds doubt as his primary means of protecting himself against irrationality. He considers reason and observation to be his only means of finding truth. His doubt allows him to believe nothing but that which is proven, but this approach is ultimately an irrational one. As the recent popularity of ancient beliefs repackaged as "New Age" has increasingly shown, one can doubt anything if he puts sufficient effort into it. Ask a Zen Buddhist who believes that reality is an illusion whether that aforementioned desk is real, and he will tell you that, like the proverbial spoon, there is no desk. Even seeing and touching the desk do not remove the possibility of doubting its existence. One can therefore see that not all doubt is a result of reason.[11]

In deductive reasoning, premises are always necessary. Before one can even begin to acquire new knowledge by reasoning, one must already know that some things are true (not the least of which is that reason is capable of finding truth at all). Reason itself therefore tells us that reason cannot be the *only* means of finding truth. Likewise, before one can accept observations as true premises, one must have some standard by which observations are evaluated (again, not the least of which is knowing that our observations have some connection to reality). Ultimately, one must

---

11. Hence the necessity of the concept of "reasonable doubt" in our court system.

know something unseen before one even begins to reason. The Christian concept of faith—the certainty of things unseen—is not only compatible with reason but is a necessary prerequisite. Once the skeptic recognizes that rational human thought requires having faith in some things, it becomes difficult to maintain the claim that all other faith is unreasonable.

Some certainties of faith are granted to everyone by general revelation.[12] These instances include knowledge such as the existence of reality, the law of non-contradiction, the fact that 1 + 1 = 2, etc. Other certainties of faith, such as "Jesus is Lord," are only provided to us by God through His Word. In all cases, people are given such knowledge as a gift. Such knowledge makes up the first principles on which all human thought depends. These gifts are not arrived at by reason, but it is certainly unreasonable to reject them. Can one be skeptical of these principles? Yes and no. For example, a person can, by an act of will, doubt the law of non-contradiction, but he can never answer the question of why. He can never have any grounds for his doubting. To say that the law of non-contradiction is false means that the law itself is therefore not true. However, making such a statement requires the law of non-contradiction itself—otherwise the statement could be both true and false in the same sense at the same time. It is impossible for a human to meaningfully deny it, because even the denial itself depends on the thing denied. He can give voice to the words, but they can never mean anything even to himself.

While we can obscure first principles with doubt (and because of sin, we often try), we have faith in them only in as much as we are certain of them. We can reason from them only in as much as we have faith in them. In light of this, it makes sense that while humans cannot attain these gifts by reason or any other means, it remains reasonable to continue accepting them once they have been given.

---

12. This will be discussed in greater detail in subsequent chapters.

2

What Is Truth?

INTRODUCTION

From a certain perspective, it seems silly to even bother defending the concept of truth. Every last person on this planet knows what truth is, and those capable of communication claim to know at least some elements of it. The first chapter mentioned that some certainties are an inbuilt part of the human mind; a basic concept of truth is one such certainty. As will be shown, one can be certain that even people who claim that there is no such thing as truth share and believe in the basic concept. How then does one explain the existence of people and philosophies that deny truth?

The first chapter described faith as a kind of certainty that is necessary for the operation of reason. It also considered unreasonable doubt—not a feeling of doubt, but a groundless effort to forget or ignore things that one really does know. Due to this practice, it is entirely possible that one may know what truth is and still attempt to confuse himself about it. Of course, simply asserting this possibility falls far short of an argument for a particular view of truth or even for the idea that everyone understands the concept. As such, merely telling a person who claims there is no truth that he is lying to himself would not only be rude, it would also represent a failure at making a reasonable case. Nevertheless, it can be helpful to keep this possibility in mind when considering the topic of truth in order to maintain a clear objective. When laying out a case for truth, one must remember that she is not teaching people something new; she is merely helping them recognize something already known. It is possible to clarify this knowledge or clear away obstructions to acknowledging it, but it is not possible to teach something already known.

CORRESPONDENCE

The basic concept of truth known to all of us has to do with correspondence. If there is a fact—a way things are—and a proposition or belief about that fact, the proposition is true if it is an accurate representation of the fact—if the two correspond. Philosophers from Aristotle to Aquinas to many modern writers have embraced this view, and it is the premise this book will work from. Aristotle described correspondence this way: "To say of what is that it is not, or of what is not that it is, is false, while to say of what is that it is, and of what is not that it is not, is true."[1] In *Summa Theologica*, Aquinas wrote more or less the same thing in different words: "truth is defined by the conformity of intellect and thing; and hence to know this conformity is to know truth."[2]

Although many attempt to deny this view of truth, doing so in any substantial way is ultimately futile. The correspondence view of truth requires three premises: that I exist, that reality exists, and that I can know about reality—that there can be a correspondence between them. By an act of will a person can deny any of those premises, but doing so is literally meaningless. One cannot deny that she exists without affirming her own existence.[3] One cannot deny that reality exists without affirming those to whom she is delivering the message, the medium through which she delivers it, and the thing spoken about. One also cannot deny that one can know anything about states of affairs without affirming a particular state of affairs (that one knows nothing).

As this analysis makes clear, two interesting things happen when anyone makes any statement about truth. Firstly, one claims that his statement corresponds to reality (i.e. that it is true according to the correspondence view). Secondly, because one claims to make a true statement, there is an implicit acknowledgement that the statement conforms to the criteria for truth that that is set forth. For example, if someone claims that there is no such thing as truth, the first thing that ought to be noticed is that he is claiming that his statement corresponds to reality—that it is true that there is no such thing as truth. Claims like this are self-referentially incoherent. Such statements cannot be accepted because they violate the

---

1. Aristotle, Metaphysics, 44.
2. Thomas, *Summa Theologica*, 65.
3. "I think, therefore I am," as Descartes put it.

law of non-contradiction. Even if the statement were true, it would necessarily make itself false.

Despite their self-contradictory nature, there are any number of such statements that are commonly accepted in our culture. For example:

- *It is impossible to know the truth.* Anyone making such a statement is claiming to know the proposition he is attempting to communicate and that the communication corresponds to reality. In short, if a person knows that it is impossible to know the truth, then it must indeed be possible to know a truth.

- *All truth is relative; there are no absolutes.* In this proposition, the words "all" and "no" are both absolute terms. Consequently, if the speaker claims that the statement is true, it means there are indeed absolutes and at least one truth that is not relative. If the statement is relative rather than absolute, it means that sometimes there are absolutes and sometimes there are not. Either way, absolutes must exist.

- *Reason is the only way we can know truth.* This statement itself cannot be proven by reason. Any attempt to prove it by reason would necessarily assume that reason is a way to know truth, part of the very proposition that the argument attempts to prove. Such an argument would be circular and therefore unreasonable. If this statement is true, it must be known by some means other than reason, and therefore reason would not be the only means of knowing truth.

- *Science is the only way we can know truth.* Because science depends on reason, this statement fails for the same reason as the prior statement: any attempt to scientifically prove this statement would be circular. Simply knowing that the statement is true implies a means other than science for knowing truth.

- *It is impossible to know anything about God.* This statement itself is about God. If it is known by the speaker, then it must be possible to know at least one thing about God.

WORD GAMES

Addressing challenges to truth is not always so simple, but unfortunately it is often this simple because of the shallow state of our intellectual culture. Our unending love of word games and inclination toward defensiveness often result in a person becoming averse to a specific word such as "truth" and simply trying to avoid using it. For example, according to Norman Geisler in *Christian Apologetics*, many agnostics try to avoid the contradiction in the phrase "it is impossible to know truth" by posing it as a question, or by saying nothing at all. He goes on to explain that these evasions merely delay the inevitable because a question such as "What do I know about reality?" demands an answer, and thoughts can be as contradictory as phrases.[4] The Zen Buddhist might also try to move away from "there is no spoon" to "what spoon?", or even to the common Zen practice of answering questions with nonsense. Of course, in practical terms, if one is answering the assertion that one cannot know truth, the assertion has already been communicated in some way. Even when they write about being silent, those who deny truth still seek converts.

It is also possible for a person to have an almost instinctive negative response to a word like truth. Perhaps such a person's experiences in life have provided the word "truth" with such a negative connotation that she stops listening as soon as the word comes up. In such cases, one can always speak in terms of "correspondence to reality" to get the message through. For some of the most ridiculous conversations, one can always call the offenders on the ridiculous behavior that (more likely than not) they would never tolerate even in themselves under any other circumstances.[5] In his Office Hours column, J. Budziszewski provides an excellent example of a dialogue including many of these points during a fictional speech:

> INTERROGATOR #1: All of your arguments about the search for truth take for granted that there is a truth to be found. I maintain that there is no truth.
>
> THEOPHILUS: My goodness. Could that possibly be true?
>
> INTERROGATOR #1: I think so. [incoherence]

---

4. Geisler, *Christian Apologetics*, 21.

5. Let us not be hypocritical about such conversations. We have likely all been on both sides of them at some point or another.

> THEOPHILUS: Then you concede that there is truth. But in that case your statement, "There is no truth," must be false.
>
> INTERROGATOR #1: Let me rephrase. I don't claim to have a truth. It is only my belief that there is no truth. [word game]
>
> THEOPHILUS: Forgive me, but that doesn't let you off the hook. A belief is about a state of affairs. To say that you believe that there is no truth is to say that it is true that there is no truth. You are still in same pickle as before.
>
> INTERROGATOR #1: But a belief isn't about anything. It's just a feeling. [ridiculousness]
>
> THEOPHILUS: If your statement was not about anything, then it could not have been about my arguments, so you have said precisely nothing.[6]

As mentioned in the introduction, this book is not about snappy comebacks or how to talk to certain types of people. It must be stressed that the purpose in reading a dialogue like this one is to illustrate a particular way of thinking—a way that includes careful listening and a reasonable skepticism. Nor should such a dialogue serve as a "look how ridiculous unbelievers are" example. People do not hold to ridiculous views because they are unintelligent, but because they believe they have a vested interest in holding them. Anyone who has ever had a fight with a spouse or parent should understand this. When tempers rise and things valued appear to be in danger, a conversation about the question of "what is right" can quickly turn into a fight over "why I am right" in which one uses any rhetorical weapon within reach. A noteworthy side effect of repenting when we find ourselves in such circumstances is that repentance opens up the possibility of understanding such traits in oneself and consequently helps one understand them in others. Apologetics often requires finding common ground, and sin is perhaps the truest common ground for fallen humanity.

---

6. Budziszewski, "Theophilus," para. 27–34.

THE STAGES OF NIHILISM

As has already been discussed, the self-referentially incoherent sort of views are not and cannot be taken completely seriously or applied consistently even by those who hold to them. It is not possible to genuinely believe that there is no truth without believing that there is truth. Consequently, such beliefs look far different in practice than they do on paper. In one chapter of his unfinished work, *The Kingdom of Man and the Kingdom of God*, Eugene Rose wrote an exposition of what he considered the primary challenge to truth as such in the modern world: nihilism. As a definition of nihilism, he uses Frederich Nietzsche's statement, "That there is no truth; that there is no absolute state of affairs-no 'thing-in-itself.' This alone is Nihilism, and of the most extreme kind."[7] Rose breaks the practice down into four different "stages" that arise from Nietzsche's simple statement. Each stage is a different manifestation of that basic kernel. The stages can certainly be considered to have a generally progressive relationship both socially and psychologically, but they do not necessarily work that way in each and every case. It is clear that the kernel is wrong because it is self-referentially incoherent, but one must also examine how it plays out in our world.

Rose refers to the first stage of Nihilism as *Liberalism*.[8] By it, he means something that is loosely connected to what most Americans mean when they use the word in the colloquial sense (without a restriction to politics). However, Rose's definition is probably closer to (although not identical with) what we refer to as relativism.[9] In this stage, the belief that there is no truth becomes manifest in a very selective way. Orthodox Christianity is certainly rejected, but it is not rejected wholesale. For example, there remain self-described Christians who hold onto some of Jesus' sentiments about helping the poor, but they deny his teachings about lust. Many like the resurrection as an inspiring story but deny its historical reality. There are denominations that say the Bible contains the Word of God but also that it can only be found in certain places within the text. Traditional wisdom is also selectively denied in many areas: murder is wrong, but

---

7. Rose, *Nihilism*, para. 9.

8. Rose, para. 39.

9. Other people may use the term "liberal" very differently, but Rose's definition will be used for the remainder of this chapter.

killing the very young is not murder; sexual morals still exist in some way but center around consent and pleasure rather than chastity.

The common element in all of these cases is that traditionally held truths are doubted, not because of conflict with a more certain truth, but in the name of expediency towards a desired goal. For example, if peace is desired, truths are held onto only inasmuch as they promote peace. Liberalism discards the notion that mankind is fundamentally flawed and cannot make it on its own. Human self-deceptions are therefore no longer regarded as such. The disagreements that persist over the basic notions of reality therefore need a different explanation: that basic notions of reality are not really known. This is where "all truth is relative" and "we cannot know anything for certain" come from. The idea is that people are not uncertain because of an ignorance that needs to be dealt with, or because of a conflict between truth and fallen human nature, but because the world itself really is uncertain; we really see things as they are.

Ultimately, the human mind can only accept such an arbitrary and contradictory mode of operation for so long (and people often have no interest in it in the first place). Consequently, many eschew Liberalism in favor of Rose's next stage: *Realism*.[10] Realists in Rose's sense of the term maintain the rejection of orthodox Christianity found in Liberalism, but do so in a much more consistent way. Rather than selectively denying spiritual truths, realists categorically deny them. Realists are typically materialists and naturalists who believe that nothing exists except matter and its properties. Science—the preeminent way of studying matter—consequently becomes the only measure of truth. Truth in reference to material reality can be trusted as absolute, but anything else can have no claim on the word at all. "There is no truth" becomes "there is no spiritual or metaphysical truth." While Liberalism and Realism are distinct, they do find common purpose. As Rose puts it, "If the Realist, therefore, shares in common with the Christian a single-mindedness and earnestness that is totally foreign to the Liberal mentality, it is only the better to join in the Liberal's attack on Christian Truth, and to carry out that attack to its conclusion: ...total abolition..."[11] For example, the New Atheists tend to have a great deal of contempt for those Rose describes as Liberals—those who seek a middle ground between taking religion seriously and discarding it

---

10. Rose, para. 66.
11. Rose, para. 74.

entirely. Nevertheless, they are often natural allies on issues such as the separation of church and state.

As with Liberalism, Realism requires self-deceptions that can only be maintained for so long. People know full well that there are truths beyond the arrangement of matter.[12] Nietzsche thought that because everything was meaningless, all one could really do is laugh or remain silent. More nihilistic nihilists have thought that laughter and silence are no more meaningful than any other options, but still consider themselves brave, intelligent, and elite for being able to accept the ugly truth.[13] Many people rightly view materialism as colorless, stifling, and narrow-minded. They therefore set off to look for spirituality once again and embrace the third stage, which Rose calls *Vitalism*.[14] While this may sound like a good development,[15] the well is still poisoned by that kernel of Nihilism and the assumption of the falsehood of Christianity and often any kind of theism. The reaction against the narrow-mindedness of realism turns into a reaction against knowledge and rationality as such. Consequently, the search for truth is left without any hope of success because divine revelation is already written off and all other tools for finding truth (such as reason) have been rejected or never practiced in the first place.

The feel-good aphorisms that come out of this view, such as "the important thing is searching for truth, not finding it," become justifications for a return to what is essentially paganism with all its stereotypical superstition and brutality. Whether or not something feels good becomes the only remaining arbiter of value. Truth is no longer something that is discovered, but something that is built—supposedly from scratch—for whatever purpose an individual has in mind. As Nietzsche put it, "The falseness of an opinion is not for us any objection to it. . . . The question is, how far an opinion is life-furthering, life-preserving . . ."[16]

Rose's fourth and final stage, *The Nihilism of Destruction*[17] is less a transition from Vitalism than it is the end result. The Vitalistic need to create a new and satisfying spirituality finds that it is necessary to destroy

---

12. The next two chapters explore this in greater detail.
13. Budziszewski, *Conscience*, xiv.
14. Rose, para. 80.
15. To be fair, in some ways, postmodernism may actually be preferable to the Enlightenment.
16. Nietzsche, *Beyond Good and Evil*, 10–11.
17. Rose, para. 109.

any other spiritualities that stand in the way. Again, as Nietzsche put it, "Who wishes to be creative must first destroy and smash accepted values."[18] Because there is no clear transition point at this stage, and because its destructive nature means that there have been very few people and even fewer ideologies who have reached this extreme, it is unnecessary to spend any more time on it. It merely stands as the ultimate death sentence for Nihilism. Rose sums it up this way:

> The spiritual eye in fallen human nature is not sound . . . we see in this life only dimly and require faith and the Grace of God to effect a healing that will enable us . . . to see clearly once more. . . . Liberalism is born of the errors of taking our diseased eye for a sound one, of mistaking its impaired vision for a view of the true world, and thus of discharging the physician of the soul . . . whose ministrations are not needed by a "healthy" man. In . . . Realism, the disease, no longer attended by the necessary physician, begins to grow; vision is narrowed; distant objects, already obscure enough in the "natural" state of impaired vision, become invisible; only the nearest objects are seen distinctly, and the patient becomes convinced no others exist. In . . . Vitalism, infection leads to inflammation; even the nearest objects become dim and distorted and there are hallucinations. In the fourth stage, . . . blindness ensues and the disease spreads to the rest of the body, effecting agony, convulsions, and death."[19]

THE NEEDS OF NIHILISM

Rose's is an interesting exposition to be sure, but it also provides a useful foundation for good practice in apologetics. As was mentioned, each stage of Nihilism is based on an incoherence and consequently cannot truly satisfy the spiritual needs of humans, who naturally recognize the necessity of truth. Each stage contains what Francis Schaeffer called "points of tension": contradictions between a person's belief system and the real world.[20] In each one of these stages, there is a genuine need—an inadequacy in the previous thought system—that leads a person or society to move onto such a point of tension. However, the presence of a contradiction means that there is also a roadblock that prevents the need

---

18. Rose, para. 110.
19. Rose, para. 116.
20. Schaeffer, The God Who Is There, 147–154.

from being genuinely met. The apologetic task is to identify these needs and remove the roadblocks.

When considering Liberalism, one can imagine those with impaired vision removing their glasses, observing how blurry the world has become, and concluding that focus was merely imposed on a blurry world by the lenses they discarded. As was previously argued, the relativism that this is based on is clearly incoherent, so what could lead a person to embrace it despite the incoherence? There is some merit to the common and easy answer of sin—that self-imposed ambiguity in knowledge enables supposedly arbitrary behavior that is actually self-serving. However, while man is indeed that sinful, he is not that simple. Nobody wakes up in the morning and considers how he might fudge important knowledge so that he can achieve selfishness. Sin is real, but it is not a motivation. Liberalism of this kind primarily derives its motivation from a particular kind of image. The image can be of a witch being burned by Puritans, a man walking down death row who was simply in the wrong place at the wrong time, or even a teenager whose creativity is stifled when she is punished for breaking her elders' dogmatic rules.

Liberalism typically seeks to prevent such suffering and therefore chases after mercy. However, because it misunderstands mercy, it can never really satisfy its desire for it. To be merciful is to give somebody better than he deserves, but Liberalism disregards the concept of dessert altogether. It instead seeks the avoidance of suffering through the rejection of justice and confuses this with genuine mercy. It is not true that if humans would just be merciful enough, then we would no longer need to worry about being just.[21] The concept of dessert is inherent in true mercy by virtue of its core of providing better than what is deserved. Any true satisfaction of mercy must therefore satisfy justice as well. Despite the popular concept of Puritans in the motivating image, Christianity does not actually stand in the way of mercy. In fact, the only true reconciliation of mercy and justice is found in Christ's atoning death. All the punishment that mankind deserve was poured out on the man, Christ. Justice was satisfied, and yet by this sacrifice we have all been given far better than what we deserve. Day-to-day applications of mercy must not only

---

21. Nor is the converse true.

proceed from this ultimate mercy[22] but also depend on the reality that there is no mercy without sacrifice.

As was noted before, people flee Liberalism for Realism because the human mind cannot indefinitely remain in such contradiction. The self-imposed vagueness of Liberalism is less than satisfying. Objectivity is what motivates the Realist. Because humanity's spiritual vision is impaired by sin, any sound spiritual judgment is difficult. While the nihilism found in Realism is still incoherent, it is a different incoherency that still allows for the illusion of objectivity. The Realist essentially declares that he is objective because he ignores any topic on which objectivity is difficult. Of course, illusion can never truly take the place of the real thing. The Realist still finds himself making spiritual judgments, but he must also hide them from himself as he makes them. As one might imagine, this can never lead to sound, objective judgments, but only to inanities that do not truly satisfy. The real thing is once again found in the person and work of Jesus Christ. Luke 5:22–24 contains a perfect example of Jesus adding objectivity to spiritual judgment. Jesus forgives the sins of a paralyzed man who is brought before Him, triggering skepticism on the part of some observers. Jesus does not ignore this skepticism or instruct the observers to ignore their doubts, but instead grounds His authority to forgive sins in something tangible. He tells them:

> "Which is easier: to say, 'Your sins are forgiven,' or to say, 'Get up and walk'? But that you may know that the Son of Man has authority on earth to forgive sins..." He said to the paralyzed man, "I tell you, get up, take your mat and go home." Immediately he stood up in front of them, took what he had been lying on and went home praising God.

Christianity is often placed in the same category with many confused and ridiculous spiritualities. However, as will be discussed in chapters 5 and 6, Christianity is unlike any other religious system because it is consistently underwritten by a spiritual authority that demonstrates itself in observed supernatural manipulation of the physical world. What is more, it is also consistent with metaphysical knowledge that people already possess.[23]

---

22. Lest mercy merely ignore those who have been wronged.

23. This metaphysical knowledge will be discussed in more depth in the next two chapters.

This once again leaves us with the Vitalist, who rejects Realism because of the stifling way in which it ignores spirituality. The motivating factor for the Vitalist, who believes that people make their own truth, is a full and abundant life. Rationality and moral rules are seen as limitations on life imposed by others that stand in the way of this goal, and so personal feelings take leadership. Unfortunately, like other needs, a full and abundant life cannot be found without the rationality and objective spiritual knowledge that are part of human beings. In fact, following one's feelings cannot even lead to a full emotional life. In the song, "It's Only Natural," the band Better Than Ezra sings about a young woman who abandons the narrative voice's bed in shame when she hears her father's approach. In the chorus, the narrative voice admonishes her for it, telling her not to fight or hide what feels good, not to listen to the voices in her head, and ultimately that her behavior is only natural for beings that are essentially monkeys.[24]

We can set aside, for now, the odd idea that humanity is apparently the only species of monkey in existence that has to be convinced to act like monkeys. The point is that while the narrative voice admonishes his subject to follow her feelings, he is simultaneously instructing her to ignore them. Were not feelings of shame the "voices in her head" that led her to act in the first place? People are filled with a wide variety of emotions. Giving these emotions the unnatural responsibility of organizing themselves means only that the strongest win, and the rest are discarded. "Following your heart" will inevitably leave you with only a small fraction of your heart.

Once the false solution is discarded, one can once again look for the fullest kind of life in Jesus Christ. "I have come that they may have life, and have it to the full," he declares in John 10:10. Christians often communicate the law in a negative way (thou shalt not), and it is appropriate to do so, but when Jesus summarized the law, He framed it in the positive "Love the Lord your God with all your heart, and all your soul, and all your mind and . . . Love your neighbor as yourself."[25] What is more, He admonishes people to act positively in a way that includes their whole selves. Only sin, that which destroys, has no place. All gods except the True God mean abandoning a part of oneself that the True God cre-

---

24. Better Than Ezra, "It's Only Natural."
25. Matt 22:37.

ated—even when one makes himself or his life his god as the Vitalist does. Jesus declares that true life cannot be found in ourselves when he says, "Whoever finds his life will lose it, and whoever loses his life for my sake will find it."[26]

TRUTH IN CHRIST

As the term itself implies, no matter how it ends up manifesting itself, Nihilism always highlights a void at the center of the human soul. We desperately try to fill it ourselves and cannot succeed. In fact, even well-meaning Christians have tried in vain to harness Christianity to fill the void amid calls to live our best lives now and expositions on how following the right moral code leads to a good life. While the temptation has often been for Christians to offer their religion for the sake of solving a person's day-to-day problems, it must be resisted. Pragmatism of that sort is what led to the abandonment of truth in the first place. The contention of this chapter is not that God can be used to provide what is missing; one cannot use as a tool someone over whom one has no power. The contention is that God Himself *is* what is missing, and the reconciliation with Him was affected only by the atoning work of Christ. Our search for truth can only end with the one who declared Himself to be Truth.[27]

26. Matt 10:39.
27. John 14:6.

3

Sin and Natural Law

INTRODUCTION

APOLOGETICS IS NECESSARILY A social endeavor, and so it naturally involves the ordinary concerns that arise in any conversation or relationship. These concerns include the fear of causing offense. As a result, there is a strong impulse to ignore the topic of sin. This impulse often comes from the fact that discussion of sin makes Christians and their audience uncomfortable or worse. Every week, each person in my church makes the unpleasant proclamation that "I am a poor miserable sinner" as a part of our liturgy; would it be better to gloss over this fact to broaden Christianity's appeal? It is inflammatory, so why would one want to alienate those to whom he is trying to make a case? However, there are factors to consider which are more important than possible discomfort and alienation.

The most crucial factor is that the idea of sin is an essential part of what is being defended. There is no Christianity if there is no sin. The Gospel makes no sense without the Law, because our violation of the Law is what necessitated Christ's sacrifice on our behalf. In order to understand the good news, we need to know the bad news. In Edward Koehler's *A Summary of Christian Doctrine*, he describes the first step in conversion as "By the Law, [the Holy Spirit] works in man knowledge of sin and contrition of heart." This step is prior to "By the Gospel, He calls penitent sinners to Christ."[1] One cannot truly proclaim or defend the Gospel without also proclaiming or defending the Law in some way. It is also worth noting that if one proclaims the Law *rightly*, he cannot help but

---

1. Koehler, *A Summary of Christian Doctrine*, 130.

proclaim the Gospel.[2] Preachers may often talk about balancing Law and Gospel, but there is no need for balance, because rightly understood they compliment rather than oppose each other.

This complementarity exists because sin is destructive. Among other things, when we sin, we damage ourselves (and usually others as well). Sin fundamentally affects us. As J. Budziszewski argues in *The Revenge of Conscience*,[3] whenever we sin it creates a need for us to try and replace what has gone missing or repair what has been damaged—a need that cannot be ignored and demands action.[4] These needs become obvious when one looks at the way we instinctively act when doing wrong. We rationalize our sin in an attempt to make evil appear good. Sometimes we try to hide what we have done from people while other times we confess it to them, but either way we do so in an attempt to maintain relationships that have been put in danger. Finally, we try to make up for our sins: We buy flowers for an offended spouse; we buy gifts for a neglected child; sometimes we even try to punish ourselves. Justification, reconciliation, and atonement are what any person naturally seeks out when he realizes he has sinned, even when refusing to admit or repent of it.

Of course, all of these needs are provided for by Christ through His life, death, and resurrection. People may try to fulfill them apart from Christ, but such attempts can never truly satisfy because humankind is not equipped to save itself. If realization of sin results in realization of need, then reminding others of sin is an important task in apologetics. Christianity is entirely about a solution for our sins; if no solution is necessary, any discussion of the subject is merely academic. This chapter therefore has two purposes. One is to clarify Christians' understanding of sin—taking advantage of Scripture's clarification. The other is to examine communication of the subject to others who do not share that advantage.

WHAT IS SIN?

This chapter will not be addressing original sin. While it is certainly an important doctrine and an appropriate topic for interdenominational

---

2. Unless he seeks to leave his hearers in despair.

3. An excellent analysis of the mechanisms and effects of sin with respect to the the conscience of man.

4. Budziszewski, *The Revenge of Conscience*, 28–32.

and doctrinal apologetics, it is usually unnecessary when defending basic Christianity. One can certainly make a strong case for original sin with the Bible; unfortunately, many people have no interest in what the Bible says. One could perhaps make a secular case, but she would reveal the necessity of the Gospel to her audience well before adequately arguing that all people are utterly depraved.[5] There is so much sin in the world that there is no need to make a harder case when a more intuitive one is adequate. What follows is not a denial of this important doctrine, but a momentary setting-aside in order to focus on the acts of sin that flow from original sin.

Christ gives the following summary of the Law: "Love the Lord your God with all your heart and with all your soul and with all your mind. This is the first and greatest commandment. And the second is like it: Love your neighbor as yourself. All the Law and the Prophets hang on these two commandments."[6] To understand these commandments, it is necessary to correct a common misunderstanding of love. Christ is not commanding us to have a certain feeling for God and neighbor. He is instead commanding a commitment to their good. It is important to note here that while the Ten Commandments are mostly phrased as "Thou Shalt Not," Christ frames the law in a positive way: "Do this." Both are appropriate ways of describing the situation, but the latter is more useful here. If one is not doing what he ought, then he is sinning.

So what is necessary to satisfy "doing what we ought"? In Erwin Kurth's *Catechetical Helps*, a companion book to Luther's Small Catechism intended for children, the first definition of sin that is offered (and the one that sounds closest to Jesus' summary) is "missing the mark." The metaphor uses an archer and a target. The mark is perfection, and any shot that misses the exact dead center is sin.[7] For a long time, I did not like this definition because I did not really understand it.

The easiest way to misunderstand this metaphor is to confuse it with perfectionism.[8] If one confuses sin with perfectionism, any time someone makes a typo he is sinning. If someone does not get straight A+'s, she is

---

5. Even synergists recognize the need for a savior, even if that need is merely for assistance.

6. Matt 22:37–40.

7. Kurth, *Catechetical Helps*, 62.

8. One might argue that the metaphor encourages that confusion, but that is a discussion for another book.

sinning. If someone does not win every race, he is sinning. If someone has to learn something, she is sinning, because if she were perfect, she would know it already. This clearly cannot be what Jesus meant. Paul writes that people are given some gifts and not others,[9] but perfectionism requires not only that everyone has them all but that everyone be the best in all. Well-meaning Christians often fall into this error in an attempt to emphasize that "all have sinned and fallen short of the glory of God."[10] Unfortunately, perfectionism of this kind trivializes sin, and given the state of fallen humanity, such bizarre lengths are unnecessary to prove the point. The misunderstanding comes from confusing actions with results. People are intended by God to be finite beings and are not responsible for the infinite goal of making all the right things happen at all times and in all places. What people are responsible for is the right use of all the gifts that God has given them. These gifts run from such ordinary functions as rationality and motor skills all the way to individual spiritual gifts. Each of these were given to us with specific purposes, and when one fails to use them as intended by God, he is sinning.

Another way of misunderstanding sin is, after rejecting perfectionism as silly, to conclude that because one need not worry about what results he accomplishes, he need only worry about what results he intends. The idea is that as long as one has good intentions, he is not sinning. The problem here is that all sin is done out of good intentions.[11] No one starts his day considering what kind of evil he will do. When an evildoer is described as acting out of selfishness or revenge, it refers to a particular twisting of the mind; it does not suggest a motivation. When people do evil, they are motivated by the good things they aim for at the expense of other good things they ignore. When a jilted wife murders her cheating husband, she is likely motivated by a desire for justice—she wants him punished for what he has done. When Peter denied Jesus, his intention was likely to keep himself safe. Clearly, these actions are wrong, but not because justice or personal safety are bad things. Peter was wrong because his actions were wrong, not because his motivation was. Once again, focusing on results (this time, intended rather than actual) to the exclusion of everything else is at the heart of the confusion.

9. Rom 12:4–8.
10. Rom 3:23.
11. As J. Budziszewski also argues in *The Revenge of Conscience*, 135.

Sin is human hearts, souls, minds, and bodies failing to be entirely committed to God; we sin when we have priorities above Him. Every power and function one has is there at the direction of the Creator. Goods like pleasure and well-being are indeed good things, but they are not to be ultimate goals placed above God or removed from the contexts in which He put them in His creation. Jesus tells us to "Seek first the kingdom of God and His righteousness, and all these things shall be added to you."[12] It is one's responsibility to do what is right rather than to cause what is right, and it is in this that we fail so shamefully. If Plato is correct when he says that one's mind is purposed toward recognizing the Good, the True, and the Beautiful, then one is sinning when he uses his mind for the evil, the false, or the ugly. If the purpose of the will is to love, then one sins any time she wills a person's harm instead of her good.

If this view is correct, then it raises a practical issue. When one is defending Christianity, it is often against those who do not share a belief in the Triune God. If morality is based on the purposes of God, then where could we possibly find common ground with those who disagree on this ultimate source?

THE NATURAL LAW

One can never discuss God's purposes for human faculties in a vacuum. While one can certainly engage in a much more precise analysis, purposes for wills and minds such as love, good, truth, and beauty are not too objectionable. However, for one to recognize these as acceptable purposes, one has to know something about what kinds of things are good and what are not. The mind and the will are clearly capable of other activities; why then does anyone say that some activities are right and some are wrong? The preceding analysis of sin was built on the concept that God only purposes our faculties towards good, but from where does this information on good come? A Christian's knowledge of good is enlightened by the Bible, certainly, and a great deal of it finds its source in the Bible. However, if it were our only source, Christians would be the only ones to know anything about goodness. This is clearly not the case.

Even in a "tolerance"-worshiping culture like contemporary America, the idea of sin is not nearly as controversial as it is often made out to be. The fact that humanity is in some way flawed is hardly subtle. This fact

---

12. Matt 6:33 (NKJV).

is the reason for every religious system ever devised: Buddhism has the eightfold path; Utilitarians have complex systems of ethics to maximize pleasure. This fact is the same reason that the problem of evil continues to be the most popular argument against theism. People may disagree over whether mankind is basically good with evil tendencies or vice versa, but everyone agrees that all is not right with the world. Even those who worship tolerance decry intolerance as evil. Even the postmodernist who does not think there is a way the world ought to be thinks everyone ought to refrain from enforcing their idea of the way the world ought to be. This universality is why an analysis of sin is in the first part of this book, not the parts that deal with the facts or implications of Christianity. One may need the Bible to get the whole picture on sin, but one does not need the Bible to tell him that humanity does not do as it ought. Even the Bible makes that clear, as will be shown later in the chapter.

Furthermore, natural knowledge of sin is not restricted to some vague impression about an abstraction like "humanity." Everyone has personal knowledge of her own sin and her own shortcomings. The past two chapters have described a number of ways in which humanity lives in confusion and contradiction. First, many believe that the Biblical kind of faith (the certainty of things unseen) is contrary to reason, while in reality, reason actually depends on the Biblical kind of faith. The second chapter covered confusion about the nature of truth and unraveled many of the popular contradictions that perpetuate that confusion. Each argument depended on concepts that any human being must know by virtue of having a normal human mind, even if they do not realize that they know them or deny knowing them. Concepts such as the law of non-contradiction, that 2 + 2 = 4, the basic nature of truth, and the fact that reality exists all fall into this category. The actions and beliefs of those who deny such things provide evidence that they really believe them even while denying them. In each case, the consequence of the denial is a web of contradictions.

Such webs are not restricted to the areas covered so far. Budziszewski points out that we find exactly the same type of behavior when it comes to moral knowledge. In an example he gives regarding abortion, he says,

> Most who call abortion wrong call it killing. Most who call it killing say it kills a baby. Most who call it killing a baby decline to prohibit it altogether. Most who decline to prohibit it think it should be restricted. More and more people favor restrictions. Yet greater

and greater numbers of people have had or have been involved in abortions.[13]

I once overheard a woman talking about her sister's two abortions. She was pro-choice, but she made an interesting assertion: While she could understand having one abortion because accidents happen, a second one really steps outside the boundaries of morality. Despite a willingness to permit abortion, the behavior of the vast majority of people outside of the extreme feminist set indicates that they still see something wrong with the procedure. Why else would the second abortion be objectionable? "Safe, Legal, and Rare" was how the ideal abortion situation was described during President Clinton's administration, but it is hard to figure out where that "rare" comes from if there is nothing wrong with the procedure.

We find the same thing when it comes to premarital sex. We are told that sexual sin is no longer taken seriously, yet at the same time, people lie incessantly about it. An experiment reported in the *Journal of Sex Research* in 2003 found that on average, the number of sexual partners reported by young women who believe they are hooked up to a polygraph machine increases by 69 percent as compared to when there was a staged threat of exposure of the data and by 29 percent as compared to a simple anonymous survey.[14] When they thought they could get away with it, the subjects reported a lower number of partners than they actually had. When they also thought somebody might find out what they had reported, they gave even lower numbers. The study chalked this up to the influence of societal norms and traditional gender roles, but it is hard to believe that these unmarried eighteen- to twenty-five-year-olds whose entire lifetime fell after the sexual revolution and whose society encourages experimentation and a libertine lifestyle are led to lie by the norms of that same society. What is more, parents who also supposedly fail to take premarital sex seriously are apparently so shy about bringing the subject up with their children that they insist the schools do so in their stead at a younger and younger age. When it comes to other people's children the culture becomes very impatient indeed about making children ready. When it comes to one's own children, "waiting" (whether until they are "ready" or "older") seems to be the mantra. It is difficult to imagine a father telling his daughter to go out there and live it up, but it apparently

---

13. Budziszewski, 26.
14. Alexander and Fisher, Terri D. "Truth," 27–35.

becomes easier if he has a teacher tell her in his stead. Jerry Seinfeld once quipped that truth and sex do not go together. If people are covering up with lies what their culture tells them to be proud of, we ought to consider the possibility that guilt remains beneath the surface.

If everyone knows these morals on some level even though their culture teaches them the opposite, they clearly know from some other source than culture. The Hindus called this source the *Rta*, the Chinese called it the *Tao*[15], and Western philosophy has traditionally referred to it as the natural law. The Bible itself attests to its existence. In Romans, Paul tells us about it:

> Indeed, when Gentiles, who do not have the law, do by nature things required by the law, they are a law for themselves, even though they do not have the law, since they show that the requirements of the law are written on their hearts, their consciences also bearing witness, and their thoughts now accusing, now even defending them.[16]

For a long time, many have held to the idea that the normal human mind either comes equipped with certain knowledge about morality or cannot help learning about it in the course of life. While there is plenty of debate over details, such as whether this knowledge is innate or if the mind is merely designed to recognize it once the component concepts are recognized (i.e. a person knows "don't hurt people" as soon as he recognizes what "hurt" and "people" mean), one can be sure that certain moral knowledge is automatically present in human beings.

The purpose of this philosophy is not to prove the content of this moral knowledge. For one thing, the natural law consists of moral *first* principles. They are not deduced from others and consequently cannot be proven. As we shall see, however, they cannot entirely be denied (although we can and do deny parts of it). As an example of this playing out in history, the revolutionary idea that "if God is dead, then everything is permitted" was really only briefly popular. Contemporary atheists are typically offended at the charge of being amoral. "I don't need your God to be good" and "belief in God stops people from being good" take the place of "your God isn't real so I can do whatever I want." The human mind is unable to give up the concept of "ought." Even cultural relativists

---

15. Which is how C.S. Lewis refers to it in *The Abolition of Man*.
16. Rom 2:14–15.

who claim there is no universal moral law tend to follow that up with the idea that we therefore ought to never impose our morality on others (which is itself a universal moral law). Like the denials of existence, truth, rationality, or faith, a denial of a universal moral law always ends up eventually depending on some part of what is denied.

Looking at it from a more positive direction, any decent ethical philosopher will begin with known moral concepts instead of weaving new ones out of thin air. For example, if one were to argue against the legitimacy of software piracy, he would no doubt begin with the concept of property and the knowledge that theft is wrong before showing how those concepts apply to the media in question. In fact, even poor ethical philosophers do this. Peter Singer, often proclaimed as "the most influential living ethicist," reaches bizarre and erroneous conclusions like the wrongness of killing cows and the rightness of killing babies, but he reaches them by starting with the correct and commonly known idea that human suffering ought not happen—that it indicates that something is wrong. Those who rationalize abortion begin with moral knowledge like the fact that children ought to be cared for before foolishly deciding that society can prevent the neglect of children by killing the ones it plans to neglect. Either way, common moral knowledge always serves as first principles when making moral judgments.

Consequently, such common moral knowledge also needs to serve as Christians' first principles when refuting moral error and making a case for sin. When denying the acceptability of abortion, for example, Christians often quote Psalm 139: "For you created my inmost being: you knit me together in my mother's womb . . . All the days ordained for me were written in your book before one of them came to be."[17] This is fine when arguing the point with those who accept the Bible as authoritative; in such a case, it is common ground and can be used as a premise while reasoning. However, this is not the case when debating the point with an unbeliever. A more profitable starting point in such a case could be the common moral knowledge that murder is wrong, from which one can make the case that abortion is murder.

---

17. Ps 139:13,16.

HOW MUCH DO WE REALLY KNOW?

Not all moral knowledge is known to all. Some things we cannot truly remove from our minds, but some things we can. Thomas Aquinas divided moral precepts into Primary, Intermediate, and Common categories. The Primary is what we all know, like the precept that gratuitously harming a human being is wrong. The Intermediate are the things that immediately follow from the Primary, such as the precept that because murder gratuitously harms a human being it is wrong. Common precepts are things that are true, but are not necessarily known to all, like Jesus' admonitions against hatred or lust—certainly true, but probably news to his listeners. As C.S. Lewis put it in *Mere Christianity*,

> Men have differed as regards what people you ought to be unselfish to—whether it was only your family, or your fellow countrymen, or everyone. But they have always agreed that you ought not to put yourself first. Selfishness has never been admired. Men have differed as to whether you should have one wife or four. But they have always agreed that you must not simply have any woman you liked.[18]

The big question, then, is this: What precepts can one really count on people knowing? How can one distinguish between true common ground and remote implications that a person may not truly be aware of? It is very likely that we all know the wrong of adultery, but do we really all know the wrong of polygamy? In the previously cited verse from Romans, Paul writes about the Gentiles doing things required by the law by nature, the voice of conscience, and thoughts on accusing and defending the law itself. One can tell what people know about right and wrong based on what people do (their common moral practices across cultures), on their consciences, and on how they justify their right-doing and wrong-doing. As John M. Cooper noted in "The Relations Between Religion and Morality in Primitive Culture," virtually all cultures agree on a number of moral precepts. They believe people ought to treat their god or gods as though they were actually gods (i.e. showing respect and honor); care for their children; refrain from murder and malicious violence, theft, and slander (at least among those in the same tribe). While sexual relationships may be different from culture to culture, marriage is always recognized and

---

18. Lewis, *Mere Christianity*, 6.

genuine adultery is universally condemned. In short, common morality agrees with a basic reading of the Ten Commandments.[19]

The Bible is also useful in discovering the contents of the natural law. It may seem contradictory that we use the Bible to figure out what everyone knows from a source other than the Bible, but this is not the case. Mankind is broken; consequently, we continuously confuse ourselves about what we know. We purposefully ignore the inscription written on our hearts, rationalizing the wrong that we do. Likewise, the world is broken. One might observe that doing right in a particular way often brings about negative consequences (e.g. admitting to infidelity to one's spouse causes hurt feelings) and erroneously deduce that such a behavior is wrong. The Bible can help cut through Christians' confusion. By way of analogy, archaeologists once recovered a remarkable ancient computational device that was sophisticated far beyond its time period. It was found at the bottom of the sea, corroded, rusted, and broken. By studying the remains, they were able to deduce a great deal about its functionality even if they could not be certain of its purpose. However, it cannot be denied that finding a copy of "The Antikytheran Mechanism For Dummies" along with the remains of the device would have been very helpful. The Bible helps us separate our misconceptions about moral law (even misconceptions we were taught from the cradle) from the real thing.

PUTTING THIS TO GOOD USE

If one can be sure that this sort of knowledge is common to all humanity, then how does one go about using it? In analyzing the different stages of nihilism in chapter 2, it was argued that people do not deny known truths for no reason at all, but because they believe they have something to gain by doing so. The same is true with respect to moral truths. A person denies a moral truth because he believes he can better accomplish another good without it. A substantial advantage that Christians have is knowing that evil is parasitic in nature; it needs good in order to have any kind of power at all. If evil is being done, one can be sure that the perpetrator is twisting a good impulse. Consequently, any denial of part of the moral law depends on the corruption of another part—on using a true moral law to support an evil action. If moral confusion is based on phony virtues, then one thing Christians can do is to show people the real

---

19. Cooper, "Relations," 33–48.

thing. If everyone knows them to some extent, there remains the chance that a person will recognize them even when in denial. The last chapter contrasted spoiled mercy with the genuine article. One could deal with spoiled love or spoiled justice in the same manner; Christ clearly demonstrated each unspoiled virtue to its fullest.

Christians can also use natural law as any ethicist does—by arguing from known to disputed moral laws. If one knows, for example, that gratuitously harming a human being is wrong, one can use that common knowledge to make a case that a particular action is wrong because it gratuitously harms another. One can also tear down common false moral systems. For example, one could easily use common moral knowledge to illuminate the flaw in the common idea that "I can do whatever I want as long as I don't hurt anybody else." A person will automatically recognize, for example, that an onlooker who stands by and watches a rape or a parent who completely neglects his children would be a genuinely evil person. Nevertheless, such a person meets the criteria of doing what they want without hurting anybody else. With a little thought, one has no choice but to reject the simplistic and false moral system.

Of course, when one leads people to conclusions that they do not like, they may spontaneously add a necessary premise to the list of moral precepts that they deny. This is especially prevalent among the highly intelligent because they see the conclusions much earlier on.[20] Denial is what it is, and so the third thing one can do is call their bluffs. This is tricky but called for in situations when one knows their audience is lying, and on some level the audience knows he is lying too. When one calls a bluff, he lets them know that he knows.

In *The God Who is There*, Francis Schaeffer describes an encounter along these lines. During a cruise on the Mediterranean, he had a conversation over dinner with an atheist who tried to be very consistent about materialism. When they retired for the evening, Schaeffer recognized that the man truly loved his young wife in a way one does not love a simple collection of atoms, and asked him if, when he took her into his arms at night, he was certain she was there. The man angrily replied that he was not certain and slammed the door.[21] Clearly he did not really believe that matter was all that existed because he treated his wife with a higher con-

---

20. A clear example of how a great ability is only good if it is oriented towards God.
21. Schaeffer, *The God Who is There*, 87.

sideration than that which was due to mere matter. Schaeffer's hope was that this man would never forget this gaping contradiction in his system of thought. One could add the additional hope that he would come to realize how much he had to lie to maintain his materialism.

But this raises an important question. How does one distinguish between a person in denial and a person who is genuinely confused? Calling a nonexistent bluff would be incredibly disrespectful. One could consider several questions in such an analysis. How basic is that which is being denied? Is the person grasping at straws—bringing up premises that he has never believed or denying ones he has never denied just to prove his point? Is his previous behavior at extreme odds with his new proclamation—is he trying to use something in his argument that he clearly does not believe to be true? A defensive person could unintentionally do many of these things.[22]

GENTLENESS AND RESPECT

Calling a bluff is tricky indeed. Schaeffer offered the following caution:

> As I seek to do this, I need to remind myself constantly that this is not a game I am playing. If I begin to enjoy it as a kind of intellectual exercise, then I am cruel and can expect no real spiritual results. As I push the man off his false balance, he must be able to feel that I care for him. Otherwise I will only end up destroying him, and the cruelty and ugliness of it all will destroy me as well.[23]

In the classic apologetics verse, Peter writes about giving an answer for the hope within us with gentleness and respect,[24] and Scripture constantly instructs Christians to love. How can one lovingly, gently, and respectfully tell a person to his face that he is lying? Even when one is not so blunt, the intended message is still clear. Most people have a vague impression of what gentleness and respect mean, but in order to practice them, one needs to clearly understand them.

Gentleness is simple enough. Its object is to treat some thing or some person in a way that avoids harm or injury. One handles a fragile vase gently in order to avoid causing damage. One also interacts with a person gently in order to avoid causing damage, whether physical, psychological,

---

22. As all of us do from time to time.
23. Schaeffer, 156.
24. 1 Pet 3:16.

or spiritual. Respect, on the other hand, is a little more complicated. Its object is to treat a thing as though it is what it is. For example, respecting a boundary means not crossing it. To cross it is to treat it as though it is not actually a boundary at all. Respecting a human being means treating him as though he is made in the image of God. Much could be said on this subject, but at the very least it means avoiding mockery and intentionally hurtful insults. At the same time, however, it means that one must not cooperate when a person wants to treat himself as less than the image of God. If a person believes he is merely a collection of atoms without any spiritual dimension or that he has no moral obligations, then respect at the very least means disagreeing with him and not treating him according to his own ideas.

It is instructive to note that both of these dispositions are different than the secular notion of niceness. To be "nice" means to be devoted to avoiding unpleasant or uncomfortable feelings—to avoid rocking the boat. However, while one certainly should not be in the business of manipulating a person's unpleasant emotions, such feelings may be triggered by one's statements without being caused by them. For example, upon being scolded for driving drunk, a person may feel guilty. However, the ultimate cause of the feeling is not the scolding but the fact of guilt. One ought not to act as though maintaining the status quo is important when the status quo is poisoning someone. A proper application of tolerance may mean that one puts up with such a status quo,[25] but actively and uncritically seeking its continuation out of fear of making waves is a failure to love.

A self-confessed bad example of calling a bluff is found in James Sire's introduction to the thirtieth anniversary edition of *The God Who is There*. Sire was giving a lecture, when a student sought to correct him by telling him that communication is impossible. Sire quite cleverly treated him as though what the student was saying was true—he acted as though he could not understand the words the student was saying to him. The student repeated himself several times, but Sire continued to play dumb. The student ended up storming out angrily and a portion of the audience did not even understand what Sire was doing.[26] Avoiding such unfruitful situations requires love, gentleness, and respect—all rightly understood.

---

25. One tolerates a bad situation when disrupting it would require sin or cause a greater evil. Chapter 13 contains a more thorough analysis.

26. Schaeffer, 19.

CONCLUSION

Sin can be a touchy subject, but God has given Christians (and all humans) the tools they need to discuss it with others. As long as people condemn others for anything at all (even for condemning others), there remains the implicit assumption that all are under a law that is both binding on and known to all. We suppress parts of it, we forget why it is there, and we try to avoid its implications. Nevertheless, even in an age as corrupt as this one, human beings cannot give up the concept of "ought" and cannot fail to recognize that they do not always do as they ought. Christians can rationally and fruitfully discuss the Law with anyone, which lays the groundwork for discussing the Gospel with anyone.

4

The Existence of God

INTRODUCTION

THE QUESTION OF WHETHER or not God exists has been batted about by philosophers for millennia. From the ontological to the cosmological to the teleological, many philosophers have put forth their arguments to prove the existence of a theistic God to those who doubt it. Of course, during those millennia, other philosophers have been equally hard at work finding flaws in those arguments and even putting forth their own arguments that a theistic God cannot possibly exist. The battle continues seemingly indefinitely with each side certain of their intellectual superiority.

Some famous arguments are not considered compelling by most today. There is, for example, the ontological argument (argument from being) put forth by Anselm of Canterbury:

> We understand God to be a perfect being, something than which nothing greater can be conceived. Because we have this concept, God at least exists in our minds as an object of the understanding. Either God exists in the mind alone, or God exists both in the mind and as an extramental reality. But if God existed in the mind alone, then we could conceive of a being greater than that than which nothing greater can be conceived, namely, one that also existed in extramental reality. Since the concept of a being greater than that than which nothing greater can be conceived is incoherent, God cannot exist in the mind alone.[1]

It basically comes down to the assertion that an existent being is more perfect than a nonexistent one; therefore a being conceived of as being ab-

---

1. Audi, *Cambridge Dictionary of Philosophy*, 697.

solutely perfect must exist. Other philosophers have noted that existence is not really a property—that there is no conceptual difference between a real hundred dollars or an imaginary hundred dollars—therefore the presence or absence of existence does not influence the mental concept of a thing. God is *defined* the same way whether He exists or not, so a definition alone cannot lead to proof of existence. This is not to say that there is no place for this argument, but rather that it is only compelling in the presence of a great many assumptions about the nature of God and man.[2]

There are other arguments as well, such as the cosmological argument, the argument from existence. We observe that things change and begin to exist. Changes have causes. The causes themselves are also changes, therefore they must also have causes. However, there cannot be an infinite regress of causes. Consequently, there must be a changeless first cause of change; just as a row of dominoes falling over one after the other requires something outside of that row of dominoes to initiate the chain reaction. Furthermore, the cause must be sufficient to account for the effect (the universe, and everything in it). To go back to the domino analogy, the first cause must be enough to actually tip over that first domino and set up all the dominoes in the first place. Critics of this argument counter that maybe there *can* be an infinite regress of causes. Others contend that there is no need for sufficient causes to account for the effect; maybe the "effects" just *are*.[3] Maybe that first domino just fell over. And so, the argument is "refuted" by pure fiat.

Another good example is the teleological argument, the argument from design. Basically, many things in nature share similar characteristics with things created by intelligent humans when it comes to complexity, purpose, and functionality. A bicycle has the purpose of moving a person; likewise a heart has the purpose of pumping blood. Since like effects have like causes, the world must be a product of design by an intelligent being. The classic analogy is that if one came across a pocket watch in the middle of a field, he would recognize the existence of a watchmaker even if he had never seen a pocket watch before. Likewise, if one came across a universe like ours, he would recognize the existence of a Creator God. Critics contend that perhaps the "like cause" is only very vaguely "like"; perhaps

2. To be fair to Anselm, he lived in a time and place in which the necessary assumptions were commonplace.

3. Audi, 697–98.

it only looks intelligent. Especially today, many would contend that the unintelligent forces of natural selection and genetic mutation create beings that appear designed. Other possibilities include the idea that there are many minor intelligent beings or that the designer merely imposed order on that which already existed (as opposed to the theistic concept of creation from nothing), and there is no true Creator at all.[4]

THE LIMITS OF ARGUMENTS

When one examines the way each argument has been debated, a pattern seems to emerge. There is something basic that was assumed by the argument, and somebody else claims it cannot really be assumed. This does not mean that they are bad arguments (although they might be for other reasons), but it does mean that they are not always found to be convincing. This should not come as a surprise after the first chapter on reason. Anything can be doubted, and consequently something must be taken on faith in order to reason at all. Because of this, there is no foolproof[5] argument that proves the existence of God beyond all shadow of a doubt. Proving anything about God to a person would require common first principles. One might cite physical evidence as his starting point, but as was seen in the brief examination of the teleological argument, physical evidence is not self-interpreting. For example, in *Christian Apologetics*, Norman Geisler makes the claim that before one can examine the physical evidence of the Resurrection, one has to prove whether God exists before drawing the conclusion that miracles point to God.[6]

So what is one to do? Strictly speaking, Geisler is correct. Even if a Christian were to demonstrate the historicity of the Resurrection, the naturalist could very well say that it was merely caused by some natural force that we have not yet understood and cataloged. Practically speaking, however, this is not usually the case. I have only encountered one claim that the miracles of the New Testament really happened, but that it did not point to spiritual authority on the part of Jesus. This claim hinged on Jesus being an alien from a technologically advanced civilization. This seems unlikely to catch on anytime soon. Even non-Christian traditions[7]

---

4. Audi, 698.
5. In the literal sense of the term.
6. Geisler, *Christian Apologetics*, 7.
7. Such as the ideas that Jesus was a guru or a Buddha.

that accept some of the miraculous events of the New Testament claim some spiritual authority for Jesus; the things his followers recorded simply have no origin in things that he actually said (i.e. the New Testament and the Church have not accurately recorded much of Jesus' teachings).

NATURAL KNOWLEDGE OF GOD

Contrary to the approach of philosophers through the ages, the Bible never sets out to philosophically prove the existence of God. Instead, it makes a far more audacious claim. In Romans, Paul writes:

> The wrath of God is being revealed from heaven against all the godlessness and wickedness of men who suppress the truth by their wickedness, since what may be known about God is plain to them because God has made it plain to them. For since the creation of the world, God's invisible qualities—his eternal power and divine nature—have been clearly seen, being understood from what has been made, so that men are without excuse. For although they knew God, they neither glorified him as God nor gave thanks to him, but their thinking became futile and their foolish hearts were darkened.[8]

Paul's claim is that everyone already knows God exists, but many deny it. If this is to be believed, then the task in apologetics is often not so much proving that God exists as it is reminding. When God speaks to Moses through the burning bush, and Moses asks how to identify him to Pharaoh, God does not instruct Moses to explain to Pharaoh that there exists an omnipotent, omniscient, omni-benevolent creator of the universe, that we are all obligated to obey Him, and that He has commanded Pharaoh to free the Israelites. God simply says, "I AM" and expects Pharaoh to understand the rest. Please do not misunderstand. This is not an argument for the existence of God. It proves nothing to anyone who does not already take the Bible as authoritative. Nor does it mean that philosophy or these famous arguments are useless. It merely indicates that one needs to understand why and how to use them.

While the claim is audacious, it also becomes apparent in the world if one looks for it. In *The Everlasting Man*, G. K. Chesterton describes a missionary's encounter with a polytheistic tribe of Australian Aborigines, who told many polytheistic stories, but immediately recognized God as

---

8. Rom 1:18–21.

preached by the missionary to be "Atahocan," somebody above all of their polytheistic gods who they recognized but had never mentioned in their stories. Chesterton goes on to note:

> There are any number of similar examples. They all testify to the unmistakable psychology of a thing taken for granted, as distinct from a thing talked about. There is a striking example in a tale taken down word for word from a Red Indian in California, which starts out with hearty and literary relish: "The sun is the father and ruler of the heavens. He is the big chief. The moon is his wife and the stars are their children"; and so on through a most ingenious and complicated story, in the middle of which is a sudden parenthesis saying that the sun and moon have to do something because "It is ordered that way by the Great Spirit Who lives above the place of all." That is exactly the attitude of most paganism towards God. He is something assumed and forgotten and remembered by accident.[9]

Situations like the ones Chesterton describes are strikingly similar to the one described by Paul.

Now, that is all well and good for the primitive pagans, but many would argue that mankind has progressed a great deal since then—that we are smarter, less given to superstition, and more scientific. Just as modern humans no longer believe in those polytheistic gods, they no longer believe in that underlying monotheistic God either. In fact, many atheists accuse theists of unconsciously sharing in their atheism. After all, both have very long lists of gods in which they disbelieve; atheists just happen to reject one more god than theists do—and usually for the same reasons. The implication here is that the rejection of all gods is the clear path that progress is taking; monotheists are simply a step behind.

But is this really the case? For one thing, a theistic God and polytheistic gods are very different concepts. It is true that the polytheistic gods changed continually and dropped away eventually,[10] but Chesterton's point is about a very different concept of God that never fundamentally changed. Just because the pattern holds with one topic does not mean it holds with a very different topic. Furthermore, while many modern people reject the notion of a personal and all-powerful God, there is

---

9. Chesterton, *The Everlasting Man*, 88–89.

10. Although, circumstances seem to predict a strong resurgence of this kind of belief in the near future.

another way in which God still makes an unacknowledged appearance. Paul Tillich identified this concept as a person's "ultimate concern." This concern unconditionally stands behind all meaning in a person's life and serves as the basis for his understanding of reality. It represents a loyalty that supersedes all others.[11] This ultimate thing, valued simply for itself, orders the value of all other things for an individual. For example, a hedonist, who holds the maximization of personal pleasure to be that which is deserving of ultimacy, might hold that life is valuable. However, life's value is contingent on the fact that life brings him pleasure. If life ceased to have that possibility, it would cease to be of value. The hedonist holds that pleasure, unlike life, needs no justification for why it is good. Good is simply what pleasure is. Pleasure, therefore, is the "god" of the hedonist.

While people may forget who God is or deny that He is a person at all, we all remain hardwired for the concept of an ultimate thing which is deserving of ultimate commitment. As J. Budziszewski notes in *The Revenge of Conscience*:

> Eventually there is something to which every knee bows. This is the person's god. As a matter of theory, one may deny that any concern deserves ultimacy. But as a matter of practice, no one escapes ceding ultimacy to something, whether it deserves ultimacy or not. Choices between incompatible urgencies are unavoidable. To prevent the rise of one or another of these urgencies to supremacy, a person would have to practice a truly Stoic discipline of contradiction—and in the end we would have to ask what urgency he served in so disordering himself.[12]

The issue here is plain. Humans do not act completely arbitrarily. If we strive for something, we surely have a reason for doing so—we attempt to justify our actions. Under close scrutiny, even those who do claim to act on behalf of nothing at all do so because they hold to some good, such as autonomy, or simply put themselves in the place of God.

The previous chapter considered the many kinds of goods that humanity recognizes by virtue of being human: truth, beauty, love, etc. What kind of ultimate concern *could* adequately order all of these? The first thing one needs to be clear on is how one would evaluate whether or not an ultimate concern is adequate. The most important criteria is that all of

---

11. Brown, *Ultimate Concern*, 1–16.
12. Budziszewski, *The Revenge of Conscience*, 51.

these goods need to be coherent—beauty cannot be false, love cannot be evil, etc. For example, aggregate pleasure cannot be god (as Utilitarians believe) because it allows for falsity in beauty or evil in love as long as a given situation contributes to aggregate pleasure. Loving your fellow man by providing aggregate pleasure could very well involve evils such as murder or theft should the situation call for it. The pleasure provided to the many could easily involve evil done to the one or the few.

One might object by denying that all these goods should be compatible. After all, there are phrases like "the ugly truth" to describe something true but unpleasant, such as a husband cheating on his wife. If a god allows for incoherence among the various things humans naturally recognize as good, then all goodness requires is achieving one of those things to some extent. As was mentioned in the previous chapter, however, all evil is done out of an attempt to achieve some moral good at the expense of another. The husband is perhaps seeking companionship or excitement with his mistress. These are good things, but it is still recognizable that what he does is wrong because he violates other goods, like fidelity and love. Ultimately, the objection falls apart because the reason the truth in this example is ugly is *because* there is some good (such as fidelity) that has been removed from the situation. The incoherence does not demonstrate that everything is fine, but precisely the opposite—that something has gone wrong.

This leads to examining the nature of a thing capable of organizing all of the goods humans recognize. The nature of the goods to be organized gives some clues to this. Any kind of interaction with beauty or truth requires an intelligent mind capable of recognizing them. Truth and beauty are not merely materialistic phenomena; things like matter and forces cannot be said to comprise them. One must also consider love—a commitment of the will to a person's good. Just as the nature of truth requires a mind to recognize it, love by its nature requires a will to practice it. Love is good, but it cannot simply float about as an abstraction unconnected to people. Because these various goods do not even exist independently of beings with minds and wills, their organization requires them to be somehow unified in personhood.

One could, of course, argue that these goods just happen to have come into existence—that a naturalistic universe inadvertently created human minds and wills in concert with these goods, and that human minds, in turn, organize them. Do we not bring order to chaotic matter when we organize stones into beautiful buildings and dead plant and animal matter into beautiful meals? Could not one simply say, as secular humanists often do, that these various goods are simply the progressive interests of human persons and that humans must organize and perfect them on their own? Unfortunately for the humanist, that would lead into Euthyphro's dilemma.

This dilemma comes from a Socratic dialog in which Socrates was grilling a man named Euthyphro about how he knows that some things are just. Euthyphro says that justice is that which is loved by the gods. Socrates asks why the gods love some things and not others. Euthyphro can only answer that they love them because these things are just (putting him into circular reasoning).[13] Despite some problems with Socrates' phraseology, the dilemma is usually applied to theism this way: either there is some good to which God Himself conforms (in which case God is not the highest thing), or God is just arbitrarily assigning things to be good in a might-makes-right kind of way and God consequently cannot meaningfully be described as good. If God is not good or is not the highest thing, then he is not what theists consider to be God. If these are the only two options, then the idea of a theistic God is incoherent. This is countered in many ways, but one of the most common is to point out that the supposed dilemma leaves out the option that God and Good are not different things at all.

Though this argument is usually brought against theism, one can apply the same dilemma to this sort of secular humanism. Either there is a good above mankind, to which mankind seeks to conform those chaotic goods that he is organizing (in which case we are organizing according to a plan outside of ourselves, and the goods are already organized by a different person); or good is defined by mankind, in which case it is completely arbitrary. Since there are substantial disagreements on how mankind ought to act, it simply comes down to the circumstances of might-makes-right, which we intuitively recognize as being morally bankrupt. The theist can escape this dilemma because the question assumes that God is a separate thing from Good, which the theist would dispute. This option is not open to the humanist, however, because no one in his right mind would ever claim that humanity is identical with good because any brief observation shows us that humans do evil on a regular

---

13. Plato, *Euthyphro*, 3–23.

basis. Such a view of humankind exists only in an idealistic hope for the future—something external to present reality.

Therefore, one is necessarily led to a being that has an intelligent mind, that has a will, is sufficient in these attributes along with power to be able to create the beings and circumstances in which we recognize these goods, and who is, Himself, identical with Good. Not only does the human mind work in a way that requires a god, the moral premises we all know necessarily lead to the existence of the theistic kind of God.[14]

SUPPRESSING THE TRUTH

Nevertheless, this conclusion, although known to all,[15] is obviously not accepted by all. In contemporary American culture, one can classify the philosophies that set themselves up against theism according to two categories. The first category is made up of the mystical kind of philosophies—pantheism, paganism, gnosticism, and the like. This chapter will not explicitly cover them because they have been indirectly addressed throughout the book. These philosophies tend to stand on basic contradictions: reality is an illusion, there is no truth, the spirituality of feelings, etc. These religions can be rejected on the basis of bad philosophy. This rejection is why many Eastern traditions deny basic elements of so-called Western thought like the law of non-contradiction. However, there is another category of philosophies that object to theism. This other kind has the claim of objective truth and rationality as well as the history of having grown out of the Enlightenment and Western civilization. This category includes agnosticism, deism, and atheism.

When dealing with objections from these quarters, the apologist must keep certain things in the forefront of her mind. Some of these include:

---

14. It has been suggested that this identification of God with Good ultimately leads to a kind of pantheism; that everything in which we recognize good must therefore be a part of God. However, this conclusion is not a logical necessity because one could develop a theory of goodness in the world based on correspondence (similar to the view of truth explained in the second chapter). According to such a view, a thing could be called good inasmuch as it reflects God in the way God intended it to reflect Him. In one sense, no one *is* Good except for God (as Jesus himself points out in Luke 18:19), but in a different sense, one can be *described* as good because he is the image of God.

15. It is the conclusion—the existence of a God who is the foundation of goodness—that is known to all, not the argument itself.

- People believe things they know are false because they have a vested interest in doing so.[16]
- Evil requires good to have any impact. Likewise, falsehoods (a kind of evil) are only believed (a kind of impact) because of the misuse of truths (a kind of good).[17]
- One cannot teach or convince people of things they already know.

If one truly believes these principles, then there are profound implications when dealing with objections to theism. Firstly, if one knows that objectors really do know that there is a God, then one must ask *what the objection is meant to accomplish*. Can it be taken at face value, or is there another meaning? What do similar types of objections usually mean when made in other contexts?

Secondly, because lies require truth to sustain them, then if a false objection is compelling to people, one knows it must be based in some way on a truth. One must then ask *what kernel of truth is it based upon*. Following from this, if a truth is being used to support falsehood, then one knows it is being misused. One must then ask *how the particular truth is being misused*. What lies are coupled with the truth?

Finally, if one cannot teach people that God exists, our object in refuting the objection should not be to teach them that God exists. *What, then, is our objective in refuting an objection?* For example, if one must lay out an argument to prove God's existence, it must be for some other goal than informing someone that God exists (e.g. perhaps it is to prove that it is reasonable to believe in God). If one is objecting to an argument that God *cannot* exist, one needs to remember that her object is only to show that he *can*, not to prove that he does. One needs to keep all these questions in mind when examining the objections of deism, agnosticism, and atheism.

DEISM

If everyone knows about a theistic God, whither all the philosophies that deny Him? In the Christian West, these philosophies grew out of the Enlightenment. When humankind declares that it can figure everything out without God, its ideas on God must change to exclude the God of the

---

16. See chapters 2 and 3.
17. See chapter 3.

Bible who declares us to be utterly dependent on Him. Deism was such a philosophical departure and focused mainly on answering the question of "Who is God" in the negative (i.e. He cannot be the Christian God). The idea of a perfect and all-powerful God remained, but the ideas concerning our relationship to that God changed. Specifically, deists believe that God created the world and then left it to its own devices. In *Christian Apologetics*, Norman Geisler makes the claim that deism is "defunct, both historically and philosophically."[18] However, there are still individuals out there who hold to it openly, and it is unofficially alive and well for many who claim agnosticism and those who identify with Christianity only in a cultural sense.[19] Geisler lists the following three central tenets of deism:

- An eternal, intelligent, all powerful creator God exists.
- God does not intervene in his creation. Miracles do not occur, and there is nothing like what Christians would call special revelation.
- God is unitarian (as opposed to trinitarian).[20]

Deism also seems to promote a generic moralistic natural religion for all people that merely has to do with being good.

With the first of the above tenets we obviously take no issue. With the third we will need to rely on special revelation, which is precluded by the second tenet. We will therefore look at several arguments for the second tenet, anti-supernaturalism.

Matthew Tindal, for example, addresses the issue of special revelation by making the argument that because God is perfect, he would offer a complete and perfect religion the first time around. Any subsequent addition would be unnecessary because a perfect religion could not be improved upon. Furthermore, since God cannot change, he could never change the religion he gave to mankind; He also must have given this natural revelation to all because He would not have shown favoritism to a particular tribe.[21]

What is Tindal's purpose in making this argument? The apparent argument is that God cannot intervene in his creation, which is intended

---

18. Geisler, 171.

19. For example, those who believe in God and identify themselves as Christian on surveys for no other reason than that their parents were Christians. The term "Christian" reflects circumstances rather than a serious belief.

20. Geisler, 166–67.

21. Tindal, *Christianity*, 3–4.

to show that the God of the Bible (or any God known apart from natural revelation) is unnecessary, and consequently that he cannot really be God. The purpose is not so much to deny God, but to claim that the God of the Bible is not needed.

Why is this argument compelling? Taken very strictly as written, it is correct. The Apostle Paul actually agrees with Tindal when he writes:

> To those who by persistence in doing good seek glory, honor, and immortality, he will give eternal life. But for those who are self-seeking and who reject the truth and follow evil, there will be wrath and anger. There will be trouble and distress for every human being who does evil: first for the Jew, then for the Gentile; but glory, honor, and peace for everyone who does good: first for the Jew, then for the Gentile. For God does not show favoritism.[22]

He proclaims this immediately before going on to explain how everyone knows right and wrong. So Christianity does claim that a perfect natural religion was handed down once and for all by a perfect God to all of mankind without exception.

How is this truth misused? Like many who take these verses out of context, Tindal mistakenly believes that this is good news. The next portion of Romans goes on to explain why it is not:

> There is no one righteous, not even one; there is no one who understands, no one who seeks God. All have turned away, they have together become worthless; there is no one who does good, not even one.[23]

In order to make Christianity meaningless, the argument for deism requires another hidden premise: that mankind is not broken. Tindal's argument concerns a religion given by God to man. However, the argument only addresses the giver and not the receiver of this natural religion. There is nothing wrong with that religion; man just does not and (now) cannot follow it. When it comes to God's immutability, one must realize that God, in the person of Jesus Christ, did not change the religion that he gave to mankind; He fulfilled it for those of us who did not fulfill it ourselves (i.e. for all of us).

Our purpose must be to deal with the goal of the argument—to demonstrate that mankind is not okay on its own. Furthermore, this can-

---

22. Rom 2:7–11.
23. Rom 3:10–12.

not be due to a deficiency in our design (which would be a fault in the Creator), but through an act of our will. We must show that we choose to do evil when we could choose to do good instead; an approach taken in the previous chapter.

Another deist alive during the same period as Tindal,[24] Peter Annet, held that miracles violated the nature of God. Because God is changeless, and he made all laws governing the universe perfect the first time, any miracles are both unnecessary because of creation's perfection and impossible because of God's immutability.[25]

What is Annet's purpose in making this argument? While the apparent argument is that a Theistic God is impossible, it is once again that the God of the Bible (or any God known apart from natural revelation) is unnecessary and thus cannot really be God.

Why is this argument compelling? The grain of truth found here is that God is perfect, and that he made a flawless universe. He certainly would not act in a particular way because he screwed up the first time.

How is this truth misused? Just because He would not act a certain way for one reason, does not mean He would not act that way for a different reason. Once again, the argument addresses God's perfection but never discusses the attributes of that to which God is relating. Firstly, the argument requires that the universe God created (including humans) remains unbroken, or at least that it is self-correcting. Secondly, the argument requires that the creation itself is changeless. A changeless God may interact with a changed creation in a different way than with an unchanged creation. Thirdly, it implies that God is inside of time going moment to moment rather than eternally outside of time interacting with every moment "at once"—that His interactions change Himself instead of His creation.

Once again, the apologist's goal must be to deal with the goal of the argument, which is to demonstrate that humankind is not fine on its own. As has already been shown, man should know by natural means about the divine attributes of God in a limited sense as well as about goodness. The problem is that even though man knows, he does not *do*. God does not interact with us by miracles and special revelation because He needs to but because we need correction.

---

24. Late 1600's; early 1700's.
25. Geisler, 161.

The deist might go on to argue that any corrective action that God might devise for a broken world should also necessarily be implicit in the original design of the world—that a perfect world would be self-correcting. For example, they might point to natural consequences of actions as God's means of correcting us. One can know *that* this is wrong because the creation is clearly *not* sufficiently self-correcting; the world is not fine.[26] Norman Geisler shows *why* it is wrong as follows:

> The deistic concept of God is built on an invalid mechanistic model rather than a personal model. On this model it is no wonder deists conclude that a "perfect" creation would be one that does not demand personal attention and miraculous intercommunication. For the more perfect the mechanic the more perfect the machine, and the most perfect mechanic could create the most perfect machine that should need no subsequent "tune-ups." However, if God is personal, as even the deistic concept of God would admit, then there is no reason why a "perfect" universe for a personal God would not be one which involves personal attention. Miraculous commerce between the personal Creator and the persons created would not only be possible, it would seem to be the most probable.[27]

The solution for a machine that goes wrong may very well be mechanical, but a solution for persons that go wrong must be personal. We find that solution only in the person of Jesus Christ.

NON-THEISM

As one might imagine, a philosophy that ultimately depends on the idea that mankind and the world are operating exactly as they are meant to by a perfect God leads to quite a bit of confusion. While one might avoid this confusion by accepting that mankind broke itself, one who will not accept such a conclusion is left with only one option: that the world was not actually created by a perfect God. And so, deism leads into atheism.

Atheism tends to come in two varieties. One is often described as "non-theism" and is simply the declaration that one does not believe in God because he has no reason to. The other sort is the claim to relative certainty that God does not exist, which will be addressed later. The non-theistic sort of atheism is often mislabeled as agnosticism. This fact reminds

26. Which goes a long way towards explaining deism's decline.
27. Geisler, 169–70.

us that when speaking to people, one is not speaking to labels. It is better to understand one's beliefs than one's self-appellation. Nevertheless, labels are quite useful when discussing specific beliefs rather than addressing specific individuals. The "non-theism" sort of atheism is usually based on the claim that the existence of God has not been sufficiently proven, and that one should not believe anything that is not sufficiently proven.

Of course, Christians know from Romans that this claim is disingenuous. This has been largely dealt with in the first chapter. If the standards of proof that non-theism typically applies to God (proof beyond *any* possibility of doubt, and without *any* faith-accepted starting points) were applied to everything else, no knowledge would be possible at all. This chapter has already shown that all recognize the reality of God whether He is acknowledged or not. Furthermore, while non-theism tries to make a distinction between "believing that God does not exist" and "not believing that God exists," it ultimately fails. God either exists or he does not, and one believes (and acts) as if either one or the other is true. One cannot wave his hands and inject middle ground into a binary choice. Middle ground may be staked out for something with little relevance to daily life, such as how many stars are in the sky. However, when it comes to whether God exists or not, one can only live as though God exists or as though does not. With all these self-deceptions, it is unsurprising that arguments from this quarter are so miserable.

RUSSELL'S TEAPOT

For example, there is Russell's Teapot. Contemporary versions of this argument involve a "Flying Spaghetti Monster" or "Invisible Pink Unicorn," but whatever the object is, the argument is more or less the same. Bertrand Russell put it this way:

> If I were to suggest that between the Earth and Mars there is a china teapot revolving about the sun in an elliptical orbit, nobody would be able to disprove my assertion provided I were careful to add that the teapot is too small to be revealed even by our most powerful telescopes. But if I were to go on to say that, since my assertion cannot be disproved, it is intolerable presumption on the part of human reason to doubt it, I should rightly be thought to be talking nonsense. If, however, the existence of such a teapot were affirmed in ancient books, taught as the sacred truth every Sunday, and instilled into the minds of children at school, hesitation to

believe in its existence would become a mark of eccentricity and entitle the doubter to the attentions of the psychiatrist in an enlightened age or of the Inquisitor in an earlier time.[28]

The basic idea is that if someone were to make a ridiculous claim like the existence of a flying spaghetti monster out in space that is all-powerful, that one must obey, etc., nobody in their right mind would believe them. So why should one believe someone who substitutes the word "God" for "Flying Spaghetti Monster?" We might possibly believe it if there were sufficient proof, but we would need something extremely compelling.

What is the purpose of making this argument? Ostensibly the purpose is to put the burden of proof on the theist. In actuality, it is to relieve the atheist of the burden of actually defending his belief. As the patterns of "refuting" the cosmological and teleological arguments for God reveal, all it takes is a declaration that any and all evidence that was presented was insufficient—the worth of the evidence with respect to evidence for the opposite claim is often irrelevant. Other purposes might include mockery—it is easier to believe something one knows is false if his opponents (God included) are cast as clowns. Ultimately someone making this argument is laying bait to try and get someone to attempt to prove the existence of God for the purposes of mockery and casual dismissal.

Why is this argument compelling? There are at least two reasons why this argument is believed by people. First of all, it is really true that one should not believe ridiculous stories just because somebody requests it. Secondly, many Christians really have presented "because I say so" or "because the Bible says so" as the best reason to believe in God. We cannot exclusively blame others if they have never heard decent reasoning from Christians.

How is this truth misused? To lead to the desired conclusion, this argument requires the incoherent claim that deductive proof is the only reason we should believe anything.[29] Secondly, it glosses over the question of what really makes a belief ridiculous—it simply asserts that belief in God is as ridiculous as belief in monsters and unicorns. Nobody believes in the teapot, monster, or unicorn. Almost everybody on the planet believes in a god, and the rest act as though a "god" exists. The non-theist

---

28. Russel, "Is there a God?," 547.
29. Refuted in chapters 1 and 2.

is the one who is actually making a claim that is contrary to all basic human standards.

We have a threefold objective in refuting such an argument: (1) to make it as hard as possible for them to believe their opponent is ridiculous; (2) to make it as hard as possible to avoid actually engaging the issue; (3) to refrain from taking the bait or giving the appearance of taking the bait. If one brings up the fact that most people believe in God in some way without being clear that he is not trying to prove God's existence, one's opponent could *rightly* point out that a thing is not necessarily true just because most people believe it.

The claim that logical proof is our only way of knowing can be refuted by logic. For the rest, when Galileo, no doubt a hero to someone who raises this kind of argument, made a claim that contradicted common knowledge, he provided profound evidence that his claim was true. What is more, his evidence rested on other common knowledge.[30] This "nontheistic" kind of argument is merely a flimsy excuse not to actually engage the issue. Sam Harris, in a debate with Rick Warren, demonstrated this when he claimed that he was open to the possibility of the divinity of both Jesus and Zeus. When Warren challenged him to look at the evidence,[31] he responded that the probability of its truth was so low that there was no need to even bother.[32] The disingenuous self-deception in this kind of "argument" should be clear.

ATHEISM PROPER

Even if successful in dealing with such excuses, eventually one must actually engage the issue and deal with open atheism and arguments that come more to the heart of the matter. Atheists' more popular arguments tend to focus on the claim that God clearly does not measure up to some standard or another. Therefore, if He exists, He is not perfect. However, the concept of God requires perfection. Therefore, the idea of God is incoherent, and He therefore cannot really exist. With this in mind, one can understand the cliché of the atheist who simultaneously claims God does not exist and curses Him for wrongdoing. In our darker moments

---

30. Mathematics, the nature of observation, etc.

31. One of the very rare instances during that debate of Warren saying something worthwhile.

32. Newsweek, *God Debate*, para. 42–45.

Christians have all done the latter, and while doing so we have no doubt wondered about the former. The good news is that while there is still self-deception, the open atheist actually struggles with God, unlike the non-theist or agnostic who tries to avoid the struggle altogether. Additionally, these arguments tend to be much more straightforward.

PARADOX OF OMNIPOTENCE

The Paradox of Omnipotence takes many forms (can God stop being omnipotent? Can he make another God, etc), but the classic question is, "Could God make a rock so heavy that he himself could not lift it?" If he could not make such a rock, then he is not omnipotent. If he could not lift such a rock, he his not omnipotent. Therefore, the only conclusion is that an omnipotent God is an impossibility.

What is the purpose of making this argument? The straightforward argument is that God cannot possibly do everything, therefore he is not God. However, if we understand that the Atheist knows God exists, we can see that the argument is not so much to prove that He does not exist as it is to prove that any god a person worships cannot really be all that he claims to be.

Why is this argument compelling? Because this argument is straightforward, we can clearly see why it is compelling. We know contradictions cannot be true, so if God necessitates a contradiction we know He cannot be real.

How is this truth misused? The question that is asked basically comes down to this: "Is God stronger than Himself?" Because God is one and is not divisible, this means that the question itself is incoherent. It is as meaningless as asking "to whom is the bachelor married?" It is not a limitation or qualification on the idea of omnipotence to say that God cannot contradict himself; it is merely a reiteration that He is real.

What is our objective in refuting it? Our purpose is likewise straightforward: to help them realize the incoherency. To paraphrase C. S. Lewis, adding the word "God" to a meaningless statement does not confer meaning upon it. One can then focus on the more productive task of helping them realize why they are so inclined towards asking incoherent questions.

THE PROBLEM OF EVIL

The Problem of Evil remains the most commonly used argument against the existence of God. The basic idea is that God is supposedly all good and all powerful. Nevertheless, there is undeniable evil in the world. If God were really all good and all powerful, He would get rid of all the evil. He clearly has not, so either He cannot or He does not want to. If the former is true, He is not all-powerful. If the latter is true, He is not perfectly good. Either way, one can conclude that a theistic God does not exist.

That would be the most basic exposition of the argument. However, it's one thing to put it in sterile philosophic terms and another to put it in a way that genuinely accesses our intrinsic knowledge. And so, we will deal with the argument in its fullest form. Some say that the best exposition of the argument was written by Dostoevsky in his novel *The Brothers Karamazov*. In one conversation Ivan gives his brother Alyosha the reason for his prior declaration that there is no God. He begins with two stories he had heard (which Dostoevsky based on actual events). This is the first story:

> "This poor child of five was subjected to every possible torture by those cultivated parents. They beat her, thrashed her, kicked her for no reason till her body was one bruise. Then, they went to greater refinements of cruelty—shut her up all night in the cold and frost of a privy, and because she didn't ask to be taken up at night (as though a child of five sleeping its angelic sound sleep could be trained to wake and ask), they smeared her face and filled her mouth with excrement, and it was her mother, her mother did this. And that mother could sleep, hearing the poor child's groans! Can you understand why a little creature, who can't even understand what's done to her, should beat her little aching heart with her tiny fist in the dark and the cold, and weep her meek unresentful tears to dear kind God to protect her?"[33]

And the second:

> "One day a serf boy, a little child of eight, threw a stone in play and hurt the paw of [a] general's favourite hound. 'Why is my favourite dog lame?' He is told that the boy threw a stone that hurt the dog's paw. 'So you did it.' The general looked the child up and down. 'Take him.' He was taken—taken from his mother and kept shut

---

33. Dostoevsky, *The Brothers Karamazov*, 224.

up all night. Early that morning the general comes out on horseback, with the hounds, his dependents, dog-boys, and huntsmen, all mounted around him in full hunting parade. ...and in front of them all stands the mother of the child. The child is stripped naked. He shivers, numb with terror, not daring to cry. . . 'Make him run,' commands the general. 'Run! Run!' shout the dog-boys. The boy runs. . . . 'At him!' yells the general, and he sets the whole pack of hounds on the child. The hounds catch him, and tear him to pieces before his mother's eyes!' . . . Well—what did he deserve? To be shot? To be shot for the satisfaction of our moral feelings?"[34]

Ivan eventually goes on to draw this conclusion:

"I understand, of course, what an upheaval of the universe it will be, when everything in heaven and earth blends in one hymn of praise and everything that lives and has lived cries aloud: 'Thou art just, O lord, for Thy ways are revealed.' When the mother embraces the fiend who threw her child to the dogs, and all three cry aloud with tears, 'Thou art just, O Lord!' then, of course, the crown of knowledge will be reached and all will be made clear. But what pulls me up here is that I can't accept that harmony. . . . I don't want to cry aloud then. . . While there is still time, I hasten to protect myself and so I renounce the higher harmony altogether. It's not worth the tears of that one tortured child who beat itself on the breast with its little fist and prayed in its stinking outhouse, with its unexpiated tears to 'dear, kind God'! It's not worth it, because those tears are unatoned for. They must be atoned for, or there can be no harmony. But how? How are you going to atone for them? Is it possible? By their being avenged? But what do I care for avenging them? What do I care for a hell for oppressors? What good can hell do, since those children have already been tortured? And what becomes of harmony, if there is hell? I want to forgive. I want to embrace. I don't want more suffering. And if the sufferings of children go to swell the sum of sufferings which was necessary to pay for truth, then I protest that the truth is not worth such a price. . . . And so I hasten to give back my entrance ticket, and if I am an honest man I am bound to give it back as soon as possible. And that I am doing. It's not God that I don't accept, Alyosha, only I most respectfully return Him the ticket."[35]

---

34. Dostoevsky, 224–25.
35. Dostoevsky, 226–27.

What is the purpose of making this argument? Ostensibly, the purpose is to prove that a theistic God cannot exist, but once again it remains certain that even the atheist knows that He does. If one does not believe the conclusion that God does not exist, the apologist should step back and examine the premises leading up to it. If he assumes the speaker knows that God exists, then he can conclude that the argument is to show that God is not up to the task of being God, that He has done a poor job, and ultimately that someone else could do a better job given God's power.

Why is this argument compelling? The truth found in this argument is the genuine value one finds in human life, family, and justice. There really is undeniable evil in the world. We know that the described treatment of those children is terrible and without excuse. The reason this argument is so universally compelling is because it directly accesses our natural knowledge of good. Many Christians answer the argument by saying that it is part of God's plan or that it is worth it in the end, as we find in Dostoevsky's exposition. These responses are meant to be comforting, but they tend to be misunderstood as claiming that God wanted and brought about such things. It is true that Jesus makes the former case[36] and Paul makes the latter,[37] but is important to note that they are making those cases to Christians, to people who trust God to some extent. The arguments are nonsensical to anyone who does not trust God at all. What is more, Jesus and Paul can both be understood as referring to the toleration and ultimately the *redemption* of suffering that should not have happened, not to the *intention* of suffering as God's means to an end.

How is this truth misused? Why is it unsound or invalid? The argument cannot be true because it is self-defeating. If one is holding a standard above God, it can only come from one place—the law written on our hearts. However, this chapter has already established how that law actually points *to* God. There are really only two options: complete materialism in the manner of Sartre and Nietzsche, or a set of organized moral goods that actually require a person behind them.

What is more, there can really be things that are worth the suffering, some of which should be easily understood. Evil does not find its source in God, but in mankind. If God were to remove all evil from the world, where would the Atheists and Christians be? Speaking for myself,

---

36. John 9:1–3.
37. Rom 8:28.

I would not exist at 12:01 if God eliminated all evil in the world at 12:00. The nature of free will is that it entails the possibility[38] of evil as well as the possibility of greater goods such as love. As long as humans will evil, removing evil altogether requires the destruction of our wills.

One must also consider the fact that physical pain is commonly understood as an indication that something is wrong. If one touches a hot stove, he feels pain and consequently pulls his hand away before it can be burned. If people felt no pain, they would suffer much more severe damage because they would have no indication that anything is wrong. We can draw a parallel from physical pain to the kind of suffering used in this argument. How could a merciful God allow us to go about our business completely unaware of the kind of horrible damage we do to ourselves and each other when we sin?

What is our objective in refuting it? We must be very careful. If an atheist's objective is to show that God has not done his job in protecting him or a loved one (or humanity in general) from something, then trying to justify God's actions in a way that says that he *mandates* pain and suffering is essentially to say that God not only failed to do anything about their suffering, He wanted it to happen. The fact is, while one can know enough to explain the persistence of evil in general, one does not know enough to explain every specific instance—and when people are truly suffering, they are often perfectly willing to give up their will, existence, or anything else just to make the pain stop. One must not confuse philosophical answers with personal ones, and the apologist must make sure others do not think he is doing so. It is very instructive to remember God's "answer" to Job's complaint about unjust suffering. Of course, if an apologist were to give an atheist God's response, which was basically, "who are you to ask such things," the atheist would rightly recognize that the apologist has no authority to treat him that way. The point is that the response God gives to Job is satisfying to him *only* because it is God's response—because of God's attention and visitation even though He never explained "why." Therefore, one's goal should usually be to show what God has actually done for us as regards evil (the Atonement made by Christ on the Cross) and God's own attitude towards suffering. Whatever reason He has for allowing particular instances of evil, He did not even spare Himself from suffering. We must know that God could wipe out all of creation in an

---

38. Not the necessity.

instant. His acceptance of even His own suffering on our behalf is proof and comfort to us that something really is worth it.

CONCLUSION

This list of arguments is very far from exhaustive, as are the approaches to each of the arguments that are covered. Nevertheless, even if one were to list every known argument, the issue would still not be closed. As long as humanity is both sinful and accountable to God, we have a vested interest in either denying our own evil or denying a God to whom we are accountable. As long as we want to deny Him, we will search for reasons to justify the denial. What is important is that Christians become as skeptical of such arguments as others are skeptical of Christianity. One must know how to refute the arguments, of course, but it is just as important to understand where the argument is coming from. Any argument against theism that can satisfy in any way must somehow be based on truth, but we know that truth belongs to God. Any argument to deny Him must eventually lead back to him as well.

II

HISTORY

Is Christianity True?

5

The New Testament as History

INTRODUCTION

So far, this book has been devoted to philosophical concerns: how reasoning and faith work together, first principles that human beings know to be true by virtue of having a normal human mind, and some of the logical implications of these ideas. However, natural knowledge, while useful, can only take one so far. Even if one were to accept the previous chapters without reservation, they would only take a person to the point of knowing that God exists, that being a good person according to His will is the most important thing for a person to do, and that he has failed miserably at this important task. This is a far cry from a Triune God, the incarnation of God as a man, and the death of that God-Man on behalf of those of us who have failed at being good persons. Furthermore, few if any would be able and willing to follow this reasoning to its end because it paints such a bleak picture—we have done evil in the face of a just God. The bad news is clear enough that we want to turn our faces away from it in the absence of a solution to humankind's dilemma. In short, philosophy and natural reason *might* lead one to accept a generic and thoroughly depressing theism.

Thanks be to God that despite this bad news, there is good news as well. However, this good news does not spring from human minds reflecting on the nature of life, the universe, and everything—no matter how adeptly they might do so. It is therefore necessary to begin looking at the core of Christianity, which needs to be learned rather than reasoned from first principles. The first step in this endeavor is a brief examination of the Bible—the book that, according to Christians, is our source of knowledge on the good news.

WHAT IS THE BIBLE?

According to classical Christianity, the Bible is "the Word of God." Chapter 7 will consider a more precise analysis of what this phrase means, but for now it is sufficient to say that it describes the communication of an omniscient and truthful God to humans and is therefore trustworthy and without error. Most of those born and raised within classically Christian churches have heard this all their lives, and for those who remain within one, it is usually the first description one thinks of when considering the Bible. This is not without reason; "the Word of God" is certainly the most important thing that the Bible is. However, Christians often fall into the trap of thinking that this is the *only* thing the Bible is. For example, well-meaning Christians will often respond to claims that Jesus was just another wise teacher by asserting, "the Bible says Jesus is the Son of God." They respond to claims that there are many roads to God by asserting, "the Bible says Jesus is the only way." These statements may be true, but they are not necessarily the most appropriate assertions in all situations. Quoting the Bible is entirely appropriate when speaking to someone who respects the Bible. Using the Bible as the final arbiter during an argument is appropriate when arguing with someone who accepts it as authoritative.

Unfortunately, fewer and fewer people respect the Bible in a meaningful way, and fewer still actually accept it as authoritative. In fact, many people stop listening as soon as the word "Bible" is mentioned. Christians may mean "Word of God" when they say the word "Bible," but different people will associate different meanings to that word. For example, someone who has intentionally rejected Christianity may think of the Bible as "an old book I'm *supposed* to believe uncritically." Christians often fail to consider the implications of applying that definition to the statements mentioned in the previous paragraph. If a Christian were to merely assert that "some old book you're supposed to believe uncritically says Jesus is the Son of God" or "some old book you're supposed to believe uncritically says that Jesus is the only way," very few—even among Christians—would expect the Christian to be taken seriously. One can therefore begin to see why many people question the "uncritically" part and ask why they should believe everything or even anything the Bible says.[1] Unfortunately, many have asked that question of their parents or pastors or friends at some point and received no real answer. If Christians do not know anything more about the Bible than that it is the Word of God, then they are not equipped to answer such questions.

A Christian can put himself in the shoes of non-Christians by imagining somebody responding to his belief that Mohammad was not a prophet by saying, "but the Qur'an says he is, and the Qur'an is the word of God." Christians are rightly skeptical of such claims about the Qur'an and should therefore expect that others will be skeptical of such claims about the Bible. As such, Christians should be thankful that the Bible can stand up to skepticism.[2] There are good reasons to believe that the Bible is the inerrant Word of God,[3] but this is an audacious claim—it requires a long time to lay out an adequate case for it and an interested listener for the case to be well-received. Derailing a conversation in order to make the case for inerrancy is usually neither polite nor useful. Consequently, it will not be the starting point in this section of the book. The inerrancy of Scripture is a concept that is absolutely fundamental to good theology and to the lives of Christians. However, that concept is not absolutely necessary in order to wrestle with the question of who Jesus is. The Bible itself, however, *is* necessary because it is the primary source of information about him. It therefore behooves one to ask the question: "Why is Scripture worth reading?" Christians need to know Scripture, but we also need to know *about* Scripture.

For now, *in this context*, it is necessary to temporarily set aside the premise that the Bible is the inerrant Word of God. Unbelievers obviously do not accept it. Most Christians have doubts about the truth of that premise at some point in their lives. Consequently, any argument to such individuals for why one should pay attention to the Bible that depends on that premise will be a poor argument. For now, the Bible will be considered from another angle. In the interests of space, this chapter's analysis will focus on the New Testament.

---

1. An entirely appropriate question for Christians and non-Christians alike to honestly ask. To be fair, however, many who ask it are uninterested in actually receiving an answer and are content to use the question alone to dismiss Christianity.

2. In contrast, the Qur'an cannot really stand up to such skepticism, but that is not the subject of this book.

3. Which will be covered in chapter 7.

The Bible,[4] as the name would imply, is obviously literature; but what kind of literature is it? Many consider it a book of inspiring stories that teach important moral lessons. There are certainly no shortage of these in the Bible: the story of Jesus' death can teach us about sacrifice, the stories of Paul's imprisonments can teach us about perseverance, and so on. Others consider it to be a book containing a list of moral precepts and instructions on how to live the best life possible. It certainly contains these as well. From Jesus' instructions to his disciples to Peter's instructions to various churches, there is plenty of such advice.[5] Others see the Bible as an anthology of historical books and letters concerning certain events and the meaning behind them. According to this view, the Bible describes the actual life and actions of Jesus, the missionary journeys of Paul, and a history of God's interactions with humanity.

Most people think the Bible is some combination of these three things; there is, after all, some truth to each of them. It is the third view of the Bible, however, that makes all the difference in the world in how one evaluates Scripture. If one believes that the Bible is *merely* a set of moral precepts or inspiring stories (whether a good one or not), he will interpret it one way; if one thinks it presumes to speak about actual events and their meaning (whether accurately or not), he will interpret it in a completely different way. It is therefore necessary to deal with the question of whether the third view has any meaning—was the Bible intended to communicate anything about history?

THE HISTORICAL NATURE OF SCRIPTURE

Many claim that it does not matter whether the stories in the Bible are historically true or not because they are merely designed to convey certain ideas. This is a very popular view in liberal denominations and within cultural "Christianity."[6] It is also common among political conservatives who find "Judeo-Christian morality" to be very useful, and among those

---

4. From the Greek word for "book."

5. Although Christians should keep in mind that not everyone would consider this advice good—especially the moral teachings that are especially foreign to contemporary America. Several of these teachings will be considered in later chapters.

6. I define "cultural Christianity" as a mere cultural inheritance rather than a religion. For example, a person who does not really know what to think about Jesus or God but goes to church because her parents did could be considered culturally Christian.

who believe that all religions are different ways of saying the same thing. But does the claim hold water?

One can begin to answer this question by looking at the text itself. If one had a book sitting in front of her, and she was curious about what kind of book it was, there are a number of very common approaches she could pursue on her own. Even if third parties said wildly different things about the book, one could still look at the introduction, or the blurb on the back cover, or simply read the text and see for one's self. All of these seem fairly obvious, but what would one find if she examined some of the books contained in the Bible this way? Luke, for example, began his Gospel with the following introduction:

> Many have undertaken to draw up an account of the things that have been fulfilled among us, just as they were handed down to us by those who from the first were eyewitnesses and servants of the word. Therefore, since I myself have carefully investigated everything from the beginning, it seemed good also to me to write an orderly account for you, most excellent Theophilus, so that you may know the certainty of the things you have been taught.[7]

John began one of his letters this way:

> That which was from the beginning, which we have heard, which we have seen with our eyes, which we have looked at and our hands have touched—this we proclaim concerning the Word of Life. The life appeared; we have seen it and testify to it, and we proclaim to you the eternal life, which was with the Father and has appeared to us. We proclaim to you what we have seen and heard, so that you also may have fellowship with us.[8]

The Gospel of John has the following summary towards the end:

> This is the disciple who testifies to these things and who wrote them down. We know that his testimony is true. Jesus did many other things as well. If every one of them were written down, I suppose that even the whole world would not have room for the books that would be written.[9]

There are also any number of places throughout the text which give a clue as to what kind of text each author intended it to be. For example:

7. Luke 1:1–4.
8. 1 John 1:1–3.
9. John 21:24–5.

> By this gospel you are saved, if you hold firmly to the word I preached to you. Otherwise, you have believed in vain. For what I received I passed on to you as of first importance: that Christ died for our sins according to the Scriptures, that he was buried, that he was raised on the third day according to the Scriptures, and that he appeared to Peter, and then to the Twelve. After that, he appeared to more than five hundred of the brothers at the same time, most of whom are still living, though some have fallen asleep. Then he appeared to James, then to all the apostles, and last of all he appeared to me also, as to one abnormally born . . . If Christ has not been raised, our preaching is useless and so is your faith.[10]

And:

> We did not follow cleverly invented stories when we told you about the power and coming of our Lord Jesus Christ, but we were eyewitnesses of his majesty. For he received honor and glory from God the Father when the voice came to him from the Majestic Glory saying, 'This is my Son, whom I love; with him I am well pleased.' We ourselves heard this voice that came from heaven when we were with him on the sacred mountain.[11]

It is very difficult for someone familiar with the book's contents to make an honest claim that it was intended to merely be an inspiring storybook without any attempt to pass the contents off as history. One does not preface a storybook with a claim to the recipient that the author has investigated these events and written up an orderly account if he wanted the recipient to think it was merely a storybook. Nor would one end their book with a claim to have personally witnessed the events contained therein unless he wanted the reader to think the contents actually occurred. Most importantly, a storybook does not claim to be worthless if read merely as a storybook. What is more, the Bible's content is focused on *what was and is done for us,* and only then does it explain what one ought to do in response. It is a rulebook merely to provide context to what was and is done for us.

This is a fairly simplistic and straightforward analysis, but one can certainly approach it with more rigor as well. As an example of what such an approach can entail, one can look at Richard Bauckham's es-

---

10. 1 Cor 15:2–8,14.
11. 2 Pet 1:16–8.

say, "Historiographical Characteristics of the Gospel of John."[12] In it, Bauckham examines a wide variety of indications that John's Gospel was intended to portray historical fact as a part of its theological message. Among other textual features, he notes the frequency with which the author provides specific names for the places at which the recorded events take place. He observes the many chronological details recorded, placing the events in relation to various Jewish festivals. Most importantly, he considers the importance of the author's portrayal of himself as an eyewitness. Bauckham argues that the author places himself within the narrative in the third person at important events, and makes himself out to be someone who could reliably know about other events. All of these features within the text indicate that it was concerned with historical detail and was intended to be taken as accurate in what it recorded.

Although the view that the Bible was intended to be read as *merely* an inspiring book is untenable, it is not difficult to see where it comes from in American culture at large. The Church itself often treats the Bible this way through the stories in Sunday School and the handful of verses read out of context every week. What is more, most people (Christians included) are only passingly familiar with the book's contents. Many people do not realize it even makes claims of historical authenticity. Finally, the Bible is more useful for purposes such as achieving political goals or as a guide to certain kinds of right living if it is treated merely as a storybook or rule book. It has been quoted profusely for thousands of years because of its many intriguing messages. Nevertheless, one of the messages it obviously tries to convey is that it is an accurate account of what actually transpired. None of this indicates that any of the historical content is accurate, but it does provide weighty evidence that the authors intended their readers to believe that the content is historical.

IS THE BIBLE A RELIABLE SOURCE ABOUT ITS SUBJECT?

If the Bible claims to be reliable about the historical details of the birth, life, and death of Christ, one must also look at whether this claim itself is trustworthy. In making a case for the historical details, one must remember that he cannot argue a person into faith in the person written about. As in the first several chapters, the Christian's task is more along the lines of defending against contrary theories (e.g. Christianity has no historical

12. Bauckham, *Testimony*, 93–112.

basis, it is pure fiction, etc.) and at the same time to make it as hard as possible to avoid an encounter with the real Jesus Christ by hiding behind such theories. To do this, one needs to know that and how it is reasonable to believe what the Bible tells us. In evaluating the Bible's claims, there are several questions one needs to consider. Because the Bible repeatedly claims to rely on eyewitness accounts, the first question is, "Are these the same books that were originally written down?" That is, are readers today actually looking at eyewitness accounts?

One of the most common claims is that the Bible is a copy of a copy of a copy and a translation of a translation of a translation. Who can say what was originally written within it? Obviously, when one is dealing with copies and translations, one is probably dealing with some degree of information loss. When one is claiming that the Bibles available today are a result of compounded copies and translations, one is claiming that the Bible contains little of the original meaning. Anyone who has played the children's game "telephone" or who has been involved in gossip understands this phenomenon.[13] At each transmission, a little bit of the original message is removed or some unoriginal message is added through simple unintentional error. When applied to the Bible, the claim is that even if eyewitnesses did write down an account of the life of Jesus, modern readers do not really have access to that account—merely to a few bits and pieces of it. Furthermore, they cannot ever be sure which bits and pieces are actually from the original; they can only speculate.

If one were to investigate whether information was lost through compounded translations, all one needs to do is compare translations to copies in the original language. Koine Greek, the language of the New Testament, has hardly been lost to the ages, nor has Hebrew, the language of the Old Testament. Most modern Bibles are not translations of translations of translations; they are merely translations, period. There are, of course, disagreements over details, but accurate translation of the Bible is as possible as translation of anything else. For theologians and pastors who require greater precision with the details, it remains possible to learn the original languages at any number of schools. Of course, translators can and often do make mistakes, but such mistakes are insufficient to

---

13. In "telephone," one person writes down a message and without showing the paper, whispers it to the person next to him. That person whispers it to the next and so on. The last person tells everyone the message he heard which is then compared to the original. There is usually very little resemblance.

support a categorical dismissal of a book's contents. If one is to allege an error, one must provide evidence for it.

The charge of information loss through frequent copying is likewise not beyond the grasp of investigation. To examine it, one need only look at the many different copies and see how much and where each manuscript differs from the others. For example, if there was one original manuscript by the author and ten copies were made, one would expect each copy to contain different errors. If ten new copies were made of each those first copies, one would expect the original errors in each to persist in the ten new copies made from each original copy. One would also expect to see new errors introduced. The end result would be that each of those hundred copies would have different sets of errors. Some errors would be common because they reflect errors made in the first copies, but few of the manuscripts would be exactly alike. If this were to happen again and again through the centuries, the end result should be many different manuscripts with many different errors. The question then becomes whether the Biblical manuscripts fit this description.

Unlike many other pieces of ancient literature for which only a handful early copies exist—and unlike the New Testament, the earliest copy is usually dated to many centuries after the original—there are 5,686 ancient Greek manuscripts of the New Testament which can be compared to each other.[14] After the time during which all those copies were made, there should be some common differences from manuscripts belonging to common branches and other errors unique to each manuscript. If the copying errors really destroyed the original message, all of those manuscripts would be in wild disagreement. In reality, this is not the case. In *Christian Apologetics*, Norman Geisler argues that the results of such a comparison show that of the 20,000 lines in the New Testament, only forty show variance. The means the New Testament copies are roughly 99.5 percent accurate with respect to what was originally written (only about 400 words are in significant doubt.)[15]

Such precision precludes a categorical dismissal of the Bible's contents due to errors creeping in over the centuries. As with translation errors, one must provide evidence that a specific part of the text is in error.

---

14. MacDowell, Josh, *New Evidence*, 34.
15. Geisler, *Apologetics*, 308.

For example, John 7:53—8:11 is almost certainly a later addition.[16] It is missing from several important manuscripts, and the manuscripts that do include it put it in different places.[17] This could be sufficient evidence for one who wanted to reject this particular story as untrustworthy, but one cannot then label the entire work as untrustworthy when the manuscripts are all in agreement on most of the rest. When it comes to copies and translations, one must remember that the possibility or probability of mistakes do not mean that a mistake *must* have happened. If someone makes such a claim, he needs evidence to support it. In light of the incomparable manuscript evidence for the New Testament, the most reasonable conclusion is that modern readers have virtually the same books that were originally written.

Once this is clear, it leads to another question: even if the Bible has largely the same content as what was originally written down, why should anyone believe the content was not false from the very beginning? The basic idea in such an objection is that inaccuracies in the account crept in through embellishment and mistakes by the authors rather than through errors in communication. In short, the charge is that the stories contained in the New Testament are legend rather than history. Jesus was a great man, and over time his followers began exaggerating their stories about him. Consequently, instead of a great teacher, modern readers hear about a miracle-working God. To establish whether such a charge is credible, there are a number of elements that must be examined.

1. When and by whom were the books written?
2. Are these witnesses believable?
3. Is the story presented in the Bible consistent with other sources?

DATING OF THE GOSPELS

It takes time for legends to develop around particular events because they tend to be hampered by people who were actually there and know what

---

16. This is the story of the woman caught in the act of adultery. She is going to be stoned when Jesus prevents it, famously saying, "If any one of you is without sin, let him be the first to throw a stone at her." The fact that it is an addition does not necessarily mean that it is false—it could be a true oral tradition written down later—however, it is not as trustworthy as the rest of John's Gospel.

17. Barker et al., *NIV Study Bible*, 1611.

really happened. It is therefore necessary to determine how close the New Testament manuscripts are to the events they describe. Who wrote them and when?

In order to date Matthew, Mark, and Luke—usually referred to as the synoptic Gospels—one must understand the relationship between them. Many of the accounts contained within them are common to all; they describe the same events in slightly different ways. Such profound similarities show that the Gospels are interdependent in some way—that some of the authors referenced a previously written Gospel when writing their own. There are, of course, disagreements among scholars over which Gospels came first and whether there are other sources to which more than one of them referred. However, just because not all questions are conclusively answered does not mean we know nothing at all. For example, it is reasonable to conclude that Luke was not written first, because in the introduction quoted earlier in this chapter the author clearly implies that he used other sources when writing.

Luke and Acts are key in dating the synoptic Gospels. These two books were written to the same person, "Theophilus," and by the same author.[18] As this author points out, Acts picks up right where the Gospel of Luke left off. Norman Geisler argues that these two books were written by Luke, the doctor who was with Paul when he wrote to the Colossians.[19] He observes that certain sections in Acts were written in the first person, indicating that the author was among Paul's companions during those missionary journeys.[20] Luke is the only one of Paul's close companions that is not mentioned by name in Acts, and is therefore the remaining candidate for authorship. Certain aspects of the work, such as the high quality of the writing and the medical terminology used, support this conclusion.[21] Luke's authorship of the two books is also uniformly supported by early church writings.[22] Nobody in the early church ever believed that anyone other than Luke wrote these books.

Acts can be pretty firmly dated at around A.D. 60-62 because the narrative ends with Paul's arrival in Rome and his imprisonment there. It

---

18. Luke 1:1–4 and Acts 1:1–3.
19. Col 4:14.
20. Acts 16:10–17, 20:5–15, 21:1–18, 27:1—28:16.
21. Geisler, 312.
22. Barker, 1532.

never mentions anything about Paul's subsequent execution in A.D. 67.[23] Because Paul was a principle subject of the book, it would have been very odd not to mention his martyrdom if it had actually been written after the execution occurred. Because Acts was a follow-up to the Gospel of Luke, the Gospel was clearly written earlier still. The Gospel of Luke can therefore be solidly dated to less than thirty years after Christ's death. If Luke used portions of the Gospel of Mark when writing as is commonly held, that would mean that Mark was written even earlier. Matthew, which also quotes Mark[24] would also have an early date.

A case can be made that the Gospel of John also stands very close to the historical circumstances. At the end of the Gospel, the claim is made that the book was written by "the disciple whom Jesus loved," a phrase used several times to describe one character in the narrative.[25] The nature of this phrase, the disciple's interesting relationship with Peter,[26] his presence at so many key moments, and the fact that Jesus entrusted his mother to this disciple's care indicate that the disciple belongs to the "inner circle" of Peter, James, and John.[27] He is obviously not Peter, and James' early martyrdom makes him an unlikely candidate. The authorship of John is also uniformly supported by early Christian writers. Among them, as Geisler notes, "the testimony of Irenaeus is crucial because only one generation stood between him and John. John's disciple, Polycarp, was among Irenaeus' teachers."[28] What is more, a fragment of the book dated to A.D. 117 was found all the way in Egypt.[29] It all adds up to a firsthand account of Christ's life by one of his closest disciples written solidly within the first century.

In addition to the four Gospels, there are also the many letters of Paul. Clearly, these must have been written prior to his death in 67. According to Geisler, there is only substantial debate about his author-

---

23. Geisler, 312.

24. Or as some argue, Matthew is quoted by both Mark and Luke.

25. John 13:23, 19:26, 20:2, 21:7, 20, 24.

26. This disciple made sure to mention twice that he beat Peter to the empty tomb in 20:4 and 8, that he relayed Peter's question to Jesus at the Last Supper in 13:23–25, and that he trailed Jesus and Peter during their final conversation in the Gospel.

27. These three share a special prominence and closeness to Jesus in the synoptic Gospels.

28. Geisler, 310.

29. Geisler, 310.

ship on 1 and 2 Timothy and Titus. Even if one were to exclude those epistles, there are still ten other letters written by Paul that attest to the major points in Jesus' life, including the most "preposterous" parts, like his divinity, resurrection, and virgin birth.[30] Paul was, of course, not one of the original twelve apostles, but he was certainly not preaching and writing independently of those who knew Jesus personally, as his letter to the Galatians attests.[31] Although much is made of his conflict with Peter, this does not prevent the other apostle from calling him a brother and referring to his letters as Scripture.[32] The book of Acts also indicates that Paul's message did not contradict that of the original apostles.

Of course, this analysis is far from exhaustive. There are many other books in the New Testament, and the details given on the books considered here are obviously not complete. This book's purpose is not to be exhaustive, and there are many good sources out there for those interested in a more in-depth study. Nevertheless, one needs to be clear that dating and authorship are not based on voodoo or the say-so of modern Christians. It is arrived at by looking at the books themselves, at what people said about them, and the circumstances surrounding them—just as one would examine any other historical literature.

So, merely from the subset of authors mentioned, there are the accounts of two of Jesus' disciples (Matthew and John), Peter's secretary (Mark),[33] Paul (who was in frequent contact with Jesus' disciples) and his companion (Luke), who closely investigated the events. What is more, not only are most of these people themselves witnesses, they also refer to many other eyewitnesses in addition to themselves. This is an excellent set of sources for any person of antiquity to say the very least.

ARE THE AUTHORS TRUSTWORTHY?

In any decent justice system, if there are witnesses to an event, it is basic detective work to investigate and evaluate whether their stories are reliable. What does such an examination say about the stories of the New Testament authors? Perhaps the most common reaction to this question is to assert that because these witnesses report miracles—something

30. Geisler, 309.
31. Gal 2.
32. 2 Pet 3:15–16.
33. Clifford, *Leading,* 18, 20, 23.

relatively few people have witnessed—they are therefore untrustworthy. However, such an assertion has nothing to do with the evidence; it is a philosophical assumption. If, as the previous chapters have argued, we have strong reason to accept a theistic worldview, then it is also an unfounded assumption. Even with such unfair objections set aside, however, the question remains whether these witnesses are trustworthy. Even if it was written by people who were familiar with the historical circumstances, what is to say these people were not lying or exaggerating? There are a number of points that make such a scenario highly unlikely.

First, the number of different witnesses provides ample opportunity for discovering inconsistencies between the different accounts. Those given in the four Gospels differ in which details are provided, but they can be easily harmonized. For example, in *Leading Lawyers' Case for the Resurrection*, Ross Clifford notes the different ways in which the four Gospels record the inscription placed above the cross.[34] Matthew records, "This is Jesus, the King of the Jews." Mark, in his typical brevity, records, "The King of the Jews." Luke records, "This is the King of the Jews," and John records, "Jesus of Nazareth, the King of the Jews."[35] Because of the differences in which details are recorded, there is no reason to believe there was a conspiracy by which the writers attempted to get their false stories straight. Nevertheless, they all complement each other by recording the same sense of the words used. Furthermore, the details are not contradictory; all four would be appropriate quotations from a sign that read, "This is Jesus of Nazareth, the King of the Jews." Also, as John notes, the sign was written in multiple languages, and so the phrasing could be slightly different between them.[36] This is exactly the sort of situation one would expect from multiple people honestly describing the same event. Some will point out different details than others or consider different details important, but they will still tell the same story. The Gospels are full of such complementary accounts—very unlikely to be the work of liars.

Second, if the Gospels were lies, their character as purported eyewitness testimony should have made the lies obvious to their original readers. They provide sufficient detail in their testimony that the accounts could have been questioned and confirmed by the readers. They mention

---

34. Clifford, 60–61.
35. Matt 27:37, Mark 15:26, Luke 23:38, and John 19:19.
36. John 19:20.

many witnesses (often by name) who could have been located and questioned. For example, Jesus appeared to different people after his death again and again. He appeared to the women at the tomb,[37] to crowds,[38] to Peter alone,[39] to the disciples together,[40] to his half-brother James,[41] and many others. Those people appearing in the Bible may often seem like characters to those of us who first heard about them in Sunday School, but these were actual people that were known in the Church. The Gospels are also specific about different locales at which the recorded events took place. As Clifford notes, whereas liars typically say as little as possible in order to avoid detection, the Gospel writers provide substantial details that can be cross-checked.[42]

Thirdly, the witnesses themselves were initially skeptical about what had occurred. Mark and Luke both record that the reports of the women who found the tomb empty were initially disbelieved by the apostles.[43] According to John, Thomas would not even believe the other ten disciples until he had actually touched Jesus and confirmed his identity by the wounds received during the crucifixion.[44] Paul had dedicated his career to hunting down and persecuting those who believed the same things he himself would later proclaim after encountering the risen Jesus. These men required proof themselves, and they record it in the process of explaining the circumstances. For example, they record that Jesus breathed on them, ate in their presence, and took other action to demonstrate his physical presence.[45] These demonstrations were sufficient that many of them underwent persecution and martyrdom because of their proclamation. As many have noted, people may die for what they believe to be true but not for what they *know* to be false. Once again, there is no reason to think they are liars.

---

37. Matt 28:9–10 and John 20:15–17.
38. 1 Cor 15:6.
39. Luke 24:34, 1 Cor 15:5.
40. Acts 1:6–11, Matt 28:16–20, John 21:4–14, and many others.
41. 1 Cor 15:7.
42. Clifford, 49.
43. Mark 16:13 and Luke 24:11.
44. John 20:24–28.
45. John 20:22, Luke 24:40–43.

ARE THE REPORTS CONSISTENT WITH SECULAR HISTORY?

Another examination that could demonstrate the falsity of the New Testament's reports is a comparison to other sources. Is the New Testament in rampant contradiction to everything else written about that time and place, or is it consistent with secular history of the time? This is not to ask whether everything in the New Testament can be reconstructed purely from secular sources as if they were the only sources that matter. This is to question whether there are sources that confirm the settings and details of Jesus' life and death or if such sources contradict the New Testament.

One can find several such references in the works of Flavius Josephus, a Jewish historian who lived in the first century.[46] For example, when Josephus talks about the Ananias the High Priest in *Antiquities of the Jews*, he writes,

> ... he assembled the Sanhedrin of the judges, and brought before them the brother of Jesus, who was called Christ, whose name was James, and some others, and when he had formed an accusation against them as breakers of the law, he delivered them to be stoned.[47]

Passages such as this one corroborate many points contained in the New Testament—in this case, the existence of Jesus, the claim that he was the Messiah, and the existence of a brother named James. Josephus' works also confirm many other minor details of the New Testament account. F.F. Bruce describes Josephus as referring to many of the political and religious leaders mentioned in the New Testament: the Herods; a number of high priests and Caesars; religious groups like the Pharisees and Sadducees; and many others.[48]

There are also pagan historians who confirm a basic outline of Jesus' life that matches what is described in the New Testament. For example, Roman historian Cornelius Tacitus (late first and early second century) wrote this about Nero's blaming of Christians for the burning of Rome:

> Hence to suppress the rumor, he falsely charged with the guilt, and punished with the most exquisite tortures, the persons commonly called Christians, who were hated for their enormities. Christus, the founder of the name, was put to death by Pontius

---

46. McDowell, 55–57.
47. Josephus, *Antiquities*, 423.
48. Bruce, *New Testament Documents*, 104.

> Pilate, procurator of Judea in the reign of Tiberius: but the pernicious superstition, repressed for a time broke out again, not only through Judea, where the mischief originated, but through the city of Rome also.[49]

The picture painted here is very compatible with that given in the New Testament, with the obvious exception that Christians did not consider their own faith to be a superstition.

Finally, there are even several sources from non-Christians who corroborate the occurrence of miraculous events in Jesus' life. Geisler[50] and Josh McDowell[51] both note a portion of the Jewish Talmud that describes the circumstances surrounding Jesus' death:

> On the eve of Passover Yeshu [of Nazareth] was hanged. For forty days before the execution took place, a herald went forth and cried, "He is going forth to be stoned because he has practiced sorcery and enticed Israel to apostasy. . ." But since nothing was brought forward in his favour he was hanged on the eve of the Passover![52]

This confirms certain events regarding Christ's death as put forward in the Gospels, but it also shows that the Gospel writers honestly recorded the arguments their opponents, the Pharisees, made against Jesus. They did not dispute that Christ performed miracles, but instead claimed that He did so by the power of Satan (sorcery).[53] Thallus, a first century historian whose work is lost except in quotations, was described by Julius Africanus as referring to the unnatural darkness surrounding the crucifixion. Thallus apparently attributed it to a solar eclipse, but Julius notes that such an explanation is impossible. The full moon occurring at the time of Passover precludes the possibility of a Solar eclipse.[54] Here there is confirmation of a miraculous event in the New Testament by someone who did not even believe it was miraculous.

There are more examples, but the general consensus among historians of the time is that Jesus was a real and extraordinary person, who was executed by Pontius Pilate at Passover, that his disciples claimed that he

---

49. Geisler, 323.
50. Geisler, 324–25.
51. McDowell, 58.
52. McDowell, 58.
53. Matt 12:24.
54. Geisler, 324.

had risen from the dead after three days, and that they followed him still. This is all very compatible with the accounts given in the Bible. There is nothing in the secular history of the time that must lead one to reject the New Testament as inaccurate.

SOME POSSIBLE OBJECTIONS

Of course, there are a number of objections to this kind of analysis. For example, the arguments for the early writing of the Gospels by eyewitnesses used the testimony of early Christian writers like Polycarp and Irenaeus. Some would argue that it is improper to use the Biblical writers or other early Christian writers as sources for the authenticity of the Bible because these people are biased in favor of Christianity. The important thing to note here is exactly what the Church is at that point in history. It is the collection of people who believe that the events recorded in the New Testament actually happened. Sources from outside the Church were exclusively those who were not convinced. To only accept convincing evidence from people who were not convinced is hardly a fair standard. Exclusively looking at evidence from those who hold the contrary viewpoint is hardly unbiased. The vast majority of evidence for an event may come from those who are convinced of it, but that is to be expected. A better method would be to compare the evidence from both sides. The dearth of evidence of falsehood from the unconvinced of the time is noteworthy; most secular mentions of Christ make it clear that they do not believe, but never make a case as to why.

There are also many scholars who dispute the early dating of the New Testament. However, according to J.P. Moreland, the case for a later date generally rests on two arguments. The first accepts what has already been noted: that it takes time for legends to develop. They then assert that the miraculous events in the New Testament are clearly legendary. The conclusion is that they must have been written later. The second argument is based on the fact that some of the gospels mention the destruction of Jerusalem in 70 A.D. The conclusion is that they must have been written after the destruction of Jerusalem.[55]

The problems with such arguments should be obvious. Firstly, they beg the question. They need to assume that the miraculous events described in the Gospels are false in order to argue that the Gospels contain

---

55. Moreland, "A Legendary Jesus," paragraph 13.

false stories because they were written later. In this context, the veracity of these events is the very point at question, and so this would be circular reasoning. One might make the deductive argument that the Gospels must be false because miracles cannot *possibly* occur or because we cannot *possibly* know if miracles occur. However, as was noted earlier, this is a philosophical argument that has nothing to do with evidence, so answering it requires approaches detailed in the first four chapters and the case laid out for a theistic world—a world in which miracles are possible and knowable.

The final kind of counterargument that is often made focuses on "maybe." Maybe the New Testament documents were simply crafted a century or more later in order to be passed off as authentic. Maybe all the evidence to the contrary was destroyed by the Church. Maybe all this "evidence" was created by Paul and Peter in a grand conspiracy to save Jewish morality. Maybe Jesus was an alien with advanced technology instead of the Sod of God.[56] The varieties of this kind of argument are endless. But refuting them usually amounts to asking the same question asked of Christians: what is the evidence for the given explanation? The case laid out in this chapter does not argue that there is no other *possible* explanation, but that the truth of these events is the *best* explanation for the facts that we possess. If somebody wants to suggest a different explanation, he needs to be prepared to back it up, just as Christians need to be prepared. It is reasonable to believe that the New Testament is historically accurate. If a person is committed to shifting again and again between various possible but ridiculous explanations, then it is appropriate to ask him why he is so afraid of the reasonable explanation.

CONCLUSION

This case is not exhaustive, either in the case for the reliability of the New Testament or the case against. Many people have spent a lot of time in close study of this subject. Most of us—Christians and non-Christians alike—are unlikely to do the same. Few are experts, and most of us probably do not intend to become experts. Nevertheless, the fact that one does not know as much as the experts need not mean that one knows less than he actually knows. One need not believe that the Bible is historical by uncritically accepting what experts say. There is no magic or voodoo

---

56. Some of these may sound silly, but I have heard every last one.

involved. Thus, one ought to be able to correct those who think that this book can only be accepted uncritically and consequently will not bother to even look at it. Christians may come to believe that the Bible is true by faith (whether as adults or children), but it is reasonable for us to believe it as well. There is no clarion call from reason or evidence to abandon Christianity. To the contrary, both suggest that Christianity is true.

6

Who Does Jesus Say that He Is?

INTRODUCTION

THE HISTORICAL FACTS PROVIDED by the New Testament raise questions that go beyond simple insight into the specifics of a certain time and place. While knowledge of history is fine, it is not in mere trivia that a person finds hope. Therefore, if Christians are to provide a reason for the hope that is within us, we must consider where the facts of history lead. In the arena of Christian apologetics, philosophy and historical evidence are ultimately without merit unless they eventually present the point of Christianity: the person and work of Jesus Christ. The information provided in the New Testament allows one to do just that.

Many people who are reluctant to accept Christianity often remain eager to have Jesus on their side in an ideological squabble. A typical Christian has probably heard of many different versions of Jesus who champion all sorts of different causes. There is, for example, the Marxist Jesus, who taught His followers all about the redistribution of wealth from the rich to the poor. There is Jesus the moral teacher who came to reform the government by denouncing vices like pornography and gambling. There is the tolerant Jesus who came to reform society by getting rid of things like prejudice and intolerance. There is the progressive Jesus whose purpose was to throw off the shackles of the old dominant religion and move forward to a more enlightened one. There is the hippie Jesus, who just wanted us all to have fond feelings for each other and get along. There is even the Jesus the political rebel who, if around today, would be up with a militia in Montana plotting to overthrow the U.S. government by force.

As bizarre as some of these are, there is at least some element of truth in each—some reason for a person to accept such an image. Jesus did instruct the rich to give their money to the poor; was found in opposition to dominant religious groups like the Pharisees and Sadducees; gave us the one Bible verse any American can quote off the top of her head, "Judge not lest ye be judged yourselves"; pronounced blessings on the peacemakers and judgment upon sinners; and refused to comply when the government gave Him instructions that were contrary to His Father's will. Of course, the same Jesus who told the rich young man to give all his money to the poor also said that the poor would always be with us. The Jesus who was concerned with moral fortitude told us His kingdom was not of this world and ate with sinners. The Jesus who opposed the Pharisees said that the foundational religious book in that culture was the word of God Himself. The tolerant Jesus, after telling us how looking at a woman lustfully is wrong, says that if a person's right eye causes him to sin, he should gouge it out and throw it away because that is better than going to Hell. The can't-we-all-just-get-along Jesus said He came to bring a sword rather than peace. The political rebel Jesus peacefully submitted to execution at the hands of the corrupt authorities. Each of these versions of Jesus is far too shallow.

Nevertheless, if such a diverse crowd wants Jesus on their side, there must be a relatively high opinion of Him in general. Jesus is far too influential to simply be ignored, and many people have picked up on and used His social commentary and teachings on morality. Consequently, the idea that Jesus was a great teacher is very common, even if one only has a simplistic knowledge of what He taught. As long as Jesus is merely an idea or a symbol who has been labeled a great teacher, it is only natural to use Him as a mascot for various causes. However, as the previous chapter has shown, Jesus is not an idea or a symbol but a well-documented man who lived in the Middle East two millennia ago. He is a participant in history who claimed to be much more. Because there are relevant and accessible historical documents concerning Him, one can know the truth of what this great teacher taught. It makes sense, then, to consider a topic on which Jesus was very outspoken: Himself.

WHO DID JESUS CLAIM TO BE?

In Matthew 16:13–15, Jesus asks His disciples who people say that He is. Their response shows that much like people today, Jesus' contemporaries had a wide variety of views on the subject. Jesus' concern stemmed from the fact that His identity was a central aspect of His teachings. In *History & Christianity*, John Warwick Montgomery contrasts Jesus with another famous man who was executed after irritating the authorities of his day: Socrates. While Socrates incessantly questioned people about themselves in hopes that they would examine their own lives, Jesus caused friction by questioning people about their beliefs concerning Himself.[1] The fact that Jesus' teachings on precisely this topic were the teachings that led to His execution[2] suggests their peculiar nature. One of Jesus' most outlandish claims is the very one most consistently denied by non-Christians today—Jesus claimed that He was God in the monotheistic sense. Perhaps the clearest example can be found in the Gospel of John in a record of a dispute over whether Jesus was the Christ.[3] At one point, Jesus tells His opponents, "I and the Father are one." They immediately attempt to stone Him for blasphemy "because you, a mere man, claim to be God." Jesus does not then explain to His opponents how they misunderstood Him and that He was not really claiming to be God, but rather speaking metaphorically. Nor does Jesus give a further nuance to His statements and say that in a sense His opponents are also one with the Father, as one might argue from a "New Age" point of view. He instead goes on to argue from the Old Testament—which His opponents ostensibly accepted as God's Word—that there is no inherent contradiction in God also being man.[4] He then goes on the argue that His opponents should accept His unique claim as true on the basis of His miracles. This was not the only time He made claims to deity. Others can be found in John 8:58, in which He calls himself by the name of "I AM," which God gave Himself in the Old Testament, and also in Mark 14:61–64 in the aforementioned record of His trial.

---

1. Montgomery, *History*, 12.
2. Mark 14:61–64 and John 19:7.
3. John 10:24–39.
4. Jesus argues based on Psalm 82:6, in which leaders are referred to as "gods" (note the lower-case "g"). He then compares this with himself indicating that he can be even more accurately referred to as God based on his relationship to the Father (being one with Him, as he said in John 10:30). Jesus' argument also precludes the idea that he was claiming to be God in some pantheistic sense (in which God is not distinct from the world and everything is a different manifestations of God). Jesus very clearly applies this to himself in a *unique* way, calling himself "the one whom the Father set apart as his very own and sent into the word" in John 10:36 as part of his argument.

If Jesus had only made a bizarre claim disconnected from His other teachings and actions, one could perhaps legitimately interpret it in a non-literal way. However, not only did Jesus make the overt claim to be God, He treated himself as God in a variety of ways. In Mark 2:1–12, Jesus is recorded as forgiving the sins of a man who was brought to Him. Not only did the religious context of the time indicate that only God could forgive sins, as those present quickly recognized,[5] but forgiving a stranger's sins is an audacious thing to do in virtually any circumstance. Jesus is also recorded as allowing people to worship Him in multiple instances.[6] One must also consider the many different ways in which Jesus referred to himself. For example, He calls himself "the good shepherd" and "the light of the world."[7] These were not simply feel-good phrases, but as Norman Geisler notes, ways of describing God taken from the Old Testament itself (Psalms 23:1 and 27:1 respectively).[8] He even calls himself "the Son of Man" regularly in the Gospels. This term comes from the book of Daniel in which a figure referred to as "the Son of Man" is described this way:

> In my vision at night I looked and there before me was one like a son of man, coming with the clouds of heaven. He approached the Ancient of Days and was led into his presence. He was given authority, glory and sovereign power; all peoples, nations and men of every language worshiped him. His dominion is an everlasting dominion that will not pass away, and his kingdom is one that will never be destroyed.[9]

This is not an appellation which somebody who merely thinks of himself as an extremely good teacher would apply to himself. Indeed, Jesus' opinion of His own teachings was exceptionally high. Chapter 7 will more precisely describe the esteem in which Jesus held the Old Testament, but for now it will suffice to note that He believed it came from God Himself. Nevertheless, Jesus took it upon himself to set His own teachings at the same level as the Old Testament. He called himself "the Lord of the Sabbath" during a dispute over the Third Commandment.[10] In the Sermon

---

5. As recorded in vs. 7.
6. Matt 14:33, 28:17; John 9:38, 20:28.
7. John 10:11, 8:12.
8. Geisler, *Apologetics*, 331.
9. Dan 7:13–14.
10. Luke 6:5.

on the Mount, Jesus repeatedly used the pattern, "You have heard it said . . . , but I say to you . . . " while comparing the Old Testament with His own teachings.[11] As highly as He valued the Old Testament, Jesus had no problem placing His own teachings alongside of it.

WHO DO WE SAY JESUS IS?

Such consistently audacious teachings are not something even a great merely human teacher should be able to utter with a straight face. Unlike other religious figures, Jesus did not claim to simply know and tell people a new way to please God and be rewarded by Him; Jesus claimed to *be* the way himself. He said, "I *am* the light of the world. Whoever follows me will never walk in darkness, but will have the light of life."[12] He said, "I *am* the gate for the sheep. Whoever enters through me will be saved."[13] He said, "I *am* the resurrection and the life. He who believes in me will live, even though he dies; and whoever lives and believes in me will never die."[14] He said, "I *am* the way and the truth and the life. No one comes to the Father except through me."[15] As was previously suggested, the charges against Him were centered solely on who He had claimed to be. Jesus was not condemned for telling everyone how to get along or for being a great moral teacher, but for the identity He claimed for Himself: the Christ, the Son of God. In light of these facts, anyone who is considering Jesus and His teachings must ask a similar question to the one Jesus himself posed: Who do I say that Jesus is?

A teacher who happened to teach a good thing now and again in the midst of a large amount of highly questionable teachings can hardly be called a great teacher. After all, even a stopped clock is right twice a day. A great teacher consistently teaches great things. The common situation in which people respond to Jesus' moral teachings apart from His statements about himself and consider Him a great teacher is what led C.S. Lewis to formulate his famous trilemma:

> I am trying here to prevent anyone saying the really foolish thing that people often say about Him: "I'm ready to accept Jesus as a

---

11. Matt 5:1–7:29.
12. John 8:12.
13. John 10:9.
14. John 11:25.
15. John 14:6.

great moral teacher, but I don't accept His claim to be God." That is the one thing we must not say. A man who was merely a man and said the sort of things Jesus said would not be a great moral teacher. He would either be a lunatic—on a level with the man who says he is a poached egg—or else he would be the Devil of Hell. You must make your choice. Either this man was, and is, the Son of God: or else a mad man or something worse. You can shut Him up for a fool, you can spit at Him and kill Him as a demon; or you can fall at His feet and call Him Lord and God. But let us not come up with any patronizing nonsense about His being a great human teacher. He has not left that open to us. He did not intend to.[16]

If Jesus was not God, then He either knew He was not God, or wrongly thought He was God. If the former is true, then it is a lie that makes Him the worst kind of megalomaniac imaginable. If it is the latter, he was the kind of person modern people would lock up for treatment and His own protection. He was not the kind of man who can be called upon to support a cause that is apart from His own.

In light of this, one could claim that Jesus really was a liar or lunatic; that (perhaps like every so-called prophet) He was completely out of His mind but also extremely charismatic; that He gathered a large following that became infected with a message born from the voices in His head. How could one know that Jesus is not a liar or a lunatic? If one ran into somebody on the street who talked like Jesus, how could one know He was both sane and telling the truth? Why would one even think to bother making an evaluation rather than just dismissing Him?

In the case of Jesus, there is a reason so many consider Him to be such a great teacher; He really was. Though the many images of Jesus presented earlier arose out of exaggerations of some of His teachings and minimizations of others, people find these images credible based on the fact that He taught profound and true insights. His compassion for the poor and the weak, His condemnations of hypocrisy, His mercy, His selflessness, His zeal for righteousness and justice all mark Him as a profoundly moral man. In *The Screwtape Letters*, C.S. Lewis observes how closely Jesus' moral teachings match other great moral teachers.[17] As the third chapter noted, humanity is able to recognize great moral teachers

---

16. Lewis, *Mere Christianity*, 52.
17. Lewis, *Screwtape*, 125.

because of the clarity those teachers provide for moral law that we already know. Jesus is almost universally recognized as such a man. Even John Stuart Mill, who was quite antagonistic towards Christianity, had this to say about Jesus:

> About the life and sayings of Jesus there is a stamp of personal originality combined with profundity of insight in the very first rank of men of sublime genius of whom our species can boast. When this pre-eminent genius is combined with the qualities of probably the greatest moral reformer and martyr to that mission who ever existed upon the earth, religion cannot be said to have made a bad choice in pitching upon this man as the ideal representative and guide of humanity; nor even now would it be easy, even for an unbeliever, to find a better translation of the rule of virtue from the abstract into the concrete than to endeavour to live so that Christ would approve of our life.[18]

It seems very implausible that such a moral man would have intentionally tried to convince people that He was God when He was not, nor that such an insightful man could have been deluded enough to believe He was God when He was not. Based on the moral insights we already have, Jesus does not appear to be a pathological liar or a lunatic. Oddly enough, then, responsibly evaluating Jesus' teachings requires serious consideration of His claims about himself.

SUBSTANTIATING HIS CLAIM

When Jesus made audacious claims, He did not expect or encourage people to believe them uncritically. When Jesus made claims to spiritual authority, He demonstrated that authority by showing His supernatural power over the material world, which people could see for themselves. For example, during the aforementioned instance in which He told a paralyzed man who was brought to Him that his sins were forgiven and the others in attendance objected to it, Jesus recognized that it was very easy to simply *say* that a person's sins were forgiven. He did not command the others to accept the claim without reason. Instead He said, "which is easier: to say, 'your sins are forgiven,' or to say, 'Get up and walk'? But that you may know that the Son of Man has authority on earth to forgive sins

---

18. MacDowell, *New Evidence*, 159.

... I tell you, get up, take your mat and go home."[19] The man who was formerly paralyzed then immediately complied with Jesus' command. In the previously mentioned instance when Jesus claimed deity, He held to the same pattern. Both before and after the audacious announcement, Jesus referred His hearers to His miracles as proof.[20] He even goes so far as to tell them not to believe "unless I do what my Father does." In Luke 7:22, Jesus tells John the Baptist's disciples to report the miracles that He has done in response to John's query about whether or not Jesus was the Christ. When Jesus made an incredible claim that was difficult to verify, He typically paired it with equally incredible actions that were easy for His listeners to verify. Because He demonstrated mastery of the physical world by non-physical (i.e. spiritual) means, it is reasonable to conclude that Jesus wielded genuine spiritual authority.

THE RESURRECTION

Jesus' Resurrection is the most important of these miracles and the ultimate vindication of His claims. If Christ never rose, then Christianity is falsified. Many modern liberal versions of Christianity see little need for a physical resurrection. However, this point of view is so foreign to classical Christianity as to make it a different religion altogether—a religion this book has no interest in defending.[21] In 1 Corinthians 15:14, Paul writes that "If Christ has not been raised, our preaching is useless and so is your faith." There are several reasons that Paul hinges all of Christianity on the actuality of the Resurrection. The doctrine of the atonement, which will be considered in more depth in chapter 8, is certainly one such reason.[22] However, there are also reasons having to do with the Resurrection as evidence for Jesus' claims. Jesus said repeatedly that He would rise again.

19. Matt 9:5–6.
20. John 10:25, 37–38.
21. Such a religion which claims the name of "Christianity" is typically a set of guidelines for bringing peace, doing good, living our best lives, etc. Propagating the guidelines usually involves dipping into Christian imagery and tradition. The guidelines may or may not be good, but as the eighth chapter will demonstrate, they are only tangentially related to the Christian religion.
22. According to Paul's theology, human death is a consequence and punishment for sin. By dying, Jesus was punished in our stead. If He remained dead, the payment He made would have been incomplete and we would still be under our deserved condemnation. The fact that death could not hold Him shows that it was satisfied and the atonement complete.

If He was wrong about that, His spiritual authority is profoundly diminished. In Luke 9:22, Jesus says, "The Son of Man must suffer many things and be rejected by the elders, chief priests and teachers of the law, and he must be killed and on the third day be raised to life." Again in 18:31 He says, "We are going up to Jerusalem and everything that is written by the prophets about the Son of Man will be fulfilled. He will be handed over to the Gentiles. They will mock him, insult him, spit on him, flog him, and kill him. On the third day, he will rise again." Matthew 20:18–19 records the same claim. One must also consider Jesus' teaching that He was God and that He himself was the way to salvation. A god who is dead and gone can hardly be the way for anyone, nor can he be much of a god. John Warwick Montgomery has detailed several instances from the period in which self-proclaimed messiahs promised miracles. Unlike Christianity, these movements fell apart after their leaders failed to deliver.[23] On the other hand, if Christ's audacious promises were actually fulfilled and He did indeed rise, then we have no reasonable choice but to count His audacious claims fulfilled as well and acknowledge His claim to Godhood.

If, as the first four chapters argued, one knows from philosophy that there is a theistic God of a particular character, then it is inconceivable that such a God would triumphantly raise an impostor from the dead and set the man in His own place for all to see. This leads to one final question: Can one conclude from the historical evidence that the resurrection actually happened? There were no eyewitnesses watching the resurrection itself as there were with Jesus' other miracles. As Ross Clifford notes, if one is to go about laying out evidence that Jesus Christ died and rose again from the dead, there are two things one must solidly demonstrate: first, that Jesus was clearly dead at one point in time, and second, that He was clearly physically alive at a later point in time.[24]

JESUS' DEATH

Jesus was certainly sentenced to death and execution. Every source from the time, both Christian and non-Christian, that was cited in the previous chapter agreed on this point. They also all agree that the sentence was actually carried out. The apostle John provides the most direct testimony to Jesus' death in His Gospel:

23. Montgomery, 74–75.
24. Clifford, *Leading*, 85.

> Now it was the day of Preparation, and the next day was to be a special Sabbath. Because the Jews did not want the bodies left of the crosses during the Sabbath, they asked Pilate to have the legs broken and the bodies taken down. The soldiers therefore came and broke the legs of the first man who had been crucified with Jesus, and then those of the other. But when they came to Jesus and found that he was already dead, they did not break his legs. Instead, one of the soldiers pierced Jesus' side with a spear, bringing a sudden flow of blood and water. The man who saw it has given testimony, and his testimony is true. He knows that he tells the truth, and he testifies so that you also may believe.[25]

From this record, along with the record of Christ's telling John to take care of His mother, we can see that John himself was a firsthand eyewitness to these events. Luke corroborates this by indicating that "all who knew him" were present at the crucifixion.[26] From their accounts, Peter (whose insights were recorded by Mark) and Matthew were also among those present. In addition, Mary, Jesus' mother, was put at the scene by John. Mary Magdalene was put at the scene by John, Matthew, and Mark. Mary, the mother of James was put at the scene by Mark and Matthew. Mark, Matthew, and Luke all mention that there were also other women watching besides the ones named. Pilate, who wanted to make sure of Jesus' death, was satisfied after consulting a centurion.[27] Joseph of Arimathea and Nicodemus could also verify that He was dead since they were the ones to bury Him.[28] This event occurred before the eyes of many witnesses. What do these witnesses describe? They speak of how He was flogged and beaten, nailed to the cross, died, was pierced by a spear, and buried. All of the available evidence from the period testifies to the fact that Jesus truly died at His execution.

There are, of course, the occasional theories from some skeptics who suggest that Jesus did not actually die. Accordingly, the witnesses misinterpreted what they saw because Jesus feigned death (possibly using a drug) or because He simply swooned. However, such theories are contradicted by too many of the simple observations of the witnesses. As Norman Geisler notes, Jesus' agony and His loud cry just before His death

25. John 19:31–35.
26. Luke 23:49.
27. Mark 15:44.
28. Luke 24:50–56, John 19:38–42.

contradict any drugging.[29] What is more, the many wounds inflicted are more than a person could plausibly survive without medical care. Jesus was flogged and repeatedly beaten the previous night, necessarily leading to heavy blood loss. Rather than being treated, He was hung on the cross from 9:00 A.M. until almost sunset.[30] Afterwards, the soldiers who recognized His death pierced Him with a spear to make sure.[31] John records that blood and water flowed out of the wound, which Geisler describes as "an indisputable medical sign of death, indicating that the red and white blood corpuscles had separated."[32] Survival would be no less improbable than a resurrection. On top of this, Jesus' actions after leaving the tomb are not those of a man who barely survived. It would have been absurd for a poor, weak, maimed man hovering on death's door to be seen as having been triumphant over death by His followers. Jesus was also extremely active in the following days, visiting many people in many places and traveling even faster than His unwounded disciples.[33]

In 1986, the Journal of the American Medical Association ran an article thoroughly analyzing the historical information in order to provide an accurate account of the physical death of Jesus. After briefly summarizing the circumstances of Jesus' arrest and trials, the article examines common scourging and crucifixion practices and their effects on Jesus:

> The severe scourging, with its intense pain and appreciable blood loss, most probably left Jesus in a preshock state . . . The physical and mental abuse meted out by the Jews and the Romans, as well as the lack of food, water, and sleep, also contributed to his generally weakened state. Therefore, even before the actual crucifixion, Jesus' physical condition was at least serious and possibly critical.[34]

As to the crucifixion, it says:

---

29. Geisler, 347.
30. Mark 15:25, 42.
31. John 19:33–34.
32. Geisler, 347.
33. Luke 24:33–34.
34. Edwards et al., "Physical Death," 1458.

> The major pathophysiologic effect of crucifixion was an interference with normal respirations. Accordingly, death resulted primarily from hypovolemic shock and exhaustion asphyxia.[35]

The article narrows the precise cause of death down to cardiac rupture or cardiorespiratory failure and draws this conclusion: "interpretations based on the assumption that Jesus did not die on the cross appear to be at odds with modern medical knowledge."[36] The historical documents and modern scientific analysis are in agreement: The best explanation for the facts of history is that Jesus physically died on that cross.

THE EMPTY TOMB

Jesus was certainly killed at that point in time. What evidence exists that Jesus was alive again at a later point? There are two important facts that need to be demonstrated to reasonably conclude that Jesus was alive after His resurrection. The first is that His body did not remain in the tomb, which would indicate (at best) some kind of non-physical resurrection. The second fact is that He was confirmed to be bodily alive elsewhere.

The tomb was confirmed to be empty by many different people. According to all four Gospels, Mary Magdalene and according to three (all except John) Mary the mother of James were among the first to witness the empty tomb. Mark mentions that Salome was also with them, and Luke records that there were several unnamed women as well. Luke records that Peter ran to the tomb, looked inside, and saw the empty graveclothes. John records that he was with Peter during that instance (and adds that he outran him). Matthew records that the guards on the tomb who had seen the angel roll away the stone also witnessed that it was empty because they went to the Jewish leaders and reported it to them. It is worth noting once again that there is strong evidence that the authors were not colluding because they all record different but compatible details—there are no contradictions. What is more, although the Jews and the Romans both tried to stamp out Christianity, there is no record of them ever showing off a full tomb to support their goal. In fact, the explanation recorded in Matthew—that the disciples stole the body[37]—indicates that there was an empty tomb that the Jewish leadership needed to explain.

35. Edwards et al., 1455.
36. Edwards et al., 1463.
37. Matt 28:13–15.

There are, of course, attempts at alternative explanations for the empty tomb. One rather creative explanation was offered in the early twentieth century by a professor of New Testament Exegesis. Kirsopp Lake suggested that the first witnesses were mistakenly looking at the wrong tomb. According to Lake, there were similar rock tombs all over Jerusalem, and the women were not in a position to be certain of which was Jesus'. He concludes:

> . . . it supplies the natural explanation of the fact that whereas they had seen the tomb closed, they found it open . . . If it were not the same [tomb], the circumstances all seem to fall into line. The women came in the early morning to a tomb which they thought was the one in which they had seen the Lord buried. They expected to find a closed tomb, but they found an open one; and a young man . . . guessing their errand, tried to tell them that they had made a mistake in the place. "He is not here," said he; "see the place where they laid him," and probably pointed to the next tomb. But the women were frightened at the detection of the errand, and fled, only imperfectly or not at all understanding what they heard.[38]

Thus, Lake considers the historical evidence ambiguous and defers the analysis of the circumstances to theology. There are, however, numerous difficulties with such an explanation. The most obvious is that Lake does not include the full record of what the "young man" told the women. In Mark 16:5–6, the author records him as saying, "Do not be alarmed. You seek Jesus of Nazareth, who was crucified. He has risen! He is not here. See the place where they laid Him." The "He is Risen" part is left out of the Professor Lake's scenario without any evidence that these words were an error or addition to the manuscript. Another problem is that empty grave-clothes were observed by Peter and John. It is unlikely that new tombs in Jerusalem came packaged with empty grave-clothes. There were also several people besides the women who watched the burial happen; any one of them could have corrected the error, and many enemies of Christianity could have then presented the body. Josh McDowell also notes that there is no cause to think that the grave was surrounded by other graves as Lake assumes; it was a personal tomb in a field rather than a cemetery.[39] With so many problems, this scenario cannot be considered

38. Lake, *Historical Evidence*, 252.
39. McDowell, 282.

to be coherent with the facts—it has to arbitrarily ignore too many of them.

Other alternative explanations follow the idea that Jesus was removed from the grave by somebody. The Achilles heel of such arguments has always been the limited number of possible identities of the "somebody." The people involved in the affair were the Jewish leadership, the Romans, and Jesus' followers. The Jews and Romans wanted to stamp out Christianity rather than encourage it—they would have no motivation for removing the body. This leaves only Jesus' followers—primarily the close ones who knew the location of the tomb early on. Jesus' disciples were recorded as being cowardly in the Gospels and as brave men only after (and because of) the Resurrection.[40] Not only would they have probably been afraid of such an attempt, it is also unlikely that they could have overpowered the guards on the tomb if they were awake, nor is there any evidence to suggest the guards were killed in their sleep. If the guards were asleep, they surely would have been awoken by the commotion of a large stone being rolled away. One must also consider that John notes that the grave-clothes were left behind folded—an odd thing for robbers in a hurry to do. However, the most damning point to consider for such a scenario is that it would mean that most of Jesus' disciples died to proclaim the truth of something they knew for certain to be false. It is not unusual for someone to die for a lie which he believes, but it is extremely unusual someone to die for the sake of a lie he knows without a doubt to be a lie. A creative mind could come up with endless conspiracy theories, but these always seem to lack evidence and ignore evidence that exists.

THE RISEN JESUS

An empty tomb may be a prerequisite for the Resurrection, but by itself it does not prove it. It is also necessary to demonstrate that Jesus was verified to be alive after the tomb was found to be empty. The New Testament contains many different eyewitness accounts of this. First, Jesus visited the women who first discovered the empty tomb; they saw Him, touched Him, and heard Him speak.[41] Luke records that Jesus visited two disciples who were traveling to Emmaus that same day as well as Peter[42]—a visit

---

40. Matt 26:56, 69–74, and Mark 6:47–50, for example.
41. Matt 28:8–10, John 20:10.
42. Luke 24:13–34

which Paul corroborates.[43] Luke and John both record Jesus appearing to ten disciples in the upper room, where they saw Jesus, watched Him eat, heard Him, and touched Him.[44] John then records another visit in the same place the next week, where the eleventh, Thomas, saw Jesus for the first time.[45] John also records Jesus appearing to himself, Peter, Thomas, Nathanael, James, John, and two others while they were fishing.[46] Matthew records His appearance to the eleven disciples at a mountain in Galilee.[47] Luke records (both in his Gospel and in Acts) Jesus appearing to a group of people before ascending into heaven.[48] Paul records his own encounter with the risen Christ, James' encounter, and an encounter at which He appeared to over 500 people at once.[49] That makes at least eleven different appearances from a variety of sources. All of these encounters involve Jesus being alive and physically present after He had been killed. In many instances He even makes a point of behaving in a way that only a physically live person can; He ate, He touched them, He breathed on them.

The transmission of the reports and identity of the authors as people who would know was established in the previous chapter. However, some would contend that they are untrustworthy because these were Jesus' friends. They may be Jesus' friends and followers, but one would expect nothing less than Jesus appearing to His followers more often than to others. One can also expect that only those who ultimately became His followers would be interested in recording such appearances. Even so, the disciples were not expecting a resurrection despite Jesus' own predictions. All of them were skeptical at first when the women told them what had happened. The two on the road to Emmaus were disappointed that Jesus was not really the Christ because He had died, but changed their minds after they were visited by Him. Thomas famously wanted physical proof before He would believe it. James, Jesus' brother, did not believe in His brother[50] at one point, but clearly did afterwards because Josephus records that he was sentenced to death by the Sanhedrin for His sake as

43. 1 Cor 15:5.
44. Luke 24:36-44, John 20:19-23.
45. John 20:24-29.
46. John 21:1-14.
47. Matt 28:16-20.
48. Luke 24:50-53 & Acts 1:6-11.
49. 1 Cor 15:5-8.
50. John 7:5.

the previous chapter noted. Paul had dedicated his life to the eradication of Christianity, but after encountering the risen Christ, he became an apostle. There is little reason to doubt all of these consistent reports from these diverse and initially skeptical people.

There are, of course, alternative explanations that attempt to make sense of these eyewitness reports. One of the most common is the claim that the experiences Jesus' followers had were simply hallucinations. As Gresham Machen put it, "it means that if there had a been a good neurologist for Peter and the others to consult, there never would have been a Christian Church."[51] The problem is that hallucinations are simply not a powerful enough explanation. Hallucinations are not magic and cannot serve as an explanation for any sensory experience in any circumstance. Like any other medical condition, they occur for specific reasons and under specific circumstances. Sir Norman Anderson, a British law professor, has noted a number of ways in which hallucinations do not fit the evidence. First, the eyewitnesses to the resurrection were variety of different people in a variety of situations and moods. Mary Magdalene was weeping at the tomb, Peter was remorseful, Thomas was skeptical, the pair on the road to Emmaus were distracted and dejected, etc. They do not all fit the certain types of people who are subject to hallucination. Second, it is unlikely that so many would have exactly the same hallucinations at the same time. Hallucinations arise out of the subconscious rather than the external senses and are therefore highly individual. Thirdly, hallucinations come out of expectation and wish fulfillment. The disciples were dejected over something they had already accepted as true. The women expected to finish anointing Christ, not find Him raised, and the disciples initially thought He was a ghost. Finally, there is no explanation for why the hallucinations suddenly stopped after forty days.[52] On top of these observations, one might add that hallucinations do not eat food as Luke records that Jesus did.[53] The disciples would likely have noticed that the fish their hallucination ate was still there. Finally, C.S. Lewis recognized just how bizarre it would be for a hallucination of Jesus to not immedi-

---

51. McDowell, 273.
52. Clifford, 98.
53. Luke 24:41–43.

ately be recognized as Jesus—something that happened on three distinct occasions.[54]

Another explanation, based on this last point, is that the person the disciples perceived as the risen Lord was in fact some other person pretending to be Jesus. After all, the disciples on the road to Emmaus did not recognize Him until He broke bread, Mary Magdalene mistook Him for a gardener, and the disciples did not initially recognize Him at the miraculous catch of fish.[55] The first problem with this explanation is that there is not even one known person with a motive, but there would need to be multiple impostors. While Jesus was appearing on the road to Emmaus, another impostor would have had to have appeared to Peter. Furthermore, these supposed Jesus impostors were still performing miraculous acts. Jesus appeared and disappeared at will, He repeated the miraculous catch of fish, and He ascended into the sky. There is also the instance of Thomas remaining skeptical until He saw the wounds Jesus received (the nail-marks and particularly the spear wound), and then being satisfied upon seeing Jesus. Is an impostor going to give himself a mortal wound—a wound that could not have adequately healed by the time of this appearance? One can hardly imagine Thomas putting his hand into an impostor's side, the wound breaking open and spilling blood while the impostor cried out in pain, and Thomas reacting by exclaiming "my Lord and my God" while falling down to worship Him. If Thomas was skeptical enough to doubt the reports of those He traveled with for three years, it is difficult to imagine skepticism immediately vanishing under such circumstances.

CONCLUSION

When one considers an actual resurrection as the explanation for the facts recorded in the New Testament and the other historical accounts, one ought to find it to be the best fit for all of the facts available. Every other explanation has to ignore a great deal of what was recorded as well as a great deal about what we know of humans in general. When closely examined, each scenario becomes a complex farce that is even more ridiculous than a resurrection. Although the charge is often made that in order to actually believe these things a Christian would have to be igno-

---

54. Lewis, *Miracles*, 153.
55. Luke 24:16,31; John 20:15; John 21:4.

rant or stupid, a closer examination of the evidence reveals that this is not at all the case. The facts of history maintain that Jesus of Nazareth is both God and Lord. Christians may be brought to believe the Jesus Christ is Lord by the work of the Holy Spirit, but they need not reject that belief for the sake of rationality. A reasoned analysis confirms the gift rather than compelling us to abandon it.

One can be sure that Jesus rose from the dead, and so one can also be sure that He is who He claimed to be—not a spokesman or mascot to convince people to listen to us, not a mere man with some moral insights, but the One to whom we must listen. Two thousand years ago, God Himself walked among humanity. This presence is history, but it is also beyond history. It is no less than factual and objective, but it is also more than historical trivia.

7

The Bible

Jesus' Inerrant Teachings

INTRODUCTION

IN THE BEGINNING OF *New Evidence that Demands a Verdict*, Josh McDowell points out many of the ways in which the Bible is a truly unique and amazing book. For example, it was written over a 1,500-year span by more than forty different authors who ran the gamut from Kings and rabbis to herdsman and tax collectors in all kinds of different settings and moods. And yet, at the same time it tells a unified story about God's plan for redemption of the world: Jesus Christ (at least if Jesus is to be believed).[1] It is the most circulated book in the world, has been translated into 2,200 different languages, and has survived through many centuries of time, persecution, and criticism.[2]

Classical Christianity, however, makes a greater claim than that the Bible is simply an extraordinary book. This chapter will examine the claim that it is the Word of God—that it is God's inerrant communication to humanity. The previous chapters dealt with two extremely important points. First, the New Testament represents a set of historically reliable documents about the life and teachings of Jesus of Nazareth. Second, the details recorded in these and other documents make the belief that Jesus Christ is God incarnate more reasonable than any alternative explanation. This makes Jesus the ultimate authority on all matters on which He

---

1. Luke 24:27.
2. McDowell, *Evidence*, 4–10.

spoke and means that everyone can trust His teachings to be completely true. Any falsehood or misinformation from Jesus is incompatible with His identity as God in the theistic sense. The establishment of these facts provides the foundation needed to explain why a person can reasonably believe that the Bible is the Word of God in addition to merely being reliable history.

A CIRCULAR ARGUMENT?

One point needs to be made clear from the beginning. This claim about the Bible depends on the Bible for its support. Because of this fact, the charge is often made that the argument represents circular reasoning: that it assumes what it tries to prove. If one were to claim that the Bible is God's Word and conclude that one can therefore trust it when it says that it is God's Word, then the charge would be correct. However, that is not the case being made in this chapter. This argument begins with the fact that the New Testament is historically reliable concerning its contents—reliability which was established in same way as for any other historical document. Its contents, however, include the teachings of Jesus—God Himself. The question to be addressed, then, is what does Jesus say about the Bible? This chapter will be using the Bible to support its divine origins not because the Bible has divine origins, but because it is historically reliable concerning a divine man and is a document worthy of respect. Consequently, the argument is not circular. It does not rely on the Bible's divine authority to recognize the Bible's divine authority; it relies on the Bible's historical authority and Jesus' divine authority to recognize the Bible's divine authority.[3]

---

3. This approach does not imply, as some Christians argue, that God needs to be verified by other sources before He can be believed. Such Christians often suggest that one *should* argue circularly because anything else puts some other authority above God. As this book has maintained throughout, faith is a gift of God, and practically speaking, no one will believe that the Bible is the word of God without that faith. The task of this apologetic is not to create faith; it is a response to unbelief in humankind—whether among Christians or non-Christians. As such, this approach merely treats the question of whether the Bible is the Word of God as an actual question. One's response cannot assume faith when unbelief is the reality. Doing so is not just poor argumentation—it is cruelty. See the introduction for more on this subject.

JESUS' RECOGNITION OF SCRIPTURE

The New Testament contains many of Jesus' teachings about the Scriptures of His time: the Old Testament. First, He taught that it is authoritative. Jesus continually quoted from and alluded to a wide variety of Old Testament books to make His points to His disciples, to human opponents, and even to Satan. As Norman Geisler argues, Jesus did not use these quotations and allusions as mere illustrations of His points, but as examples of divine authority behind His points.[4] When Jesus frequently says "it is written" before referencing the Old Testament, He is not informing His audience that the Scriptures exist on paper—the phrase is intended to convey the authority of what He is about to say. Furthermore, in one instance, He tells His listeners that they are wrong specifically because they do not know the Scriptures.[5] In another, He prefaces His quotations of Exodus with "God said" before condemning His opponents for having ignored what was written by telling them they "nullify the word of God for the sake of . . . tradition."[6] Jesus uses the Old Testament, not as a means of saying "consider the thought presented in this literature," but as a means of saying "you ought to believe and practice these things."

Secondly, Jesus considered the Old Testament to be not just morally or spiritually accurate but historically accurate. He often mentioned specific events recorded within it as being true. These events include even the most incredible stories that are most often the targets of skeptics today. Jesus cited the Flood and the destruction of Sodom as explanations of what His second coming will be like.[7] In order to explain how God originally designed marriage, Jesus brought up the creation of Adam and Eve.[8] Jesus brings up Jonah having been eaten by a great fish when explaining His coming resurrection.[9] Not only does Jesus refer to these and many other miraculous events, He cites them in ways that preclude simple allusion to fiction, as will be explored later on.

Thirdly, Jesus considered Scriptures to be accurate even to the smallest degree. When He explains to the crowd listening to the Sermon on

---

4. Geisler, *Christian Apologetics*, 356.
5. Matt 22:29.
6. Matt 15:1–6.
7. Luke 17:22–30.
8. Matt 19:3–6.
9. Matt 12:39–41.

the Mount that He is not abolishing the Law or the Prophets, He says, "I tell you the truth, until heaven and earth disappear, not the smallest letter, not the least stroke of a pen, will by any means disappear from the Law until everything is accomplished."[10] This was not mere hyperbole, but Jesus' actual practice. For example, when He refuted the Sadducees' denial of the resurrection, He based His argument entirely on a verb tense in Exodus—a small detail that many readers would miss and yet which Jesus considered to carry the weight of God's authority.[11]

Finally, Jesus confirmed the audience of the Old Testament. He did not consider it to be merely a record of what God said in a particular cultural context but that God spoke through the Scriptures to His contemporaries. As was previously mentioned, He prefaces His citation of the Fourth Commandment and another part of Exodus with "God said . . ." (Matthew 15:4). When He argued to the Pharisees that the Messiah they expected would have to be God, He refers to a Psalm by saying that David was "speaking by the Spirit."[12] When Jesus refuted the Sadducees, Matthew records Him saying, "Have you not heard *what God said to you*, [emphasis added] 'I am the God of Abraham, the God of Isaac, and the God of Jacob.'" The clear implication is that while the verse in Exodus He quoted was a record of God speaking to Moses, the written account ought to have been considered God speaking to them centuries later. It is true that this implication is not necessarily made in the parallel accounts of this event in Mark and Luke.[13] However, it is important to note that Christians do not typically claim that the Gospels always record the exact words of Jesus.[14] The Gospels were written in Greek, which is probably not what Jesus would have been speaking in. The claim is that having been written by Jesus' students, they carry the informational content of Jesus' words. In this case, we would say that Matthew simply recorded different but compatible content as compared to Mark or Luke.

A very common objection to this analysis is that Jesus was merely accommodating false but popular Jewish beliefs about the Old Testament

---

10. Matt 5:18–19.
11. Matt 22:31–32.
12. Matt 22:41–45.
13. Mark 12:18–27 & Luke 20:27–40.
14. Although they may be in some cases and they certainly are in specific instances where they are quoted as such—for example, Jesus' cry of "Eli, Eli, lama sabachthani" in Aramaic in Mark 15:34.

in His teachings. The claim is that He used the Old Testament as a tool to make His own teachings accessible to His hearers, but did not actually affirm the authority or historical accuracy of the Old Testament. While this may seem initially plausible, applying it to specific instances is very difficult. Consider, for example, Matthew 12: 38–41 in which Jesus mentions Jonah:

> Then some of the Pharisees and teachers of the law said to him, "Teacher, we want to see a miraculous sign from you."
>
> He answered, "A wicked and adulterous generation asks for a miraculous sign! But none will be given it except the sign of the prophet Jonah. For as Jonah was three days and three nights in the belly of a huge fish, so the Son of Man will be three days and three nights in the heart of the earth. The men of Ninevah will stand up at the judgment with this generation and condemn it; for they repented at the preaching of Jonah, and now one greater than Jonah is here."

If Jesus was alluding to an allegory, then He was inferring by His comparison of "just as" that His resurrection would also be allegorical—something which the previous chapter demonstrated was not actually the case. There is also no reason to think Jesus did not believe in the final judgment He mentioned so often. Could Jesus really be saying that people from a fictional account would stand up at the judgment and condemn those to whom He spoke? What is more, if He was claiming to be greater than an allegorical symbol when He says "one greater than Jonah is here," then it was hardly a claim worth making. No one would refer to *Pilgrim's Progress* and say, "Now one greater than Christian is here." This would be an utterly ridiculous comparison if Jesus did not believe He was referring to a real event.

One can see an example of the same phenomenon in Matthew 19:3–9, in which Jesus quotes the book of Genesis:

> Some Pharisees came to him to test him. They asked, "Is it lawful for a man to divorce his wife for any and every reason?"
>
> "Haven't you read," he replied, "that at the beginning the Creator 'made them male and female,' and said, 'For this reason a man will leave his father and mother and be united to his wife, and the two will become one flesh'? So they are no longer two, but one. Therefore, what God has joined together, let man not separate."

> "Why then," they asked, "did Moses command that a man give his wife a certificate of divorce and send her away?"
>
> Jesus replied, "Moses permitted you to divorce your wives because your hearts were hard. But it was not this way from the beginning. I tell you that anyone who divorces his wife, except for marital unfaithfulness, and marries another woman commits adultery."

Jesus' argument makes no sense if He is referring to an untrue myth. "It was not this way in the beginning" is very different from "it was not this way in this story." The former indicates that Jesus was referencing a point in history.

One can understand "accommodation" in two ways. The first is merely to adapt one's message to particular circumstances. The second is to reconcile one's message to those circumstances or agree with them. If Jesus were accommodating when He used the kind of language recorded above, it could only be in the second sense, which means He was agreeing with error. When Jesus went so far as to tell His hearers that "God said" when God had not, then He would have been flat out lying. Jesus would not do such things, particularly in light of the fact that Jesus was hardly reluctant to refute error. His disagreements with the religious authorities of the time are well-known. If Jesus, the Son of God, is to be believed, then one must conclude that the Old Testament is the inerrant Word of God Himself.

APOSTOLIC AUTHORITY

Such an approach is appropriate for the Old Testament, but Jesus could hardly say such things about the New Testament because it was written after He ascended. Nevertheless, this does not mean the New Testament was written apart from Jesus' divine authority. Jesus said enough to authorize the New Testament as the Word of God, equivalent to the Old Testament while He was still with His disciples. Jesus' twelve apostles were merely the means by which the New Testament was delivered. For example, after the Last Supper and after Judas had departed, Jesus spoke to the disciples at length about what would happen after He had gone away and informed them about the coming of the Holy Spirit. In John 14:24, Jesus says, "But the Counselor, the Holy Spirit, whom the Father will send in my name, will teach you all things and will remind you of everything I have said to you." In 15:16, He says, "You did not choose me, but I chose you and appointed you to go and bear fruit—fruit that will last." In 15:20, He says, "Remember the words I spoke to you: 'No servant is greater than his master.' If they persecuted me, they will persecute you also. If they obeyed my teaching, they will obey yours also." In 15:26, He says "When the Counselor comes, whom I will send to you from the Father, the Spirit of truth who goes out from the Father, he will testify about me. And you also must testify, for you have been with me from the beginning." In 16:12, He says,

> I have much more to say to you, more than you can now bear. But when he, the Spirit of truth comes, he will guide you into all truth. He will not speak on his own; he will speak only what he hears, and he will tell you what is yet to come. He will bring glory to me by taking from what is mine and making it known to you. All that belongs to the Father is mine. That is why I said the Spirit will take from what is mine and make it known to you.

This is not the only discourse in which Jesus spoke about this kind of authority. In Matthew 16:18–19, He says to Simon, "And I tell you that you are Peter, and on this rock I will build my church, and the gates of Hades will not overcome it. I will give you the keys of the kingdom of heaven; whatever you bind on earth will be bound in heaven, and whatever you loose on earth will be loosed in heaven." After the resurrection, In John 20:23, Jesus visited His Apostles and, ". . . he breathed on them and said, 'Receive the Holy Spirit. If you forgive anyone his sins, they are forgiven; if you do not forgive them, they are not forgiven.'" At the end of Matthew, He instructs them to "Go and make disciples of all nations, baptizing them in the name of the Father and of the Son and of the Holy Spirit, and teaching them to obey everything I have commanded you." From these teachings of Jesus, one can conclude that Jesus gave His Apostles a special authority to proclaim Him and His teachings.

At Pentecost, as recorded in Acts 2, these promises were fulfilled, these men were filled with the promised Holy Spirit and the authority that Christ described, and they began to preach. Not only that, but these men also validated their testimony by miracles the same way Jesus did. In the book of Acts, Luke records a number of instances of this. In 2:43 he writes, "Everyone was filled with awe, and many wonders and miraculous signs were done by the apostles." In 5:12–16 he writes,

> The apostles performed many miraculous signs and wonders among the people. And all the believers used to meet together in Solomon's Colonnade. No one else dared join them, even though they were highly regarded by the people. Nevertheless, more and more men and women believed in the Lord and were added to their number. As a result, people brought the sick into the streets and laid them on beds and mats so that at least Peter's shadow might fall on some of them as he passed by. Crowds gathered also from the towns around Jerusalem, bringing their sick and those tormented by evil spirits, and all of them were healed.

In 6:8, he mentions that "Stephen, a man full of God's grace and power, did great wonders and miraculous signs among the people." Luke also provides specific examples, such as Peter's healing of a crippled beggar[15] and Paul's raising of a young man named Eutychus whom he had inadvertently killed through boredom,[16] among others miracles. It is clear from these signs that the authority that Jesus had promised to His Apostles was actually delivered and remained with them.

The New Testament is a collection of books and letters that were written by these same men and by people accredited by them (e. g. Mark, Luke, James, and Jude). Not only that, but the Apostles themselves recognized these new writings as being Scripture. For example, in 2 Peter 3:15–16, Peter writes,

> Bear in mind that our Lord's patience means salvation, just as our dear brother Paul also wrote you with the wisdom that God gave him. He writes the same way in all his letters, speaking in them of these matters. His letters contain some things that are hard to understand, which ignorant and unstable people distort, as they do the *other Scriptures* [emphasis added], to their own destruction.

Peter not only referred to Paul's letters as Scripture but did so in a way that indicates his audience had already been well aware of that fact. Those receiving the letter already understood that Paul's letters were Scripture, and Peter was aware that they believed it. Far from correcting this belief, he showed that he shared it. Likewise, in 1 Timothy 5:18, Paul writes, "For the Scripture says, 'Do not muzzle the ox while it is treading out the grain,' and 'the worker deserves his wages.'" Here, Paul quotes both

---

15. Acts 3:1–7.

16. Acts 20:7–12. Eutychus fell asleep and out of a third story window during a particularly long talk of Paul's.

Deuteronomy and the Gospel of Luke and calls them both Scripture in the same breath; once again he does so in a way that indicates that Paul and his audience already recognized that both were Scripture in the same sense. The Apostles, whom Jesus had authorized to teach in His name, clearly recognized the New Testament books as Scripture.

It is also clear that these writings were meant to be and were widely circulated in the early church that sprang out of what these men taught. In the closing of his letter to the Colossians, Paul instructs them to pass the letter on to Laodicea.[17] Revelation was addressed to seven different churches.[18] James is addressed to "the twelve tribes scattered among the nations."[19] Peter's first epistle is addressed to "God's elect, strangers in the world, scattered throughout Pontus, Galatia, Cappadocia, Asia and Bithynia."[20] All this indicates that these were not merely letters to specific people in specific contexts, but that they intentionally carried true instruction from the Apostles to all Christians. Outside of the New Testament itself, the early church fathers also recognized the New Testament writings as Scripture. According to Josh McDowell, Athanasius was the first to record all twenty-seven books of the New Testament as Scripture in 367 A.D. (followed soon after by identical lists from Augustine and Jerome).[21] Before that, however, church fathers like Polycarp, Irenaeus, and Justin Martyr all quoted from various New Testament writings as Scripture.[22]

In light of these facts, it becomes clear that the Church did not elevate mundane documents by calling them the Word of God. The appearance within the Church of additional documents falsely attributed to the Apostles and written centuries after their deaths[23] eventually necessitated that the Church officially proclaim certain books to be Scripture. However, this process of canonization did not represent the introduction of a new category of holy writings or the introduction of new non-Apostolic texts. As F.F. Bruce writes, "when at last a Church Council—the Synod of Hippo in A.D. 393—listed the twenty-seven books of the New Testament, it did

---

17. Col 4:16.
18. Rev 1:4.
19. Jas 1:1.
20. 1 Pet 1:1.
21. McDowell, 23–24.
22. McDowell, 24.
23. Such as the so-called Gospels of Thomas and Judas.

not confer upon them any authority which they did not already possess, but simply recorded their previously established canonicity."[24] While evaluating the inclusion of each document is beyond the scope of this book, categorically denying the divine authority of the New Testament involves denying Jesus' authorization of the Apostles. Similarly, watering this authority down is a failure to take seriously the previously detailed teachings of the Son of God. Once again, the most reasonable conclusion is that these books are indeed the Word of God in the same way that the Old Testament was considered to be by Jesus; that God Himself is speaking inerrant truth to us using human authors.

CONTRADICTIONS AND MISTAKES

If this claim to inerrancy is true, it would mean that the original manuscripts of the New Testament had no errors. However, errors and contradictions in the Bible are frequently alleged by skeptics. The fact that the claim of inerrancy is about the original manuscripts rather than a blanket statement for all possible copies and translations explains the occasional typographical or copyist error.[25] Obvious figurative language taken literally sometimes accounts for others. An example of this is the psalmist referring to "the foundations of the earth" and a skeptic claiming he intended to communicate that the earth is flat.[26] However, these explanations are not catch-alls that explain every supposed error. Many claim that the Bible is erroneous in a variety of ways. Some claim that it makes claims that contradict the world we observe—that it makes factual errors. When Jesus asks, "I have spoken to you of earthly things and you do not believe; how then will you believe if I speak of heavenly things,"[27] those who make such a claim would respond in the affirmative: "That is correct. The Bible is not credible on earthly topics, and so it is not credible on heavenly ones either." Others claim that it contradicts even itself—that the Bible is incoherent in some of its teachings. If such claims are true, then inerrancy is indeed washed up, as is the notion that the Bible is God's

---

24. Bruce, *Books*, 111

25. As chapter 5 argued, the transmission of the New Testament text is 99.5 percent accurate, but the other .5 percent does exist.

26. Ps 102:25. To be fair to the skeptic, there are Christians who take figurative language literally in other places (and also those who take literal language figuratively).

27. John 3:12.

Word. God could not be ignorant of the world He created, nor could He contradict Himself. If the Bible has these characteristics, then it simply cannot be His Word. There are many different alleged contradictions that are trotted out as examples; a work as large and complex as the Bible provides plenty of material for the imagination to work with. However, these alleged errors tend to follow certain patterns. In lieu of the impossible task of covering every possible objection, this chapter will consider only several examples of different patterns of objections.

MAKING UNWARRANTED ASSUMPTIONS

Approaching any text with a false assumption can easily lead to misunderstanding it. The New Testament itself contains a good example of this kind of occurrence. In the Gospel of Luke, the Sadducees attempted to demonstrate the absurdity of the resurrection of the dead by putting together a scenario that ostensibly showed that if the resurrection actually occurred, following the law would also necessitate breaking the law.[28] The law of Moses required a man to marry his childless brother's widow in certain circumstances in order to maintain the family line. The Sadducees suggested that if an unlucky woman were to be widowed multiple times, she would be married to seven different men at the resurrection. Jesus refuted this argument by pointing out that they were making an unfounded assumption: that men and women would be married at the resurrection. Skeptics sometimes attempt to disprove the inerrancy of the Bible in similar ways, and so Christians need to be ready to refute them as Jesus did—by pointing out the unfounded assumption. In this case, Jesus was able to go further by indicating with His unique knowledge how things would actually be at the resurrection. Christians may not have that advantage but can still suggest plausible alternatives.

A verse that inexplicably but frequently draws this kind of attention is Matthew 4:8: "Again, the devil took [Jesus] to a very high mountain and showed him all the kingdoms of the world and their splendor. 'All this I will give you,' he said, 'if you will bow down and worship me.'" Some claim that this event could only be possible on a flat earth. Even on the highest of mountains, one would not be able to see the opposite side of the globe. The conclusion, therefore, is that the Bible implicitly supports a proposition that modern people clearly know to be false. This sugges-

---

28. Luke 20:27–35.

tion is perhaps made more plausible by the idea that it was common to believe this falsehood in different times and places. Nevertheless, the assumption that line-of-sight is the only means of viewing a kingdom is not only unnecessary, but silly. I can see all the kingdoms of the world and their splendor without leaving my living room simply by turning on the History Channel. While I am not suggesting that Jesus and Satan had satellite television on the mountaintop, even a limited imagination can suggest plausible alternatives. A supernatural being like Satan could surely provide something more impressive than line-of-sight and a pair of binoculars.

Another alleged error can be found in Mark 8:22–25:

> "They came to Bethsaida, and some people brought a blind man and begged Jesus to touch him. He took the blind man by the hand and led him outside the village. When he had spit on the man's eyes and put his hands on him, Jesus asked, 'Do you see anything?' He looked up and said, 'I see people; they look like trees walking around.' Once more Jesus put his hands on the man's eyes. Then his eyes were opened, his sight was restored, and he saw everything clearly."

Some skeptics read this passage and claim that Jesus had to heal the man twice because he failed to do it right the first time. If Jesus can make such errors, then His teachings are surely not entirely trustworthy. Even if this passage is somewhat mysterious, the assumption that Jesus made a mistake should be doubted even from a casual reading. Why would an author who claims the deity of his subject invent a story that makes it appear as if his subject were making a mistake? Another explanation for the events is that Jesus healed two distinct problems. As Russel Grigg argued in his article "Trees Walking," the other problem was almost certainly *visual agnosia*. This condition, often occurring after sight is restored to a person who has been blind for a very long time, is a result of the brain failing to properly interpret visual information. In these cases, the mind has either never learned or "forgotten" how to make sense of what is seen, and those affected cannot readily identify objects.[29] Such symptoms seem remarkably similar to what Mark describes in these verses. Jesus healing blindness and then healing a consequence of the blindness seems a better explanation than Jesus making a mistake in His miraculous healing. This

---

29. Griggs, "Trees Walking."

also adds the interesting wrinkle that in his narrative, Mark describes a condition resulting from healed blindness many centuries before blindness was being healed by conventional medical techniques. It is a story that could not have been faked at the time it was written. This itself is powerful evidence that Mark is simply recording what happened rather than inventing stories as he goes.

People sometimes claim that Christians are not playing fair with these alternative explanations because they are adding information to the story until it makes sense. There are two problems with this line of thinking. The first is that the skeptic is *also* adding information to the story: the assumptions. Matthew does not mention line-of-sight, nor does Mark comment that Jesus made a mistake. Conceiving explanations of this sort is merely a normal part of interpreting any piece of literature. The second problem is that the Bible makes no claim to be exhaustive.[30] Indeed, there is no literary work of any kind throughout all of history that contains literally all knowledge—even on a single subject. No such book could ever be printed or read. Nevertheless, no one claims that every book ever written is in error or untrustworthy as a result. Inerrancy means that the Bible is completely true in what it affirms. Limiting the judgment of a book's truthfulness to "what it affirms" is not a clever rhetorical device that Christians made up to maintain an outdated claim that the Bible is God's Word. It is the same standard a sensible person would use on any other book.

PRECISION

Another common pattern of alleging mistakes confuses precision with accuracy. We can see this in complaints that some make about 1 Kings 7:23. The author records the designs of a certain furnishing in Solomon's Temple: "He made the Sea of cast metal, circular in shape, measuring ten cubits from rim to rim . . . It took a line of thirty cubits to measure around it." If one can recall grade school geometry, he will remember that the circumference of a circle is equal to *pi* multiplied by the diameter. In this case, that would mean that according to the Bible, $30 = \pi \times 10$. If we solve for *pi*, one finds that it is equal to three, which is obviously not the case. *Pi*

---

30. On the contrary, John ends his Gospel by asserting that he did not and could not include everything Jesus did.

is actually equal to 3.141592653589793238462643383279.... The claim is therefore that the Bible is wrong on the subject of mathematics.

The problem, of course, is that the number given above is not equal to *pi* either. *Pi* is an irrational number. Despite many digits being calculated, its exact value has never been found or recorded because it does not have one. For the Bible to record it exactly would mean that it is an infinitely long book.[31] This does not mean the Bible contains an error anymore than it means math textbooks contain errors because they are not infinitely long. This is a matter of precision rather than accuracy. For an irrational number, 3, 3.14, 3.14159, etc. are all accurate values because approximations are all that can be offered. The difference between them is in the precision with which one approximates. This does not mean that there can be no inaccuracy in recording *pi* or that any given number will do. For example, 4, 3.17, or 3.14152 would all be inaccurate because they offer incorrect digits. Nevertheless, accuracy does not depend on an infinite number of decimal places. In engineering, the precision used is always a function of the precision needed. No designs for anything circular *ever* require the complete value of *pi*. One may need more digits when designing a satellite, but a single digit should be sufficient for the reservoir described in 1 Kings.

A similar example can be found in Leviticus 11:13 and 19: "These are the birds you are to detest because they are detestable: the eagle, the vulture, the black vulture ... And the stork, any kind of heron, the hoopoe and the bat."[32] In our scientifically enlightened age, everyone now knows that bats are not birds, but mammals. The Bible, however, calls them birds. Does this mean that the Bible has made a scientific error? The reason the English word "bat" includes the classification of mammal as part of its definition is the system developed by Carl Linnaeus in the eighteenth century. Moses, writing several thousand years beforehand, was obviously not using this system. The alleged error is merely an imprecision in translation. The ancient Hebrew word for bird is obviously not going to mean the same as a modern English word that is based on a particular classification system. The consequence is that there is no more precise translation than the one given in most Bibles. This does not mean that the Bible is wrong. It merely means that ancient Hebrews classified their

---

31. Specifically, it would mean that the given diameter or circumference would require infinite decimal places in order to make the equation work.

32. See also Deuteronomy 14:11 and 18.

animals differently than we do. The Linnaean system itself is constantly changing as new species with different characteristics are discovered. It is accepted because of it is a useful way of classifying creatures, not because it is the only way or because it is objective truth.

IGNORANCE OF CONTEXT

In addition to contradictions between the Bible and common knowledge, there are also alleged contradictions within the Bible itself. As was mentioned in the first chapter, the law of non-contradiction states that a proposition and its opposite cannot both be true in the same sense at the same time. It was likewise mentioned that this law cannot possibly be false. Consequently, if the Bible does in fact contradict itself, then it must contain a falsehood. Of course, when people find supposed contradictions in the Bible, they often forget the modifying clause, "in the same sense." The sense of a proposition in the Bible or any other literature is highly dependent on context—something that can be easily overlooked or ignored.

For example, in Matthew 5:16, Jesus says, "Let your light shine before men, that they may see your good deeds and praise your father in heaven," but in Matthew 6:1, He says, "Be careful not to do your 'acts of righteousness' before men, to be seen by them." Is Jesus really so sloppy that He is contradicting himself in the same discourse? Is Matthew so sloppy that he garbles Jesus' teachings that badly? If these explanations seem implausible, then one must examine the sense in which Jesus is making each statement. In this case, it is not even necessary to look at the wider context in Matthew. In 5:16, Jesus attaches a purpose to His instruction—so that onlookers will praise God. In 6:1, He attaches a different purpose to doing good works in front of people—merely to be seen by men. Even a small application of reading comprehension skills reveals that Jesus wants people to see His followers' good works so that they will praise God, not so that they will praise His followers. That anyone could consider this a contradiction borders on hilarity.[33]

---

33. Lest anyone claim I am setting up a straw man and attributing to skeptics an embarrassing argument that no intelligent person would ever make, this claim, while showing up in many places, can even be found on the "Scary Bible Quotes" website of Dr. Michael Huemer, a philosophy professor at the University of Colorado and educated man who presumably knows how to read. To put the best construction on everything, there are also Christians who read the Bible without discernible comprehension. Perhaps

A better example can perhaps be found in John 14:27. The author quotes Jesus as saying, "Peace I leave with you; my peace I give you." Nevertheless, in Matthew 10:34, Jesus says, "Do not suppose that I have come to bring peace to the earth. I did not come to bring peace, but a sword." In one book, Jesus says He brings peace, and in another, He says He does not. Is Jesus therefore contradicting Himself? To answer this, it is necessary to understand the nature of peace. When one brings peace, it implies some kind of cessation of hostilities between two or more parties. Peace in this sense has at least two objects. Properly understanding Jesus' words necessitates identifying the different parties Jesus has in mind. If one were to look at the wider context in John, Jesus gives the statement after the Last Supper when He tells His disciples He is about to go away to His death. The peace He is leaving them with is that achieved by His death: peace between God and Man.[34] In Matthew, however, Jesus is sending His disciples out as missionaries and warning them about what they will encounter. In the next verses He explains:

> For I have come to turn "a man against his father, a daughter against her mother, a daughter-in-law against her mother-in-law—a man's enemies will be the members of his own household." Anyone who loves his father or mother more than me is not worthy of me; anyone who loves his son or daughter more than me is not worthy of me.

The peace He speaks of here, the kind He is obviously not bringing, is between people and other people.[35] The context therefore makes it clear that Jesus is being consistent with Himself and with what is taught throughout the Bible. He came to reconcile us with God through His death; He did not come to set up a utopia on Earth.

One more example can be found in Matthew 16:28. Jesus says, "I tell you the truth, some who are standing here will not taste death before they see the Son of Man coming in his kingdom." The claim is sometimes made that Jesus was predicting that His Second Coming would occur before some of those listening to Him had died. Almost 2,000 years later, with His disciples nowhere to be seen, it is safe to conclude that this is not

---

Dr. Huemer is merely responding to what he erroneously believes is the Christian way of reading.

34. See chapter 8 for more on this gospel message.

35. It is likely that Jesus uses family relationships as a metaphor because they are the closest bonds one has.

the case. Did Jesus therefore give an inaccurate prediction? The first thing one must address is what Jesus means by "the Son of Man coming in His kingdom." In this particular case, it is instructive to remember that the chapter and verse separations were not part of the original manuscripts.[36] If one keeps reading in the unbroken narrative, Matthew skips the next six days and proceeds to write about the Transfiguration, when Jesus was shown in His glory.[37] It is likely that the coming Jesus spoke of was His transfiguration. In support of this is, it can be noted that the wider context involves Jesus rebuking Peter for having in mind "the things of men"—good things happening in this world. It is unlikely that Jesus offered His Second Coming (when all the problems of this world will be ended) as a contrast to what Peter was considering. It is also interesting to consider 2 Peter 1:16–18. In these verses, Peter recalls the Transfiguration and speaks of it in terms similar to those Jesus uses. It is very likely that Peter, one who was actually there, did not think Jesus was referring to His Second Coming.

DEATH BY A THOUSAND QUALIFICATIONS?

Refuting these allegations of mistakes has involved a number of clarifications on what inerrancy means. It does not mean that the Bible contains all information. It does not deny the necessity of interpreting the Bible. It does not mean every statement is infinitely precise. It does not mean one can remove a statement from its own context and apply it to all others. Some would argue that as such qualifications pile up, the concept of inerrancy becomes meaningless because there is no way in which it can be practically applied. However, the clarifications given in this chapter are merely the functional details of a single qualification: the Bible is a book. While this chapter obviously contends that it is unlike any other book in the sense that it is the Word of God Himself, that Word remains in the form of a book. It must be read, and the rules of reading comprehension therefore apply to the Bible as much as to any other book.

The key difference in the way skeptics read the Bible and the way Christians ought to is harmonization. For example, The Bible says that the Father is God, the Son is God, and that the Holy Ghost is God. It also says that there are not three Gods, but one God. One could look

---

36. They were added later for reference purposes.
37. Matt 17:1–13.

at these claims and call it a contradiction, or one could reconcile these apparent contradictions by recognizing the doctrine of the Trinity—that God is three in person and one in essence. Harmonization is not a magical process that Christians made up so that they can still call the Bible the Word of God despite its problems. One practices harmonization in virtually any kind of communication. This is even the case in something as modern and non-religious as video games. In *Xenosaga Episode I*, there is a character (an android named KOS-MOS) who typically has red eyes. However, at several points in the story when she is doing something particularly amazing, she has blue eyes. The player has two possible interpretations. He can either suggest that the animators made a mistake in some of those scenes or that the change in eye color reflects an internal change that allows these extraordinary feats. The latter, of course, ends up being the case in the story. Even in something of this nature, one initially assumes harmony instead of contradiction according to the respect one has for the work. This book has listed many reasons one might have for respecting the Bible—from its historical reliability to the way the Son of God Himself held it in such high esteem. As such, Christians have good reason to search for harmony instead of assuming error.[38]

CONCLUSION

If the inerrancy of the Bible cannot be rejected on the grounds of contradictions and mistakes, then the case made in this chapter remains. Jesus Christ, the Son of God, was reliably recorded as endorsing the divine authority of the Old Testament and authorizing His Apostles to provide His teachings in the New Testament. When one holds a Bible, she is holding a book that can be trusted over and above the opinions of humankind—a book that came from God Himself and is without error. In some ways, this idea is as bizarre as the claim that the man Jesus Christ was also God. Nevertheless, this extraordinary conclusion is where the facts of history lead. Far from reducing the Bible to the ramblings of ignorant priests and religious nutcases, a reasonable analysis confirms Scripture to be the Word of God.

38. Even when one may not know how to harmonize a particular passage, it is still entirely reasonable to believe that said harmony exists but is not yet understood. This does not mean one must keep harmonizing in the face of ongoing and inexplicable contradictions—it merely means that one does not casually throw out an esteemed piece of literature.

8

The Genuine Gospel

INTRODUCTION

ONCE ONE KNOWS HE has a book authored by God, the natural follow-up is to consider the point of it. The bad news that mankind is sinful and in denial about that sin has been dealt with from both a Biblical and philosophical perspective. It is also clear that Jesus saw Himself not just as knowing the way by which this problem is solved but as being the way by which it is solved. The New Testament is therefore primarily concerned with the Gospel, the Good News, brought by Jesus in solution to the Bad News caused by mankind. He tells His disciples that the Old Testament was primarily concerned with Himself as well.[1] But how did Jesus solve the problem of our sinfulness? Just what is the Good News?

FALSE GOSPELS

Unfortunately, even among professing Christians there seem to be countless different answers to that question. "Jesus died for your sins" has become almost a meaningless slogan, and so people fill in the meaning with all kinds of nonsense. Some claim that God gained some insight through Jesus' life and death—that, for example the Good News is that now that Jesus suffered and died as a human, God can understand how hard it is to be human so that He is able to help us now that He realizes we have it so hard. Some claim that the Good News is that because of Jesus' death, God gives us a second chance to live a good life, or sometimes as many chances as it takes provided the time between your last confession and your death does not involve any truly "bad" sins. Some claim that the Good News

---

1. Luke 24:25–27

is that Jesus finally provided the ultimate example to everyone on how to live—perhaps how to care for the poor or how to be tolerant so that our society will eventually become perfect because we finally know how to be good. Some claim that the Good News is that instead of the rigid and difficult requirements of the Old Testament, Jesus has given us the supposedly easier task of loving God and our neighbor. Some claim that the Good News is that by His crucifixion, Jesus showed that God loves people, that all are unconditionally accepted by Him, and everyone will be okay now that we finally understand His love. As usual, there is some element of truth in all of these, but every one of them misses the point of the Gospel.

In a world that is hostile to God, this sort of confusion inside the Church inevitably sows a different kind of confusion outside the Church. Christianity is mocked and dismissed for reasons that have no bearing on the real Gospel. They think that God sends people to Hell for having the misfortune of being born a Muslim or Buddhist. They are indignant that remote tribes who never heard the name of Jesus are going to Hell simply because they had the misfortune of never hearing. They think that "having faith" is a new imperative forming the basis of a new code of ethics and recognize that it is a rather odd redefinition of "being a good person." They think it is senseless to say that one religion is the exclusive way to heaven. I recall an episode of *South Park* in which a group of dead souls of different faiths are ushered into the afterlife, and what takes place is essentially a drawing where it is announced, "and the correct religion is . . . Mormonism! Sorry, everyone, Mormonism was the right choice."[2] Then, like folks who had the wrong lotto number, everyone else is sent to Hell. Such conclusions are ridiculous, but they do logically follow from various false gospels. However, they do not follow from the true Gospel.

DEFENDING THE GOSPEL

Therefore, both inside and outside the church, Christians need to stand ready to make a defense of the Gospel itself. One of the supposed Biblical contradictions that shows up from time to time is in God's plan for salvation. After all, in Ephesians 2:8–9, it says, "For it is by grace you have been saved, through faith—and this not from yourselves, it is the gift of God—not by works, so that no one can boast." But in James 2:24, it says

---

2. This is a paraphrase.

"You see that a person is justified by what he does, and not by faith alone." In Revelation 22:12, Jesus says, "Behold, I am coming soon! My reward is with me, and I will give to everyone according to what he has done." And so, some say that the Bible simultaneously teaches that we are saved by faith alone, that we are saved by faith and works, and that we are saved by works alone. Is the confusion in the Church caused by the incoherence of Scripture?

The previous chapters have touched on some principles of interpreting the Bible, but there is another one not yet mentioned: using Scripture to interpret Scripture by analyzing the unclear passages in light of the clear ones. If one passage that is very cryptic seems to contradict another passage that is very clear, one interprets the cryptic part so that it is consistent with the clear part. Once again, this is exactly how you would interpret any book worthy of respect—not just the Bible. What some consider to be the clearest and most systematic explanation of the Gospel is found in the first eight chapters of Paul's letter to the Romans. In many of his letters, Paul is addressing a specific error or need of the recipients. In Galatians, he angrily refutes the error that Christians must follow the ceremonial practices of the Old Testament in order to be saved.[3] In 1 and 2 Timothy, he is advising a young pastor. In Philippians, he is commending and encouraging a church he knows well. In Romans, however, debate continues over the occasion for the writing. There is no obvious problem that Paul is refuting, and so many believe he is simply laying out the Gospel to a church which he had tried and failed to visit and preach to in person. The theology Paul systematically lays out here is in some ways an easier place to get the main idea than the scattered verses that are often used to support various false gospels (verses that we will address later). Of course, this is by no means the only place in the Bible where the Gospel is taught; it is merely a place where it is very well explained.

ROMANS

After his greetings and introduction, Paul begins laying out his case in 1:18 with an explanation of the bad news—that "the wrath of God is being revealed from heaven against all the godlessness and wickedness of men who suppress the truth by their wickedness."[4] He expounds on the plight

---

3. Or indeed any law, but that is exegesis for another time.
4. Rom. 1:18.

of mankind, declaring that our problem is not ignorance about God, but an unwillingness to acknowledge Him as such.[5] This unwillingness manifests itself in all sorts of immorality, including a vice list that most readers would join in condemning. Paul then turns to the reader to show that each one is guilty under the same law used to condemn others. In light of this, he points out that God will judge all people by what they do. To those who do good, God will give eternal life. To those who do evil, there will only be wrath and anger.[6] Paul then addresses the common objections from Jews and Gentiles. He reminds the Gentiles of the law of God written on their hearts, while he takes time to note that this situation is no different for Jews, whose mere possession of the Law (in a more explicit form than mere natural law) gives no exemption from following it.[7] He concludes with a series of quotations from the Old Testament to drive his point home:

> "There is no one righteous, not even one; there is no one who understands, no one who seeks God. All have turned away, they have together become worthless; there is no one who does good, not even one." "Their throats are open graves; their tongues practice deceit." "The poison of vipers is on their lips." "Their mouths are full of cursing and bitterness." "Their feet are swift to shed blood; ruin and misery mark their ways, and the way of peace they do not know." "There is no fear of God before their eyes."[8]

The argument Paul is making is that while a person might hypothetically earn heaven by living a righteous life, there is not a single person who has ever done so. We need to be righteous to escape God's wrath, but if we are honest, our attempts at following the law only show us how much we fail at achieving righteousness through following the law.

Now that he has shut out all of the false hopes we self-righteously cling to, Paul changes the subject to the Good News. He writes,

> But now, a righteousness from God, apart from law, has been made known, to which the Law and the Prophets testify. This righteousness from God comes through faith in Jesus Christ, to all who believe. There is no difference, for all have sinned and fall short of the glory of God, and are justified freely by his grace through

5. Rom. 1:19–23.
6. Rom. 2:1–8.
7. Rom 2:12–29.
8. Rom 3:10–18.

> the redemption that came by Christ Jesus. God presented Him as a sacrifice of atonement, through faith in his blood. He did this to demonstrate his justice, because in his forbearance he had left the sins committed beforehand unpunished—he did it to demonstrate his justice at the present time, so as to be just and the one who justifies those who have faith in Jesus.
>
> Where then is boasting? It is excluded. On what principle? On that of observing the law? No, but on that of faith. For we maintain that a man is justified by faith apart from observing the law.[9]

The Gospel does not mean that humans no longer need to be righteous to stand before God, but rather that the source of this righteousness is no longer our own actions but Jesus Christ. Paul makes it clear that this righteousness is imputed to us through faith and not earned through following the law.

In the following chapters, Paul further develops this basic message. He emphasizes the role of faith by means of a long example concerning Abraham in chapter 4. In chapter 5, he begins examining the objective consequences of this message. The conflict between God and men that Paul described in the first couple chapters is now over. Our debt to God has been paid by Christ's blood, our punishment was poured out on Him, and so God's righteous wrath has been satisfied and is no longer directed at us. The war is over and we are now reconciled with God. He also makes it clear who Christ achieved this new righteousness for: "While we were still sinners, Christ died for us."[10] He did not do this for the good people while the bad ones get what they deserve; Paul made it clear that all are bad people. Instead, God demonstrated His love by providing righteousness for the very same sinners at whom He was wrathful. Love and Justice, irreconcilable because of our deserved punishment now come together; justice is satisfied and God still provides us what justice alone never could. Children often operate under the misconception that "my parents don't love me because they yell at me and tell me I can't do things I want to do." In a culture that often refuses to grow up, this misconception has great staying power. Nevertheless, Paul shows here that God's love and God's wrath are not as incompatible as many make them out to be.

---

9. Rom 3:21–28.
10. Rom 5:8.

Paul then goes on to address what this means in our lives. The first misconception he addresses is that of assuming license. "What shall we say then? Shall we go on sinning so that grace may increase? By no means!"[11] He then proceeds to explain the mechanism by which this comes to be. He does *not* state that we need to stop sinning or else we will lose our new righteousness. He instead explains that in Baptism, we are united to Christ in His death and therefore also in His resurrection. This sacramental reality is what changes us. Paul explains that Christians now struggle with sin instead of living in it—that there are "two laws at work in us." There is a change in that we now have a need to do good and avoid evil, but this need is indicative, not imperative. "I am a poor miserable sinner" is a direct contradiction of "I am fine the way I am and do not need to change." Any understanding of the first that makes the second compatible with it is an understanding that precludes the Gospel that Paul has pointed out. As Paul writes,

> Therefore, there is now no condemnation for those who are in Christ Jesus, because through Christ Jesus the law of the Spirit of life set me from the law of sin and death. For what the law was powerless to do in that it was weakened by the sinful nature, God did by sending his own Son in the likeness of sinful man to be a sin offering.[12]

The ultimate result of God's work is that we will share in Christ's eternal life and be raised from the dead.

THE FINAL JUDGMENT

If this is the true Gospel, then what is one to make of the comments and verses throughout the Bible that seem to support one of the other "gospels" mentioned at the beginning of this chapter? There are no shortage of verses that speak of a final judgment in which good people are rewarded and evildoers are punished. Revelation 22:12[13] comes to mind again, as does Matthew 25:31–46.[14] If the Bible's message of salvation is no more complicated than this, then the only role this seems to leave Jesus is as

---

11. Rom 6:1–2.
12. Rom 8:1–3.
13. Quoted earlier in the chapter.
14. The judgment of the sheep and the goats. Those who cared for "the least of these brothers of mine" go to eternal life. Those who do not go into eternal fire.

an example for how somebody ought to act in order to pass through this judgment to eternal life. However, passages like these can be reconciled quite easily with the Gospel preached by Paul. Paul himself mentions the final judgment in Romans 2:5–8. However, as was already described, he does not mention this event in order to comfort us—he goes on to say that no one qualifies on their own.[15] The Final Judgment will indeed take place, but we will survive it only by the imputed righteousness of Christ of which Paul speaks.[16]

JESUS' INSTRUCTIONS

The Final Judgment can be read in a way that is consistent with what Paul taught, since Paul also taught the Final Judgment. Nevertheless, these are not the only passages that can appear to teach a salvation that comes from works. Jesus seems to explicitly teach salvation by works in a number of places of which Matthew 19:16–22 is one example:

> Now a man came up to Jesus and asked. "Teacher, what good thing must I do to inherit eternal life?"
>
> "Why do you ask me about what is good?" Jesus replied. "There is only One who is good. If you want to enter life, obey the commandments."
>
> "Which ones?" the man inquired.
>
> Jesus replied, "Do not murder, do not commit adultery, do not steal, do not give false testimony, honor your father and mother, and love your neighbor as yourself."
>
> "All these I have kept," the young man said. "What do I still lack?"
>
> Jesus answered, "If you want to be perfect, go, sell your possessions and give to the poor, and you will have treasure in heaven. Then come, follow me." When the young man heard this, he went away sad, because he had great wealth. Then Jesus said to his disciples, "I tell you the truth, it is hard for a rich man to enter the kingdom of heaven. Again I tell you, it is easier for a camel to go through the eye of a needle than for a rich man to enter the kingdom of God."

It certainly seems as though the rich man asked how to be saved and Jesus told him to perform a list of good works in order to enter the kingdom

15. Rom 3:9–18.
16. Rom 3:21–22; 4:5–8.

of heaven. Is this therefore salvation by works? If it is, then we are all in trouble, because no one but Jesus Himself does what He describes here. This is consistent with Paul's teaching on earning one's way into heaven. The disciples clearly got this message, because their response was not, "Phew! Good thing we're not rich and that we did give up everything to follow you." They ask, "Who then can be saved?"[17] Peter goes so far as to complain that they will not be getting anything for leaving everything to follow Jesus.[18] Jesus prefaced His answer with "There is only One who is good." The rest should make it clear that the One is not the rich young man (or any of us).

The Sermon on the Mount should also make this last fact abundantly clear. "Unless your righteousness surpasses that of the Pharisees and teachers of the law, you will certainly not enter the kingdom of heaven."[19] "Anyone who is angry with his brother will be subject to judgment."[20] "Anyone who looks at a woman lustfully has already committed adultery."[21] "If your right hand causes you to sin, cut it off and throw it away. It is better for you to lose one part of your body than for your whole body to go into hell."[22] And it goes on and on. Do not divorce, do not lie, turn the other cheek to those who strike you, give even more than is demanded to anyone who sues you, love your enemies, do not do anything for praise from men, do not worry,[23] do not judge hypocritically, do to others what you would have them do to you. The list goes on and on before culminating in, "Be perfect as your father in heaven is perfect."[24] Jesus is indeed talking about earning one's way into heaven here, but this is not good news! Jesus' standards are why Paul tells us that no one will be saved by their works. No one can honestly look at her life and think she has perfectly done all of these things. The good news is that immediately

---

17. Matt 19:25
18. Matt 25:27.
19. Matt 5:20.
20. Matt 5:22.
21. Matt 5:28.
22. Matt 5:30.
23. This verse is often quoted as good advice, and it is, but it is a command as well. However, one can discern the presence of the Gospel even in these passages if Jesus tells us not to worry even in light of this heavy burden of law.
24. Matt 5:48.

before delivering the law, Jesus said that He had come to fulfill it.[25] Jesus meant exactly that when He said, "There is only One who is good." Paul's teaching that the righteousness of that One is imputed to us by faith is the only way this can be good news.

The Gospel is the only way to reconcile Jesus' strong teaching of the law with His forgiveness of adulteresses and tax collectors, His insistence to His followers who wanted Him to keep making food for them that they eat His flesh and blood instead, and His parable of the Pharisee and the tax collector in which the repentant sinner goes home justified. Paul's letter to the Romans does not invent a Gospel that Jesus never taught, it explains that very same Gospel outside of a historical narrative. Jesus was laying out the same bad news as Paul in verses like the ones above. He also laid out the same good news in passages such as Matthew 20:28 in which He tells His disciples that "the Son of Man did not come to be served, but to serve, and to give his life as a ransom for many" or in John 3:16, when He tells Nicodemus that God so loved the world that He gave His only begotten son, that whosoever believes in Him shall not perish, but have everlasting life.

There is a great section in John in which Jesus explains the Gospel to a particularly stubborn group of people (6:15–59). After Jesus miraculously fed a crowd of over 5,000 people, that crowd wanted to make Him king by force (6:15). They were looking for another leader for Israel like Moses. Their miraculous meal made them think of the days when the Israelites were given manna from heaven (6:30–31), and they wanted Jesus to bring those days again. Jesus told them that bread is unimportant compared to the eternal life He offers (6:26–27) through belief in Him. They return to the subject of manna from heaven. He says that the true bread from heaven is the one who came down from heaven. They say, "Great, give us this better bread."[26] Then Jesus explicitly tells them that He is the bread of life (6:35). They continue grumbling because they know His earthly parents but not His heavenly Father. Jesus finally tells them flat out that if they want to eat something, they need to eat His flesh and His blood which He is to sacrifice for our sins ("This bread is my flesh which I will give for the life of the world." 6:51). Jesus is explaining that the important thing that He came to do is to do His Father's will and be sacrificed, but

---

25. Matt 5:17.
26. This is a paraphrase.

the crowd refuses to accept this—not because they are too unintelligent to understand Jesus' message but because they willfully refuse it because they are focused on something else—an earthly kingdom. Paul did not make up the Gospel—He received it from Jesus who taught exactly the same thing. All the important points in Romans—man's inability to live up to God's law, Christ's sacrifice as an atonement for those sins, and the receipt of Christ's righteousness by belief in Him—are all taught by Jesus as well.

FAITH AND WORKS

So if salvation by works is clearly out, then what about the third option of some combination of faith and works such as Christ's imputed righteousness giving us a chance to earn heaven by achieving our own inherent righteousness? There is no shortage of Biblical examples of people who completely changed after their conversion. Paul himself is perhaps the most obvious: a Pharisee who hunted down and executed Christians and then made an apostle after his encounter with the risen Christ. There are also the many moral precepts listed in both the Old and New Testaments—virtually all the epistles include exhortations for the recipients to behave in a way that is worthy of the Gospel and give some detail on what that entails. Beyond this, there are a number of passages that some would claim state that we need works in addition to faith to be saved. In Romans, Paul says that we are saved by faith and not by works, but some would suggest that instead of reading other Scripture in light of Paul, we need to read Paul in light of these other passages of Scripture. Both approaches could be considered "using Scripture to interpret Scripture,"[27] and so it makes sense to examine whether or not our understanding of Paul should be modified by other passages. Could we reconcile Paul's teachings about faith with other writers' teachings about works by making both necessary elements of salvation?

One of the most commonly used passages that is said to teach faith and works is found in the second chapter of James, a portion of which was quoted earlier when posing the supposed contradiction in God's plan for salvation:

---

27. A principle of Biblical interpretation that indicates that if something in the Bible is unclear, one should look to other parts of the Bible for clarification—a good general rule for reading any book.

> What good is it, my brothers, if a man claims to have faith but has no deeds? Can such a faith save him? Suppose a brother or sister is without clothes and daily food. If one of you says to him, "Go, I wish you well; keep warm and well fed," but does nothing about his physical needs, what good is it? In the same way, faith by itself, if it is not accompanied by action, is dead. But someone will say, "You have faith; I have deeds." Show me your faith without deeds, and I will show you my faith by what I do. You believe that there is one God. Good! Even the demons believe that—and shudder. You foolish man, do you want evidence that faith without deeds is useless? Was not our ancestor Abraham considered righteous for what he did when he offered his son Isaac on the altar? You see that his faith and his actions were working together, and his faith was made complete by what he did. And the scripture was fulfilled that says, "Abraham believed God, and it was credited to him as righteousness," and he was called God's friend. You see that a person is justified by what he does and not by faith alone.[28]

After an initial read, it seems difficult to reconcile this with what Paul says. James even uses the same example of Abraham to reach what looks like a conclusion opposite to Paul's. Surely, there is the temptation to conclude that Paul is teaching that we are saved by faith while James is teaching that we are saved by faith and works and therefore reconcile these two teachings by concluding that Paul was only telling half the story and James tells the rest of it: that we are initially saved by faith but must finish the job ourselves by doing works—that we are cleansed from original sin by Christ's righteousness, but must earn our own inherent righteousness as well in order to be ultimately justified before God.

In order to take Paul seriously, however, one must recognize that he makes it very explicit that we are saved by faith *and not works*.[29] If James is then really saying that we are saved in the same sense by some combination of faith and works, there is a genuine contradiction between the two. Since we have good reason to believe that the Bible is the communication of a non-contradictory God, however, this is not an acceptable conclusion. And so, a closer examination of James is warranted.

> 2:14: *What good is it, my brothers, if a man claims to have faith but has no deeds? Can such a faith save him?*

---

28. Jas 2:14–26.
29. Rom 3:21–2, 27–8.

James begins by rhetorically questioning the worth of a situation. However, the situation is not that a man has faith but has no deeds; it is that a man *claims* to have faith but has no deeds. James is leaving open the question of whether this hypothetical man has "faith" at all. The second question also contains an overlooked word: "such." James does not pose the question of whether faith can save this man but whether a faith of a particular character can save him. But what is the character to which James refers? So far, all the reader knows is that it is possessed by a man who has no deeds, but James will become more specific later on. Likewise, he will also make clear to whom the man is making his claim.

> 2:15–17: *Suppose a brother or sister is without clothes and daily food. If one of you says to him, "Go, I wish you well; keep warm and well fed," but does nothing about his physical needs, what good is it? In the same way, faith by itself, if it is not accompanied by action, is dead.*

The first thing to note is that James is not here instructing his reader on how to treat people in need. He assumes his reader already knows this. As verse 17 makes clear with the words, "in the same way," James is making an analogy between the claim of faith on the part of one without action and the claims of well-wishing that are not accompanied by action. The clear implication is that people whose actions do not line up with their words are liars—their words are ultimately empty. James has therefore called the claim of faith a falsehood; the man has faith of a sort, but a dead one rather than one that possesses life.

> 2:18: *But someone will say, "You have faith; I have deeds." Show me your faith without deeds and I will show you my faith by what I do.*

In this verse, James makes it clearer to whom the man is claiming to have faith. This takes the form of a hypothetical dialog between the man and James, but James is not putting himself in the stead of God. The claim of faith is being made before men and it is James, a man, asking for the evidence.

> 2:19: *You believe that there is one God. Good! Even the demons believe that—and shudder.*

Here, James begins to clarify the sort of faith he is proclaiming to be empty. As the author of Hebrews writes, faith is "the certainty of things unseen."[30] The only unseen thing in this man's faith is God—it is a faith consisting only of basic monotheism. Monotheism is true, but rather than being identical with saving faith, it is something even the demons recognize. James' example describes a faith whose object is insufficient for salvation. This insufficiency is indicated to others by a lack of works but is not itself a lack of works. While faith is "the certainty of things unseen," a lack of works *can* be seen as James has already pointed out.

> 2:20: *You foolish man, do you want evidence that faith without deeds is useless?*

Because it has already been established that James is criticizing an insufficient type of faith, one must read this verse without concluding that a sufficient type of faith is also inadequate without deeds. What one *can* conclude is that an essential element of faith must always result in works. The rhetorical question, then, indicates that James is about to give evidence that the saving kind of faith is accompanied by works.

> 2:21: *Was not our ancestor Abraham considered righteous for what he did when he offered his son Isaac on the altar?*

Once again, the key question to ask is, "Considered righteous by whom?" The immediate context remains claims of faith before men, and so one cannot simply assume James is saying Abraham was considered righteous before God for what he did. Likewise, the larger context of Genesis (which James will quote a few verses later) precludes such an interpretation. Years before Abraham offered up Isaac (Gen 22:10), "Abraham believed the Lord, and he credited it to him as righteousness" (Gen 15:6). Both the immediate and wider contexts require one to read this verse to say that Abraham was considered righteous by those who read about him because of his obedience.

> 2:22: *You see that his faith and his actions were working together, and his faith was made complete by what he did.*

James does not explicitly state what faith and actions were working together to do, so the context must determine it. In light of what has been read so far, one must read this to mean that faith and actions worked together to show men that Abraham had a sufficient faith. Faith is then made complete in this sense: it would be implausible to suggest to a reader

30. Heb 11:1.

that Abraham truly believed God if Abraham had no inclination to obey Him. Surely there are effects caused by both faith and works, but this does not automatically mean that justification is the effect James is speaking about.

> 2:23: *And the scripture was fulfilled that says, "Abraham believed God and it was credited to him as righteousness."*

A superficial reading of this verse could result in the interpretation that God's imputation of righteousness to Abraham in Gen. 15:6 was only made real and effective when Abraham obeyed. A closer examination, however, shows that James, while referencing that verse, is *not directly quoting it*. Whereas Genesis makes it active "he [the Lord] credited it to him [Abraham] as righteousness," James changes it to a passive voice "it was credited to him [Abraham] as righteousness." As was argued in the previous chapter, respect for the literature prevents one from jumping to the conclusion that James is deceptively misquoting Moses. He is referencing Genesis, but intentionally adapting it to his own message. The nature of the change, therefore, is part of the message James is communicating. He specifically removes God as the actor from crediting righteousness to Abraham. Therefore, the reader *must* not read this to mean that God's crediting was fulfilled by Abraham's actions. With one actor separated from the situation, the actor supplied by the context must take His place. Once again, James remains consistent in speaking of fulfillment before men.

> 2:24: *You see that a person is justified by what he does and not by faith alone.*

The verse that initially seemed to so blatantly contradict Paul no longer has that appearance. The consistent context requires reading this as meaning that a person is justified before men by what he does and not by faith alone. James' message in these verses is to instruct his reader that not everyone who claims to have faith actually has it. A sufficient saving faith results not only in justification but also in works, just as an exploding firework results in both light and sound. Works do not result in justification, but the sufficient faith that does save also results in works. As Luther famously declared, a man is justified by faith alone but not by a faith that is alone.

When read carefully, James is indeed compatible with Romans, not because Paul's context is "the beginning" of the Christian life where we are saved by faith and James' context is the mature Christian life where we remain saved by works. It is compatible because Paul is explaining *that* we are saved by faith and James is talking about discerning *whether* a generic person *has* saving faith. When James speaks of fulfillment and completion, he means the substantiation of the claim, not the actualization of God's imputation of righteousness. It is not the book of Romans, but careful reading of James which saves one from this error. One cannot read "What good is it . . . if a man claims to have faith but has no deeds? Can such faith save him?" as though it said, "What good is it if a man has faith but no deeds? Can faith alone save him?" In the same way, one cannot read "work out your salvation with fear and trembling"[31] as if it said "work *for* your salvation with fear and trembling."

DEAD FAITH

There remains, however, one question that was not answered by James. What is the missing element of faith that he implied in 2:19–20? He was clear that it is essential to saving faith—that a faith that does not include it is not the kind of faith that delivers salvation. We also know that the presence of this unseen thing is accompanied by obedience. But what essential "thing" could cause the effect James describes? When a man *claims* to have saving faith but actually has an insufficient faith as in the situation James presents, what missing thing is making him a liar? An answer can perhaps be found in 1 John.

Truth and lies are a major theme in 1 John, in which John talks about the same topic that James does: How does one discern a genuine faith? He begins by setting out the truth of his claims about Christianity based on what he has seen and heard. Then throughout the letter he makes statements such as:

> If we claim to have fellowship with him yet walk in the darkness, we lie and do not live by the truth.[32]

---

31. Phil 2:12.
32. 1 John 1:6.

> If we claim to be without sin, we deceive ourselves and the truth is not in us.[33]
>
> If we claim we have not sinned, we make him out to be a liar and his word has no place in our lives.[34]
>
> The man who says, "I know him," but does not do what he commands is a liar, and the truth is not in him.[35]
>
> Anyone who claims to be in the light but hates his brother is still in the darkness.[36]
>
> Who is the liar? It is the man who denies that Jesus is the Christ. Such a man is the antichrist—he denies the Father and the Son.[37]

Many of these statements involve contrasting a person's declarations with his actions in order to verify the truth of those declarations—if someone says A, but does B, he is a liar. John focuses particularly on claims about one's relationship with God. However, there are two quotations out of the ones cited that simply say if a Christian[38] says A, he is a liar. The last one listed is one such, making belief in Jesus' office as the Messiah an obviously essential element of saving faith. The other is, "If we claim we have not sinned, we make him out to be a liar and his word has no place in our lives." The knowledge that we are sinners is an essential element of saving faith. As was mentioned in the chapter on sin, the first step in conversion is that the Holy Spirit works knowledge of sin and contrition over it through the Law. The Gospel is literal nonsense without that knowledge; "Jesus died to pay for our sins" becomes a fill-in-the-blank: Jesus died to pay for a nebulous "something" or perhaps simply, "Jesus died." Apart from the bit about sin, there is no reason to consider Jesus' death good news.

The knowledge that we are sinners fits the first criteria that James laid out for his missing unseen thing; it is an essential element of saving faith. Does it match the second? Does its lack necessarily result in an absence of works? The answer is simple. "I am a sinner" and "there is nothing I

---

33. 1 John 1:8.
34. 1 John 1:10.
35. 1 John 2:4.
36. 1 John 2:9.
37. 1 John 2:22.
38. John always says, "we" in this letter.

ought to do differently" are literal contradictions. If one understands the former in any way that allows the latter, she does not understand it in the way the Bible means it. To say "I am a sinner" is to say "I do not do good." However, "I ought to do good" is a truism—"what ought to be done" and "good deeds" are identical concepts. Therefore, if one believes "I do not do good," and "I ought to do good" is literally undeniable, then the only possible conclusion is "I ought to change what I do." To deny or fudge the meanings of these words enough to deny a contradiction is to deny part of the essential content of saving faith as given by Scripture.

A person might be able to simultaneously believe that the moon is made of green cheese and that the moon is not made of green cheese for his entire life provided he never needs to plan a mission to land on the moon. Nevertheless, where they touch our lives, contradictions cannot last forever because a person can only act as if one or the other is true. Ideas on "what we ought to do" obviously touch our lives in such a way. That may be different for another species in another universe, but it is unavoidable for humans in our own. The contradiction between "I am a sinner" and "there is nothing I ought to do differently" *must* eventually break down. And so, one is brought back to Romans once again, where Paul describes the conflict between our sinful and regenerate natures, and eventually describes victory over them by continually putting the sinful nature to death.[39] Saving faith creates an indicative (not an imperative) need to change. It is a hunger that God gives us, not merely a command that we must carry out "or else."

James may have had other essential elements in mind while describing an insufficient faith. His example, an intellectual acknowledgment of monotheism, was pretty bare, after all. However, knowledge of our sinfulness fits the bill very well. Luther acknowledged that we are saved by faith alone, but not by a faith that is alone. However, like James, the problem Luther describes is in the content of our faith. The content of one's actions merely provides clues to the content of one's faith. Salvation comes, not by faith in something, but faith in the atoning sacrifice of Jesus Christ for sinful humans.

With this understanding, one can also answer those who use verses like 1 John 3:4–10 to argue salvation by works:

---

39. Rom 8:1–17.

> Everyone who sins breaks the law; in fact, sin is lawlessness. But you know that he appeared so that he might take away our sins. And in him is no sin. No one who lives in him keeps on sinning. No one who continues to sin has either seen him or known him. Dear children, do not let anyone lead you astray. He who does what is right is righteous, just as he is righteous. He who does what is sinful is of the devil, because the devil has been sinning from the beginning. The reason the Son of God appeared was to destroy the devil's work. No one who is born of God will continue to sin, because God's seed remains in him; he cannot go on sinning, because he has been born of God. This is how we know who the children of God are an who the children of the devil are: Anyone who does not do what is right is not a child of God; nor is anyone who does not love his brother.

It is simple to see that John does not intend to communicate that upon becoming a Christian, one can again never sin without ceasing to be a Christian. This is the same letter in which the same apostle says, "My dear children, I write this to you so that you will not sin, but if anybody does sin, we have one who speaks to the Father in our defense—Jesus Christ, the Righteous One. He is the atoning sacrifice for our sins, and not only for ours but also for the sins of the whole world."[40] One can be sure that whatever John is saying, he is not blatantly contradicting what he said earlier. John gives no timetables for not "continuing to sin." One should conclude that John is writing about a change in our lives that *will* occur, not saying, "You had better not do anything else wrong or else." This change is something that the Christian can have faith that God will bring about in him.

CONCLUSION

There is no contradiction within Bible's message of salvation. Christians need not take all these passages and calculate some kind of average between them in order to find a coherent message. We need not "find the right balance" between Law and Gospel as if they were somehow contrary to one another. We need not divvy up the contributions towards our salvation between God and ourselves and simply disagree over how much or what kinds of our own effort are required. Everyone can read the mes-

---

40. 1 John 2:1–2.

sage for themselves without having a priest as an intermediary.[41] The bad news may be worse than we would ever admit on our own, but the Good News is better than we could ever imagine. It is by Christ's merits alone that we are saved from justly deserved punishment—saved by grace alone through faith alone in Christ alone.

---

41. Provided one reads carefully, honestly, and continuously.

III

LIFE

If Christianity Is True

9

Science vs. Christianity

The Root of the Problem

INTRODUCTION

THE FIRST CHAPTER OF this book considered the apparent conflict between faith and reason. Both inside the church and out, there are many who erroneously claim that the two are incompatible with each other. It characterized faith and reason (focusing on deductive reasoning), the nature of the supposed conflict (that deductive reasoning cannot allow a contradiction and faith depends on contradictions), and found that accepting contradictions is not an essential element of Biblical faith. The author of Hebrews described faith as the certainty of things unseen, not the certainty of things contradictory.

It is not only with regards to deductive reasoning and contradictions, however, that there is friction between faith and reason. There is also a great deal of angst over a conflict between religion and science. In the Western world, this nearly always takes the form of a conflict between Christianity and science. Beyond the question of whether faith interferes with deductive reasoning, there is the question of whether it interferes with our ability to understand the physical world. Galileo is often offered as the quintessential example of this conflict. He, of course, promoted a heliocentric view of the universe in which the Earth moves around the Sun. The Church, as the story usually goes, persecuted Galileo because of passages in the Bible such as, "the world is firmly established, it cannot be moved"[1] and "the sun rises and the sun sets, and hurries back to where it rises."[2] In so doing, they denied the clear evidence put forward by Galileo in favor of blind adherence to an old book and consequently held back science through dogmatism. Of course, others argue that the conflict resulted from adherence to Aristotelian astronomy rather than adherence to the Bible. One could also point out that the necessity of describing motion within a frame of reference renders the question moot anyway. When people speak about sunrise or sunset, they are not being inaccurate, they are merely using the earth as a frame of reference to describe the motion. Regardless of its foundation in fact, the usual story certainly captures the idea held by many that scientific progress is necessarily held back by religion. This conflict is probably most clearly seen today on the question of origins. There are controversies over the public school curriculum, petitions against intelligent design in universities, allegations of discrimination against intelligent design advocates, and so forth.

Unfortunately, many of the popular and simple means of setting aside this conflict are inadequate. For example, many claim that there really is no conflict because science and religion are two completely different domains of thought—that science tells us the "how" and religion tells us the "why" when it comes to the world. This may be plausible for some religions, but not for Christianity. As this book has demonstrated, Christianity is based on actual occurrences in the actual world—the same subject that science addresses. In his miracles, Jesus tied his spiritual authority to physical phenomena that occurred by supernatural means. The need for the Gospel rests on the Fall in Genesis being an actual event in history. People, events, lineages, histories—these are all things that occur in the same physical world that science studies. This attempted resolution goes back to the same separation of faith and reason debunked in the first chapter—that faith is in the realm of the irrational and science in the realm of the rational. This, in turn, leads to the modern conceit that science is the only way one can know truth.[3] Resolution cannot be found in separating facts from meaning and value as many suggest.

In order to appropriately address the conflict, it is necessary to examine its nature. This chapter will take a similar approach to the first

---

1. Ps 93:1.
2. Eccl 1:5.
3. Shown to be self-referentially incoherent in chapter 2.

chapter's analysis of the conflict between faith and reason—characterizing the two sides and finding the source of the conflict. This time, however, the focus will be on abductive reasoning rather than deductive. Unlike deductive reasoning, which applies logical rules to known premises to reach inescapable conclusions, abductive reasoning looks at facts and finds the best explanation for them out of many possible explanations.

ABDUCTIVE REASONING

When I taught this topic at my church, I drew a picture of a cake on the white board and asked the class to figure out why it was there. There were two theories we considered. The first was that the Evangelism committee drew it while planning refreshments for the upcoming talent show. The second was that I drew it so that I could make a point about abductive reasoning. I then asked the class to give me some facts about the drawing that might help us. They observed that the picture was indeed drawn by a person (of questionable artistic talent),[4] that we were in an apologetics class discussing abductive reasoning, and that it was important to me that they figure out why it was there. However, they also observed that we were meeting in the very room that the Evangelism committee had used earlier that week to discuss the talent show and that they were discussing refreshments. Eventually my wife and the other committee members present all denied that the picture was present at the meeting; and we observed that they were all honest people. Unsurprisingly, we arrived at the correct conclusion that I drew the picture to give a concrete example of an abstract point.

That conclusion was the best one because it was the simplest solution that explained all of the relevant facts. It was better than the explanation that the Evangelism committee was planning a celebration because that explanation was a poor fit with the fact that everyone in the meeting denied it. In order to be true, that explanation would require a conspiracy of lies from people known to be honest—a situation with no evidence to support it. It is a possible explanation, but not the best explanation. Of course, with different facts put into the mix, a different conclusion might end up being the best one. For example, if I had introduced the observation that I had seen our pastor draw a picture that morning, it

---

4. A quick thank-you to Mike for pointing out that it did not look like a toddler had drawn it because there was the impression of depth.

would have been good to reconsider our theory. Such a change would not result from a mistake that was made, but from new information relevant to the analysis.

The presence or absence of different facts can lead to very different conclusions even when one follows the same reasoning process. Because of this, abductive reasoning does not and cannot offer certainty. Nevertheless, simply because it can be wrong does not mean that one should ignore it or dismiss it without cause. If there were a situation in which the question of who drew the picture would make a difference in one's behavior, one ought to act according to the best information available. The same holds true for inductive reasoning. Generalizations can be incorrect, but despite the claims of many modern people, generalizations are an essential part of life. That is why Christians should not find themselves saying, "I do not need to believe in evolution because it is only a theory, and theories might be wrong." There may be plenty of other reasons to doubt a particular theory, and its theoretical nature might make it possible to doubt, but as chapter 5 argued when addressing the historical reliability of the Bible, the fact that there may be another explanation is not by itself reason to doubt an accepted explanation. One ought to use the best explanations available.

THE NATURE OF SCIENCE

Nevertheless, because of the possibility of falsehood, one should be interested in ways in which the abductive reasoning process could be made more reliable. In the example of the drawing, the class was simply using facts that were readily available, either because we happened to observe them directly or because someone mentioned them. However, if one were to go after facts in a targeted manner, one would have a better set of information, and consequently a better chance at arriving at a better explanation. Because of this, many people throughout history have propagated techniques that a person could use to minimize the possibility of drawing a wrong conclusion. The Scientific Method is one such body of techniques. The very basic version of the Scientific Method is divided into four stages:

- Characterization
- Hypothesis

- Prediction
- Experiment

First, one characterizes the observation (e.g.: there is a drawing of a cake on the blackboard). Next, one suggest a hypothesis—a possible explanation for what has been observed. Then, one makes a prediction—if the hypothesis were true or false, what would the consequences be (i.e. what else would be true or false as a result)? Finally, one performs experiments to verify whether or not the prediction is indeed accurate. If it is, one has acquired new evidence for her hypothesis; if not, she may or may not have evidence against it depending on what was being tested.

Of course, science becomes a great deal more complicated than that as there are many variations and ancillary techniques to further improve on this basic method. For example, there is repeatability: Repeating the same experiment again and again helps reduce the possibility of a mistake in the experiment leading to an erroneous result. There is also peer review, the concept in which other qualified people can look at how the process was followed and point out flaws in reasoning or method and offer ideas for improvement. There is the concept of control, by which one creates a situation in which the influence of one factor can be isolated from the influence of other factors. These techniques and others help refine abductive reasoning to minimize the chance of mistaken conclusions.

Of course, science is iterative as well, meaning that the results of one step are fed into the next step. For example, once one has adequately supported a theory, it can be used as evidence for or against other hypotheses. This adds a couple of advantages. First, it allows the possibility of correction—one might discover that a supported theory may be in conflict with a theory with even greater support, and so the first theory is modified to make it consistent with the second or discarded entirely if it cannot be salvaged. Secondly, iteration allows the exponential growth in knowledge that has come about as a result of science. Each fact learned is not only an addition to what humans know, but also becomes another tool to help us learn more.

The word "science" is used in a number of different ways, but all definitions revolve around this method. Science could mean the method itself. It could mean the current body of knowledge achieved by all the iterations of this method. It could mean the opinions of the community of people who openly practice this method. Nevertheless, in all these cases, the foundation of science is an enhanced method of abductive reasoning.

THE CONFLICT

If this method sounds good, that is probably because it is. The benefits of science should be fairly obvious to all of us. Therefore, it does and should give us pause that something ostensibly good is in conflict with Christianity in our culture. How can this be if Christianity is true? This brings us back to our original question about the nature of the conflict, especially where it concerns origins. To understand the objections that science often makes against the idea that the universe was created by God, a good place to start is to look at some of what has been written against the Intelligent Design movement[5] by scientists. For example, the faculty of Iowa State University drafted a petition[6] on the subject in late 2005 signed by 124 professors in order to "reject all attempts to represent Intelligent Design as a scientific endeavor."[7] The statement identifies three problems with claims that the complexity of life and processes can only be explained by an intelligent creator: "(1) the arbitrary selection of features claimed to be engineered by a designer; (2) unverifiable conclusions about the wishes and desires of that designer; and (3) an abandonment by science of methodological naturalism."[8]

The first two of the three objections are unsubstantiated within the statement itself. The first, the supposed arbitrary nature of alleged design features, provokes some interesting questions, but not ones which will be covered in this book. The second objection has already been considered—at the very least the wishes and desires of the designer can be investigated by philosophy, history, intuition, and revelation. These questions cannot be outside the realm of reasoned judgment. The statement, however, dwells on the third: "an abandonment by science of methodological naturalism." It states,

---

5. This movement argues that the evidence shows that life is the result of action by an intelligent agent (often identified with God).

6. This petition is no longer available on the Iowa State website, but the full text can be found via website archive sites' record of the cited address.

7. Iowa State faculty, "Statement," paragraph 1.

8. Iowa State faculty, paragraph 2.

> Methodological naturalism, the view that natural phenomena can be explained without reference to supernatural beings or events, is the foundation of the natural sciences. The history of science contains many instances where complex natural phenomena were eventually understood only by adherence to methodological naturalism.[9]

This same point can be found in a similar petition drafted by University of Iowa faculty:

> Methodological naturalism, the view that natural phenomena can be explained without reference to supernatural beings or events is, by far, historically the most successful research strategy of the natural sciences. The goal of science is to form hypotheses to explain the natural world around us. Scientific hypotheses must be falsifiable and tested by the evaluation of evidence obtained through observation and experimentation. The history of science contains many instances where complex natural phenomena were eventually understood only by adherence to methodological naturalism. However, we know of no instance in which a competition between two theories, one naturalistic and the other supernaturalistic, has been in the end won by the latter.[10]

"Methodological naturalism" is another approach that the scientific method, as popularly practiced, has added to optimize abductive reasoning. To put it in the simplest terms, any observed phenomena in the physical world must be explained *exclusively* in terms of observed natural forces. To be fair, this idea has indeed been extremely helpful in explaining the world around us, as was claimed in the petition. While "God did it" is possible in many instances, that certainly does not always mean it is the best explanation.[11] In operational science, the study of how the world presently works, it makes perfect sense to restrict theories to natural forces. In most cases, there is no reason to think that a supernatural power is interfering with experiments, and methodological naturalism provides an effective check on and motivation to question superstition.

However, as this book has argued, every bad thing is a good thing that has been corrupted by being taken out of its proper place, and any

---

9. Iowa State faculty, paragraph 3.
10. University of Iowa faculty, "Statement," paragraph 1.
11. The fact that it is also a very easy explanation has likely contributed to some of its historical misapplications.

good thing over which sinful humanity has power can be corrupted. Science also can be and is spoiled when it is removed from its proper context. Obviously science works well when studying the way the world works, but when it comes to origins (the way the world came about), the area of study is not how things work now, but how things happened in the past. There is a historical element to the subject. If philosophy, revelation, and intuition all indicate that humans live in a theistic universe, then the world came about not purely through natural causes, but through the actions of God—that is, to some extent through supernatural causes. A method that can only entertain natural causes cannot be the sole arbiter of events that are likely to involve supernatural causes. This is another example of why the notion that science is the only way we can know truth is problematic.

The nature of the flaw can indicate something about the consequences. The best naturalistic explanation for a supernatural event can never be the true explanation; it must be deficient to some extent. The response of many Christians to this deficiency is to simply add God into the current scientific theory. After all, if science is merely ignoring God, then should not adding God be all that is required? Unfortunately, simple addition does not account for the complete nature of the error. Science is oriented around finding the best naturalistic explanation. Consequently, there is a corollary to the first consequence. If there is a supernatural cause and a material effect (as there is in any miracle), science must substitute the most plausible false natural cause for the true supernatural cause.[12] As was mentioned earlier, one ought to act as though the best explanation is true. If "the best explanation" is perverted into "the best naturalistic explanation," then it becomes apparent that in cases where God's action is present, science must propagate a false naturalistic story as true. Simply adding God to a false story does not a true story make.

Imagine going through the exercise with the cake again, only with the restriction that the picture must have a non-human cause. Very different explanations would be offered. One would have to look for other

---

12. Of course, one can argue over the extent of the effect of the supernatural cause for any given miracle. For example, in the parting of the Red Sea, on could argue that God moved the water, or caused wind that moved the water, or perhaps some more subtle or sophisticated means. Nevertheless, no matter what the theory, if one is talking about a miracle, there must be some point at which matter is affected by the supernatural rather than by the natural.

Science vs. Christianity 151

ways that pictures could be drawn, suggest them as possible explanations, and then target the search for evidence to support those scenarios. Facts that could be interpreted as evidence for the true scenario would be reinterpreted to fit a false scenario. Someone might observe that gorillas have been trained to draw (or at least to wield drawing implements against paper), and offer as a hypothesis that a simian of some kind drew the picture. Any artists present in the class could certainly have put forward the evidence that the picture looks like it was drawn by a monkey in support of that theory, even though it could also be interpreted as meaning that I am a terrible artist. Someone else might observe that machines can draw pictures, so he might hypothesize that the picture was already printed on the board when it was manufactured. No matter how many other enhancements one might add to the process of discovering the origins of the picture, one could never actually find the true origin if the process itself precludes it. As a consequence, a person following the method and committed to explaining the observation must also "discover" a lie to be the truth.

This characterizes the problem, but it does not offer any solutions to it or alternative explanations to the scientific theory of origins. For now, the extent to which science's conclusion is in error has also been left unanswered. Nevertheless, one can be certain that it is in error. In speaking with unbelievers, Christians probably ought not to go much further. What has been accomplished here is a demonstration that rejection of the current scientific theory—even purely on religious grounds—is not necessarily a rejection of reason or even of science in general. It is a rejection of the application of the scientific method to the exclusion of all others with respect to certain topics.

Of course, Christians can and should go further. If the Bible is really the Word of God, then we have access to information that the naturalist does not and can go into greater detail in proposing alternative theories and pointing out errors in the body of scientific knowledge. Nevertheless, that is a conversation that ought to be among Christians while we ourselves remain in substantial disagreement on the issue.[13] While Christians

---

13. Does this necessitate two sciences—a Christian and a secular? Perhaps even one for every religion? This is a complicated question beyond the scope of this book. To answer briefly, I find such a split distasteful. My inclination is that it would be unnecessary in operational science, but may be an unfortunate necessity when it comes to certain topics such as origins and cosmology. Having different beliefs about where the world

should not hide their views on the subject, there is often little point in debating evolution and creationism with the unbelieving world. For example, virtually any case for a young earth is going to depend on information found in Scriptures that unbelievers do not accept. Acceptance of these Scriptures is going to depend on acceptance of Jesus as the Son of God—something found only among Christians. Without that common ground, we would merely be arguing in circles (as is typically the case in the rare debates between creationists and evolutionists). Christians must certainly reject the false idea that Christianity is broadly anti-scientific or irrational. Depending on a given Christian's beliefs about origins, there may also be situations in which we must defend the possibility of a relatively young earth.[14] After all, one could argue that if the Bible is certainly wrong on history, then it cannot be the Word of God.[15] However, Christians should not try to convince a non-believer that the earth is 6,000 years old and that he therefore ought to become a Christian; there is no point to it.

GOING FURTHER

There is a great deal of disagreement among Christians over the extent to which science is wrong, and there are intelligent people of goodwill on many different sides. Nevertheless, Christians who disagree over this topic often engage in unprofitable arguments that tend to miss the point. The most obvious examples are those that claim the other side either ignores the facts presented by the world around us or the facts presented by the Bible. Both of these allegations ignore the reality that both the Bible and the world need to be interpreted.[16] Of course, while these allegations are assumed far too often, they often have some basis in fact. There are Christians who fit each description. However, neither of these approaches is adequate. The fact that Christianity is a historical faith taking place in the physical world has two implications: (1) the physical world cannot be considered inherently deceptive and (2) the Bible can inform us about the

---

came from is the status quo for humanity. The idea of all of humankind progressing until we all unite behind a single idea seems less plausible every day.

14. Without being too dogmatic about a specific age.

15. The other option, of course, is to argue that the Bible says nothing of the kind. However, as the chapter will consider, this approach often causes as many problems as it solves.

16. However, despite what many people believe, the necessity of interpretation does not remove the distinction between good and bad interpretations.

physical world. Simplistic attempts to deal with the disagreements dodge the real issues and make the conflict harder than it has to be. While it is entirely appropriate to choose a side and argue for its truth, it is inappropriate to oversimplify the issue—the debate is real.

THE EXTENT OF THE ERROR

Because of its commitment to methodological naturalism, science must necessarily be (or will eventually come to be) in error when it answers questions of origins. Because of this philosophical flaw, one cannot simply trust the authority of what mainstream science tells her on subjects where she has good reason to believe that God was involved. However, this still leaves the question of the extent of the error. Many take what is essentially a deistic view of creation in order to minimize the difficulties with science. In this case, God, at a single point in time, set the entire universe in motion—"God caused the Big Bang" is a popular Christian explanation. Subsequent points at which God intervened in physical life on earth were more localized and personal phenomena—changing the course of human history, certainly, but not profoundly changing the way the universe works. In such a scenario, there would be merely one occurrence for which science substituted a natural cause for a supernatural cause. It may even be an occurrence so far back in the chain of events that science has not theorized about it yet. In such a case, any error in mainstream science would be minimal.

But is this instantaneous creation consistent with how the Bible describes creation? That depends on how one interprets the relevant passages. The case this book has made for Christianity involves the Bible using different types of literature, some more figurative than others. Knowing what kind of literature a portion of Scripture is makes all the difference in how to interpret it. In modern times, it is very frequently claimed that the creation account in Genesis is basically poetry,[17] and consequently, the only thing the reader is meant to take out of it is that God created the world, that he made humans in His image, and that humankind sinned. Everything else is just what the reader adds to it. The problem with this explanation is that even if Genesis is poetry, that is not how one should interpret poetry. Nobody reads Psalm 23 and claims that the only thing we can take away from it is that God took care of David. Even a cursory

17. Or another highly figurative genre.

examination of the various images in the psalm reveals the different kinds of needs God supplies, the completeness with which he supplies them, and God's utter trustworthiness. Even if the first chapter of Genesis is a poem (and I am not claiming it is), one's goal should be to get as much as possible out of it, not as little as possible. Even if the days are merely poetic devices, the repetition of this device surely means something. The phrase, "and there was evening, and there was morning—the [nth] day" is used again and again in the chapter.[18] The repetition of "God said . . . and it was so," in describing all the new things being added to the world surely means something as well. Even as a poem, Genesis 1 does not describe a God setting things in motion and watching them play out, but a God who is actively involved until he finished. It describes a God repeatedly intervening, changing, and adding to the world by supernatural means. It describes a God directly involved in the creation of life, the formation of the earth, the stars, and everything else. No matter how Genesis is read, one is left with God repeatedly causing wide-reaching physical phenomena by supernatural means. A deistic interpretation is a poor one.

This repeated activity of God means the potential extent to which science is in error is vast. As was mentioned earlier, science is iterative. One theory can be used as evidence for other theories, which can be used for still others and so on. While this is a great strength, it can also be a great liability. A false theory may have influence on many other theories. If there are multiple situations in which supernatural causes had far-reaching physical effects, as Genesis implies regardless of genre, then errors could be compounded even further.

ATTEMPTED RECONCILIATIONS

As one evaluates the different explanations for all the facts—both physical and Biblical—that are in front of Christians on this topic, there are several points that an appropriate analysis must adhere to.

- Firstly, it must include facts from the Bible in the discussion. It has already been shown that one cannot place the Bible into a completely different realm of thought, so it must be on the table. While it is not purposed as a science textbook,[19] Christians

---

18. Gen 1:5, 8, 13, 19, 23, and 31.

19. This is a frequently misused contention. The fact that the Bible is not a science textbook has to do with its precision on what it describes, not the issue of whether it

have it on good authority (Christ's) that it is inerrant in what it affirms. Any true explanation of origins must not only fit the facts presented within just as it must fit what we observe in creation, the facts within should actually inform our theories about creation.

- Secondly, as the prior consideration of abductive reasoning implied, the analysis must recognize that facts do not speak for themselves; they need to be interpreted by a rational mind. That interpretation may come in such a way that it is without conscious thought, but it is still an interpretation. Even when one reads the Bible, one interprets the text. The same is true of the physical evidence.

- Thirdly, one cannot enter the analysis with the assumption that everything science affirms is true. As has already been argued, it must be in error to some extent, and there is reason to believe that the extent could potentially be very large indeed.

How does this work together? The purpose of the Christian scientist is not to come up with an explanation that fits both the Bible and current scientific theories about the world. The purpose must be to come up with an explanation that fits both the facts presented in the Bible and our actual observations of the world. Many Christians approach the problem by acknowledging that the Bible itself is non-negotiable but also consider popular interpretations of the physical evidence to be non-negotiable. As a result, interpretations of the Bible are forced to adapt to current scientific theories—theories that may change and ultimately make the interpretations appear very foolish. Unfortunately, when one marries Scripture to the spirit of the age, it inevitably becomes a widow. As has already been demonstrated, the popular interpretations of the physical evidence also need to be called into question, and whether by Christians or not, they eventually will be. One must not ignore reality, but one may need to interpret his observations differently than contemporary science in light of the additional information that Scripture brings to the table.

There are many different proposed reconciliations between Scripture and scientific theory, but this book will only consider three of the most popular in America. There may also be countless variations on each of these three, but not every variation can be addressed in this space.

---

describes historical occurrences in the physical world.

THEISTIC EVOLUTION

Basic theistic evolution is perhaps the most popular reconciliation among modern Christians. The idea is that God designed the world in such a way that it includes the process of evolution which would ultimately produce humanity. Just as we can say that God causes the rain to fall on the just and unjust alike while still understanding that the immediate cause of rain is the water cycle, one can say that the immediate cause of evolution is natural selection and genetic variation while God is still the ultimate cause. Because God set a particularly designed universe into motion and guided it, the emergence of life is happening exactly as God planned it. Evolution following the Big Bang is merely the means that God used to create the world.

At first glance, this would appear to be the easy solution to the problem. It puts God back in the role of creator but allows one to be in full agreement with the scientific community. There is no more conflict because the theory is completely consistent with modern scientific theories. This is often considered a mark in its favor, but based on our analysis of the source of the conflict, it is actually detrimental. Certain branches of science—namely biology, cosmology, and geology—should not be entirely correct in their version of history because at some point they must substitute a natural cause for a supernatural one. That is the first problem with theistic evolution—it proposes a solution that completely glosses over the source of the conflict.

One must also consider the implications it has for the philosophical underpinnings of Christianity. The most substantial implication is for answering the problem of natural evil.[20] Why would a good God allow disaster, disease, starvation, and the like—evils that do not appear to proceed from a will besides God's, but from the world itself? Evolution depends on survival of the fittest, but its corollary is death of the unfit. If, by evolution, giraffes acquired long necks to reach food in higher places, then it follows that many of those similar species without such an advantage starved to death before they were able to procreate. If a species acquired a mechanism that helped defend against a predator, then those without are frequently killed by predators. Evolution's functionality depends on things like starvation and violent death. Furthermore, the fossil record shows evidence not just of death, but sicknesses and deformities.

---

20. As opposed to the problem of moral evil considered in chapter 4.

Likewise, disasters—hurricanes, floods, earthquakes, etc—are considered by mainstream science to have always been around. How does one reconcile this with Genesis' account (even a poetic account) that God saw that His creation was "very good?" Are starvation, disease, violence, and disaster very good things?

This view of history precludes the classic Christian answer to the existence of natural evil—that such things are the result of the Fall. Adam's sin did not just damage humanity, but God cursed the earth as a result.[21] All these things existed well before any species like man was around to sin.[22] If they are not the result of something having gone wrong, then they are present because God created the world this way. He does not merely tolerate but actually mandates natural evil. With the classic explanation removed, a new one is necessary, and theistic evolutionists have offered a variety of them. One popular explanation is that God did not create a perfect world, but the best possible world. There are good things in this world that depend in some way on such evils existing. Perhaps evil needs to exist so that people can recognize goodness. Perhaps virtues such as self-sacrifice could not be realized without evil. If God removed the evils, there would also be less good and the world would be worse off.

But are goods which are contingent on evil plausible—especially in light of God being identical with goodness as covered in chapter 4? Ultimately, one can arrange the possibilities into two sets of binary options. The first is that God Himself is either the foundation of the good that depends on evil or He is not. If He is, then there are once again only two options: Either God Himself is also the foundation of the evil on which that good depends, or He is not. If God is the foundation of the good but not of the evil, then God—Goodness in Person—is a contingent being. He needs something outside of Himself to be all He can be. This contradicts the very idea of a theistic God. On the other hand, if God is the foundation of the evil, then it makes no sense to identify Him as good. He is instead beyond good and evil. If God is not the foundation of the evil-contingent good, then the Euthyphro dilemma applies once again. He is not identical with goodness, and there is either a standard above

---

21. Gen 3:17–19.

22. Even if one were to completely write off the suffering of animals as irrelevant, the fact remains that according to evolutionary theory, man suffers from these problems for the same reasons animals do—it is from the animals that man inherited his susceptibility to such things in the first place.

Him to which God himself must submit (in which case He is not really God at all), or He is just arbitrarily making up the difference between right and wrong. In this case, He is not only once again beyond good and evil rather than good as the Bible describes Him, but He even designed goodness in such a way that it must depend on evil.

What then is one to make of virtues that seem to depend on evil? Although many intelligent Christians believe otherwise, describing self-sacrifice or courage as dependent on evil is not a logical necessity but a failure of imagination. Christians worship a God in three persons. Each person of the Trinity gives Himself to the Others so completely that They are only one being. While not intuitive, the Trinity represents complete and perfect self-sacrifice without loss. To see the same picture painted in the finite world, one need only imagine marriage uncorrupted by sin. Both husband and wife concern themselves only with each other, and yet each are completely provided for without loss or suffering—that love then results in offspring who themselves enter into this sacrificial love. Of course, no such marriage has existed after the Fall, but that is because something is wrong, not because all is as God intended. Courage, as it turns out, does not depend on the necessity of evil either, but only of the possibility. God could bravely create a world in which evil was possible by means of free will while knowing what the possible actualization of evil would cost Him when He redeemed it. Likewise, a man on horseback could bravely leap a small gully, trusting his own skill and the soundness of his horse without a guarantee that he would make it but also without actually failing. If mere human creativity can discern plausible ways in which such virtues can exist without evil, then how much more can divine creativity?

There are many wise and intelligent Christians who believe otherwise—that natural evil was created for the sake of good in some way. Some of them I have even quoted in this book. Nevertheless, this does appear inconsistent with the simple observation that pain is intended to indicate that something has gone wrong. One can certainly remain a Christian while accepting theistic evolution. However, when a skeptic starts asking why God loves smallpox and cancer so much, theistic evolutionists have the unenviable task of explaining why instead of placing the origins of such suffering in the Fall.

In addition to philosophical concerns, theistic evolution has strong implications for how one is able to read the Bible. First, one must reconsider the Bible's view of death. According to theistic evolution, it is the very engine of creation as the less adapted die in favor of the better adapted according to God's plan. However, the New Testament is consistent in considering death as an enemy over which Christ was victorious. In Romans, Paul describes death as entering the world through Adam's sin[23] and as "the wages of sin."[24] In 1 Corinthians 15:26, when speaking about Christ's resurrection, Paul calls death "the last enemy to be destroyed." Paul hinges the Gospel itself on a connection between sin and death. Adam brought death into the world (and to all of mankind) by sinning. Jesus saved us from sin by submitting to that death though he did not deserve it. If death was a natural part of creation, then Christ deserved to die by virtue of his perfect humanity the same way we all do. If death and sin have no connection, then Christ's death and our sin also have no connection. One may certainly argue that the death of certain creatures is a necessary part of creation—digestion and many other essential and clearly designed functions require it. In light of this, Paul's description of the Gospel requires a different view of human death than of animal death[25]—a distinction that many theistic evolutionists embrace. However, under theistic evolution, there can be no distinction between human death and animal death. Humans die because of what we inherited from our animal ancestors, as God supposedly intended.

Secondly, theistic evolution does not allow the option of interpreting the first several chapters of Genesis as historical narrative. However, this approach to the text is highly suspect. Genesis is clearly narrative because it is consists almost entirely of statements that one person took a particular action, and then something else happened, and then another person took another action and so on. Furthermore, the characters involved in the story must all be historical figures. In his Gospel, Luke traces Joseph's lineage all the way back to Adam, whose father he then identifies as God.[26] If the Gospels are intended to be historically accurate,[27] then Joseph must have been an historical figure. Historical figures, of course, must have historical parents, not fictional ones. Furthermore, the procreative activity

23. Rom 5:12–19.
24. Rom 6:23.
25. Exactly where one ought to draw this distinction will be considered later on.
26. Whether or not it contains gaps, it clearly is intended to describe real people.
27. As argued in chapter 5.

must have been in history. Consequently, one must conclude that Adam and Eve were actual people who actually had the actual descendants detailed in Genesis and repeated in Luke. Therefore, Genesis is certainly a narrative about historical people. Likewise, as was argued in chapter 7, Jesus refers to certain events, including Adam and Eve's creation as well as the flood, as actual historical occurrences, so Genesis is a narrative about historical events as well as historical people. What is more, like Luke and John in their Gospels, Moses tells us in Genesis itself what kind of literature he is writing. In 2:4 it says, "This is the account of the heavens and the earth when they were created." The same phraseology is used many other times throughout the book in reference to genealogies, to Abraham's father, to Ishmael, Issac, Esau, Jacob etc.,[28] which all Christians believe are historical. The same kind of reasoning that reveals the Gospels to be historical narrative reveals the same about Genesis.

Reading it as narrative, of course, means that "God formed the man from the dust of the ground and breathed into his nostrils the breath of life, and the man became a living being." It also means that "The Lord God made woman from the rib he had taken out of the man." While figurative language may still used (just as it is used in the Gospels), Genesis clearly describes God's direct intervention in the various stages of creation, and especially that of humans. These details appear to be incompatible with theistic evolution, which must maintain that both men and women were not created by direct divine intervention, but through gradual changes in creatures who were very much like humans, but nevertheless not humans. If one uses theistic evolution as an apologetic when the Bible is challenged by mainstream science, then one needs to take a different approach to apologetics than the one considered in this book, including finding a different way of explaining why we ought to read the Gospels as historical narrative.

Although this theory is often very casually offered as a solution to conflicts with science, it has far-reaching implications on important matters. It may be a simple means of reconciling science with deism but becomes much more complicated when it comes to Christianity. As Hank Hanegraaff put it, "Under the banner of 'theistic evolution,' a growing number of Christians maintain that God used evolution as His method for creation. This, in my estimation, is the worst of all possibilities. It is

---

28. Gen. 11:27; 25:12 and 19; 36:1; and 37:2.

one thing to believe in evolution; it is quite another to blame God for it."[29] Christians often imagine that if one simply interprets Genesis in a non-historical way, the Bible's stance on creation can be adapted to any theory that comes around, and we have an easy means of reconciling Christianity with science forever. Unfortunately, things are far more complicated than that.

PROGRESSIVE CREATIONISM

The second common theory to consider is progressive creationism. This view accepts Genesis as history, but as a very imprecise history which uses a great deal of figurative language. Genesis 2 begins after 15 billion years of creative activity on God's behalf. According to this view, the "days" of Genesis 1 are actually very long overlapping ages. Life was created directly by God's hand, but God did so only occasionally during that time. "Let there be light" was the Big Bang. The second and third days describe the slow formation of the earth from the results of that explosion and the creation of plants. The fourth day describes not the creation of the stars, but the dissipation of something[30] blocking the earth's view of them. The last two days involved God directly, but only periodically, creating different animal species on the earth. There was a historical Adam and Eve who were the actual parents of the entire human race who did cause mankind to fall into sin. Evolution is denied as an acceptable explanation for the development of life, and so mainstream biology is called into question, but there are no major changes when it comes to geology or cosmology with respect to the origins of earth and the universe.

This approach does either eliminate or lessen some of the difficulties encountered by theistic evolution. It is willing to question some of the conclusions of science—often on the basis of methodological naturalism's inadequacies. The inconsistencies with the Gospel message are also eased, as human death and suffering are not inextricably linked to animal death and suffering; it can be a result of a Fall occurring in history as the Bible describes. For the same reason, the problem of natural evil (at least when it comes to humans) can still be answered in the traditional way.

Nevertheless, even though the details of this explanation do superficially answer the theological, philosophical and scientific problems

29. Hanegraaff, "Ask Hank," 54.
30. Often a dust cloud of some kind.

arising from theistic evolution, the answers do leave something to be desired. The answers do not involve logical contradictions, but they do involve many incongruities. Firstly, the Bible's imagery quickly becomes very odd. For example, most Christian thinkers have held that the Old Testament sacrificial system was a foreshadowing of Christ. The idea of a lamb without blemish being sacrificially killed for the forgiveness of sins is perhaps the most obvious element of this. Nevertheless, because progressive creationism accepts the mainstream interpretation of the fossil record when it comes to timing the arrival of new animals, it must also accept the presence of death, disease, and deformity among them. If this is true, the concept of a lamb without blemish becomes almost nonsensical. The "blemishes" described in the sacrificial code would be a normal part of God's very good creation rather than a result of the Fall and hence not blemishes at all. There are any number of similar oddities.[31] Confusing imagery does not falsify Christianity or progressive creationism, but it does seem to interfere reading the whole of Scripture closely.

The acceptance of the vast majority of prehistory produces similar oddities in the classic answer to the problem of natural evil. While earthquakes, hurricanes, and the like would surely be part of God's perfect creation, an imaginative person could come up with suggestions for ways in which a perfect humanity could avoid suffering in such situations. The same could be said of diseases and sickness. However, what are we then to make of animal suffering? While one could argue that in modern times there is a great deal of inappropriate anthropomorphism with regards to animals due to the animal rights movement, it is hard to credit that compassion towards suffering animals is a completely human invention. We are inclined towards putting suffering animals to sleep and condemn people who abuse their pets. However, progressive creationism implies that by God's design, all animals were suffering well before man appeared on the earth. Progressive creationism reduces animal suffering from being less important than human suffering to completely irrelevant.

Finally, the reconciliation with science also retains some oddities. While the absence of God from mainstream biological explanations is typically questioned, His absence from cosmological and geological explanations typically is not. Because Christians also hold that God created the earth and the universe, it seems odd that these fields would not also

---

31. For example, the Bible seems to imply vegetarianism before the Flood even if it does not state it outright.

come into question. The result is interpretations of both the Bible and the physical data that often seem very strained. Even if the days in Genesis are not literal, their order still describes the Earth existing before the Sun and stars, plants before the sun, birds before land animals, and so on. All of these contradict mainstream prehistory. If the theories behind this prehistory are unquestioned, it seems presumptive to arbitrarily reject the conclusions these theories lead to. On the other hand, if mainstream prehistory is accepted, then Genesis must be a very odd historical narrative indeed. Even if "evening," "morning," and "day" are figurative language, they are clearly meant to convey the ending of one period, and the beginning of the next. Reconciling a historical Genesis with mainstream prehistory means overlapping "days" of various lengths that do not seem supported by the text itself. Even if the text does technically allow such interpretations, it seems odd that the reader could never arrive at the correct one until thousands of years after it was written—even in historical narrative.

The other substantial problem with progressive creationism (which is problematic for theistic evolution as well) is that it forces an interpretation of the Genesis Flood as local instead of worldwide. After all, one would think that a global flood destroying all breathing animals would leave some kind of evidence behind. If one does not count the many layers of sedimentary rock laid down all over the entire globe filled with quickly buried dead things, the marine fossils even in the highest mountain ranges, the water covering the majority of the planet, the prevalence of universal flood myths, etc. then there really is not much evidence. The progressive creationist would necessarily explain these facts in the same way as mainstream science; features slowly created over billions of years—features that existed well before anyone named Noah could have. As such, Noah's flood is interpreted to refer to an event that killed all humans except for Noah and those on the ark, but affected only the relatively small geographic area to which humans had spread.

Does the language of Scripture indicate a local flood? Local flood proponents tend to argue that while it sounds global in English, it does not in the original Hebrew.[32] For example, the Hebrew words for the "high mountains" which Moses describes as being covered in water[33] is

32. Essentially that these chapters have never been competently translated into English.
33. Gen 7:19.

allegedly much more generic—it could mean "anything from 'a small hillock' to 'a towering peak.'"[34] Furthermore, no matter what language one uses, Moses' "all the earth" language is seen as figurative. Figurative use of such language certainly occurs elsewhere in the Scripture. Paul writes of people talking about the faith of the Roman church "all over the world," but he does not literally mean the entire globe.[35] All the kings of the earth seeking an audience with Solomon probably did not include every last tribe on the planet.[36] This kind of interpretation is entirely reasonable in such contexts.

But is this kind of interpretation reasonable in the case of the Genesis flood? In addition to simply referring to "the earth" constantly, Moses uses phrases that seem to refer to the entire earth ("the face of the earth," "wiped off the earth," "under the entire heavens," etc) at least six times during the flood narrative.[37] He uses phrases that refer to all animal life as being subject to the events of the flood at least twenty-six different times.[38] While there are modifying clauses for the extent of destruction to animal life (unlike the earth), they all modify by type, not by extent.[39] This goes a little bit beyond simple hyperbole. If Paul had used that kind of language when referring to the Romans' faith, I would say he meant the entire planet as well.

Moses also mentions all of the "high mountains" or as others argue, the generic "elevated places" being covered to a depth of over twenty feet.[40] If this is figurative language, it ranks right up there with the old example of "he was as tall as a six-foot two-inch tree" when it comes to literary quality. What does this kind of statement mean for the interpretation of the generic high places? If, as local flood proponents insist, the high places were not the mountains (which remained uncovered), then they are simply some indeterminate places of middling height—higher than the plains but presumably lower than the mountains. There is nothing in the text to indicate that Moses was referring to a specific landmark. A

34. Ross, "The Waters of the Flood," paragraph 3.
35. Rom 1:8.
36. 2 Chr. 9:23
37. Gen 6:7; 7:4, 11, 19, and 23.
38. Gen 6:7, 17; 7:3, 14, 15, 16, 21, 22, 23; 8:17, 19, 21; 9:10, 11, 15.
39. For example, Moses excludes marine animals by writing "Everything on dry land that had the breath of life in its nostrils died" in 7:22.
40. Gen 7:19.

significant strike against the local flood interpretation is that a statement like "all of the indeterminate places of middling height under the entire heavens were covered to a depth of over twenty feet" is not in any way meaningful. It says absolutely nothing to illustrate how deep the water is—the very thing Moses is describing. If the Hebrew does not refer to all the high mountains (indicating that the highest elevation was covered by twenty feet of water) or some other specific feature, it ceases to have any relevance as a frame of reference.

One must also consider God's promise at the end, which explicitly includes animal life.[41] Never again will all life be cut off by the waters of a flood; never again will there be a flood to destroy the earth," and also, "Never again will the waters become a flood to destroy all life."[42] As many have pointed out, if these promises were in reference to a local flood and "all life" referred to some local subset of life, they were broken during hurricane Katrina, the 2004 tsunami that hit Indonesia, and countless other local floods since Noah. Some counter that "all life" refers only to corrupt humans. For example, Greg Neyman of Answers in Creation, uses a different translation of Genesis 9:15 that reads, "and I will remember My covenant, which is between Me and you and every living creature of all flesh; and never again shall the water become a flood to destroy all flesh." Neyman claims that "all flesh" is defined in 6:12, which could refer to humans alone.[43] However, there seems to be little need to go back three chapters for a definition, when the cited verse itself explicitly attaches "all flesh" to "you and every living creature." Contradicting the immediate context in favor of an earlier context that happens to give a preferred interpretation is extremely poor technique.

Progressive creationism initially seems like a reasonable compromise between science and Christianity. It has fewer difficult issues to resolve with respect to Christianity and philosophy than does theistic evolution. It also has fewer strong disagreements with mainstream science than does young earth creationism while still acknowledging the problem of methodological naturalism. At the same time, it seems odder than the other two alternatives. The willingness to question mainstream biological history is an odd contrast with the apparent implicit trust of mainstream

41. Gen 9:10.
42. Gen 9:11 and 15.
43. Neyman, "God's Broken Promise," paragraphs 4–7.

geological and cosmological history even though they should both be subject to the same skepticism. Likewise, while there is no contradiction in its interpretation of Scripture, the Bible seems much muddier as a result—the account of the Flood in particular becomes almost nonsensical. None of these facts conclusively eliminate progressive creationism as a possibility, but it remains a very ugly one.

YOUNG EARTH CREATIONISM

This theory has been the predominant view of the Church (with a few notable exceptions) until the past few centuries. According to young earth creationism (YEC), Genesis must be read as straightforward historical narrative, and so the conclusion is that God created the universe in six twenty-four-hour stages. If one traces the genealogies in the Bible (and depending on whether one considers any gaps in them), this occurred roughly between 6,000 and 10,000 years ago. After the Fall and the subsequent curse placed on the Earth, the way in which the world functioned was profoundly changed, and nature has been degenerating ever since. Later, a catastrophic global flood reshaped the face of the planet. These events are considered history learned from an infallible source, and consequently attempts are made to explain observations of the world around us in a way that is consistent with these events. The YEC view represents a major paradigm shift from mainstream science because many different theories about the past are reconsidered with the additional information brought to the table by the historical account of Scripture.

Having been the predominant view for so long, the few allegations that this view contradicts Scripture can be relatively easily answered. The classic example is the question of who Cain's wife was.[44] If Adam and Eve were the only people that God created, and they were the parents of all people, who could their children have married? The classic solution is that their children could have married each other. The Biblical command against incest was not given until the time of Moses, while the issue of physical deformities resulting from incestuous relationships has a simple answer as well. These deformities arise because parents have genetic errors that they pass on to their children. Usually, if a part of the genetic code is damaged in one parent, that same portion of the code is fine in the other parent, and the child is consequently protected from the damaged code

44. Gen 4:17.

actually being implemented. On the other hand, if two people have the same parents, there is a high likelihood that they have the same genetic flaws. As a result, there is no protection against their implementation in the children. However, for Adam and Eve's children to have common genetic flaws inherited from their parents, Adam and Eve would have had to have been created by God with genetic flaws. With no common flaws to pass on and those flaws only accumulating over subsequent generations, there would have been many generations before deformities would become a problem. One might also raise the issue that the Bible does not mention any people other than Adam, Eve, Cain, and Abel existing until that point. However, Genesis is not exhaustive in its details and Cain's banishment could have been as many as 130 years after the Fall. Abel's murder by Cain was the latest event mentioned before Cain laying with his wife. The next dated event was the birth of Seth when Adam was 130.[45] He seemed to be viewed by his parents as a replacement for Abel,[46] and so Cain leaving with his wife after the murder probably occurred around the same time.

The other common objection is that because the Sun was not created until the fourth day, the first three days could not possibly be literal. However, it can be pointed out that while the day is defined by the Sun, Genesis was written by Moses well after the meaning had been established. As something of a geek, I have certainly spent days without seeing the sun, and yet the same amount of time had still passed. Finally, Genesis explicitly mentions God separating day from night apart from the sun on the first day.[47] This particular objection provides no necessity and little motivation to read the days as figurative.

Ultimately, reconciling this view with Scripture is very easy; the Church has had millennia to practice. The far more difficult task is reconciling this account with what has been observed about the world. As is typical in this debate, the simple solutions are completely inadequate. Some suggest that just as God created a mature Adam and Eve who would have had the appearance of age although they were quite young, He also created a mature universe with the appearance of age. This view, however, comes so close to making God deceptive that there may not be any dis-

45. Gen 5:3.
46. Gen 4:25.
47. Gen 1:5.

tinction at all. While the Bible indicates that Adam and Eve were created mature enough to speak and act, it indicates no such thing about the universe. Furthermore, this would still leave the young earth creationist with the problems of death and suffering, because a mature universe includes a great many dead things buried in the ground. Finally, it has implications for the stars. Starlight takes a long time to travel to Earth (longer than the young earth creationist believes the earth has been around), and yet this light clearly has reached earth. A variety of workarounds for this have been suggested,[48] but the idea that God created light in transit would indicate that most of the celestial motions we observe are merely a picture show of things that never happened—coming perilously close to making the universe an illusion.

Sophisticated young earth proponents recognize the need to actually deal with rather than explain away the physical data. To return to the example of the starlight problem, they have proposed a variety of solutions. A common suggestion is that the speed of light was actually much faster in the past than it is now, so that light from distant stars could have reached the earth in much less time than is supposed. A unique relativistic cosmology proposed by Dr. Russel Humphreys suggests that time did not run at the same rate everywhere in the universe during the creation week. Without getting bogged down in the technical details of gravitational time dilation, the end result is that while the Earth is very young, distant stars may actually be very old even though they were created on the fourth day of what was a literal week on Earth.[49] Do theories such as these adequately explain both the Biblical and physical data? Unfortunately, an evaluation of the technical details of such theories is beyond the scope of this book, because it is beyond the expertise of this author.

Because most people are in the same position, questions of this nature are typically determined by the consensus of experts in the field—a consensus that does not support any particular YEC theory. There are several factors, however, that make this approach inadequate for the question at hand. The first factor has already been established—the current scientific consensus includes the inappropriate application of methodological naturalism. The second is that these theories question other widely held beliefs. For example, Dr. Humpheys' model rejects the Copernican

---

48. Although none seem to have been settled on as of yet.
49. Tyler, "Review of A Young-Earth Relativistic Cosmology," paragraph 14.

principle—that the Earth has no special place in a universe which is essentially homogeneous on large scales.⁵⁰ The idea that the speed of light has changed rejects the idea of uniformitarianism—that the only physical laws and forces that have ever been acting upon the world are the forces that are observed now. These ideas probably arose for very good reasons, just as there was a reason for adherence to methodological naturalism. Nevertheless, they are not rejected arbitrarily. They are rejected because of the Biblical data that has been brought to the table—data that includes extraordinary changes like creation events, global floods, and curses. While the Bible is certainly not so precise that it clearly supports a change in the speed of light or contradicts the idea that the universe has no real center, it does provide sufficient incentive to question these kinds of assumptions. At this time and on this subject, experts are unreliable—not because of some conspiracy against God, but because of a consistent and pervasive methodological problem. If popular assumptions among experts are reasonably questionable, then the consensus of experts is of limited utility.

Unfortunately, the most popular argument against YEC is merely that it contradicts a large number of conclusions garnered by the scientific method—creationism ignores things that have been proven time and again, it was disproved long ago, etc. This is true; it contradicts many theories about the past in geology, cosmology, and biology. When compared to progressive creationism, mainstream science is in the same ballpark. When compared to young earth creationism, however, it is not even playing the same sport. There is an extremely wide gap between a 4.5-billion-year-old earth and a 10,000-year-old earth. Nevertheless, YEC cannot be dismissed for this reason alone; it remains within the possible extent of error. Consequently, by itself, this argument demonstrates nothing. One ought to be willing to consider the possibility that mainstream science really is that far off.

YEC is seldom engaged by the mainstream scientific community because as far as the mainstream is concerned, the question was considered settled long ago. Unfortunately, as has already been demonstrated, it was settled without ever appropriately settling the root problems that methodological naturalism poses. The questions that need to be asked about YEC are not along the lines of, "Does this match up with current

---

50. Tyler, "Review of A Young-Earth Relativistic Cosmology," paragraphs 9–10.

scientific knowledge?" They are along the lines of, "Does this match up with actual observations of the world around us?" While passing time can be directly measured, age cannot. When considering history that nobody was timing, age must be inferred from other observations and measurements. YEC represents not just a modification of current scientific theory, but a major paradigm shift that changes the way some issues are even approached. This is not how it is usually treated. The majority of criticisms fall short because they criticize YEC as either a piecemeal modification of certain theories or an utter rejection of abductive reasoning. It is neither.

Can young earth creationists provide alternative biological, cosmological, and geological theories of origins that plausibly fit the physical data as well as they fit the Biblical? Ultimately, answering this question means examining that data—an endeavor that is ill-suited for a chapter that has tried to stay within the category of philosophy of science rather than science proper. It should be clear, however, that it cannot be written off as unreasonable as many modern Christians are eager to do. There is, of course, a lot of junk in many creationist circles that Christians need to be careful of. Nevertheless, a brief glance at the history of certain areas of science (such as medicine in the 1700's) demonstrates that the presence of bad theories at some point in history does not mean that an area of science has no future. Science has always been about discarding worse theories in favor of better ones, and a version of science that drops methodological naturalism and embraces Scripture as history is no different. The lack of severe Biblical and philosophical problems is a strong point in favor of YEC, and addressing any scientific problems it may have requires serious engagement rather than the casual dismissal it usually receives. When one avenue of inquiry (such as the consensus of experts) is inconclusive, it is appropriate to depend on others—including a thoughtful analysis of the Bible. While one typically does not know as much as an expert, it does not mean that one necessarily knows less than he actually knows. At the same time, however, young earth creationists have not even reached an internal consensus on many of the difficult issues. Until this happens, one cannot truly consider the issue closed.

TOWARDS A SOLUTION

Theistic evolution and progressive creationism are both relatively young theories. While a Christian idea of a young Earth is older, seriously seeking to reconcile this idea with the physical world is also a relatively young endeavor.[51] It is only natural that none will stand out as *the* obvious solution from all angles. The problems with the first two theories seem more severe, but to be fair, it is also true that this author is unqualified to adequately evaluate the scientific problems with particular young-earth theories. That must be left to scientists who understand the root problems. What can be said, however, is that the YEC side of the conflict is the side whose overall approach is most appropriate. It is more willing to allow facts from a plain reading of Scripture to inform the analysis and is more willing to question the conclusions of the scientific method where methodological naturalism and other assumptions make them suspect. Time will tell whether these questions have good answers. Whatever solution ends up being true, this kind of approach is most likely to find it.[52] Given the problems of modern science, open-mindedness is more essential than ever.

Consensus among Christians on this issue does not seem likely anytime soon. Nevertheless, the implications of methodological naturalism do not mean that science has dealt a critical blow to Christianity, and the acceptance of traditional Christian ideas on origins does not require accepting critical blows to reason or rejecting the prospect of studying the physical world. Likewise, the problems with theistic evolution and progressive creationism should give Christians pause before embracing them for the sake of saving Christianity in a scientific age or science in a Christian age. Tension between science and religion will be part of a Christian's life for some time, but we need not fear it. There needs to be a conflict in this time and place. Science must not be elevated to a superhuman level, and Christians must not forget that the Bible can be interpreted badly despite its inerrancy. The issue remains one in which human judgment and interpretation must play a role in the here and now. Christians should approach the conflict with love, charity, and all of our faculties.

---

51. One with an unfortunate history of attempts to establish the viewpoint by fiat and ignore difficulties with the physical data.

52. Those readers who do not subscribe to YEC views are invited to consider this to be helpful criticism rather than condemnation.

10

Abortion and Other Life Issues

INTRODUCTION

ABORTION IS ONE OF the primary topics on which Christianity is unfortunately at odds with modern American culture. I say "unfortunately" not simply because the culture happens to be wrong, but because there is nothing uniquely Christian about the idea that it is wrong to intentionally kill innocent human beings. As a basic part of the natural law, the knowledge of murder's wrongness is a moral insight that every person in every culture throughout history has possessed. Nevertheless, the pro-life movement has been tied almost exclusively to Christianity in this country.[1] With that perception comes the perception that one can only argue against abortion from religious authority. I once had a short e-mail dialog with a conservative but pro-choice commentator. Knowing that he was agnostic when I responded to his column advocating legal abortion, I wrote in a way that argued only from the common belief we shared that murder was wrong; I did not bring God into the discussion. Interestingly enough, in a very bizarre non-sequitur, he responded to me as if I had not only mentioned God but based my entire argument on His revelatory commands. It was not that he failed to read my argument—he responded to the e-mail point-by-point, quoting me as he went—I think he was simply unable to respond to any other kind of pro-life argument.

If he really was unable to do so, it was probably because he did not routinely hear arguments that do not involve the Bible. Pro-life Christians often quote Psalm 139 in the debate: "'For you created my inmost being: you knit me together in my mother's womb . . . All the days ordained for

---

1. This is not to say there are no pro-life individuals who are Muslim, Jewish, agnostic, etc. This is merely a generalization.

me were written in your book before one of them came to be."² There is nothing wrong with quoting the Bible when one is speaking with a person who cares about what it says. Furthermore, chapter 7 lays out a case for why a person should care about what it says. There is a place for those approaches. Nevertheless, on issues where there is already sufficient common belief, it is often more profitable to begin with that common belief.

The basic pro-life argument is that abortion should not be allowed because it is murder. As was argued in chapter 3, it really is common knowledge that it is wrong to intentionally kill innocent human beings. Therefore, in order to justify abortion against such a charge, there are only five options:³

- Abortion is not intentional.
- Abortion does not involve killing.
- The subjects of abortion are not innocent.
- The subjects of abortion are not human beings.
- Sometimes wrong ought to be done.

ABORTION IS NOT INTENTIONAL

The idea that abortion is not intentional usually comes up only as a plea for sympathy. "With the situation she was in, she simply had no choice." Sympathy will be considered later in this chapter, but for now it is sufficient to note that abortions do not simply happen. Claims like this usually come down, not to no choice at all, but to a selection of undesirable choices with abortion being the most tempting. The pro-abortion movement has always celebrated choice and does not seem likely to begin claiming women do not have adequate faculties for exercising their "reproductive rights" any time soon. People may claim that abortion is the best choice, but only the most unthinking sentimentalist claims there is no choice.

ABORTION DOES NOT INVOLVE KILLING

There was a time when people claimed that abortion does not really involve killing. The "uterine contents" were described as blood clots to

---

2. Ps 139:13,16.

3. This is a variation on J. Budziszewski's argument in *The Revenge of Conscience*, 33. Budziszewski does not include the third point and quickly dismisses the fifth.

make the procedure easier for mothers to swallow. However, this option could never work once the issue was tied so tightly to "women's health." Examination by modern medicine cannot help but result in the realization that the various characteristics of life such as metabolism, reproduction, and so on are all there. With modern medical technology, particularly ultrasounds, it has become clear that whatever the fetus is, it is certainly a living thing. As William Saletan of Slate.com put it,

> Pro-lifers are often caricatured as stupid creationists who just want to put women back in their place. Science and free inquiry are supposed to help them get over their 'love affair with the fetus.' But science hasn't cooperated. Ultrasound has exposed the life in the womb to those of us who didn't want to see what abortion kills. The fetus is squirming, and so are we.[4]

Consequently, modern claims that abortions do not involve killing are not rationalizations or arguments at all. They are simply lies and ought to be treated as such. As abortion practices become more abhorrent, this fact will only become more obvious. Take, for example, the newer practice of "selective reduction," which in the case of twins, triplets, and so forth allows the parents to bring the number of babies down to a more manageable level by killing the least desirable ones. An article in the *Washington Post Magazine* reported on couples carrying multiple children who were considering the procedure. One couple wanted twins instead of the triplets they were actually carrying. The article related a preliminary ultrasound appointment. After the sonographer related the age of the fetuses, she showed the image to the mother and began interpreting it:

> Greenbaum [the sonographer] turned the screen toward the patient. "That's the little heartbeat," she said, pointing to the area where a tiny organ was clearly pulsing. "And there are the little hands. There's the head. The body."
>
> "Oh, my God, I can really see it!" the patient cried. "Oh, my God! I can see the fingers!"
>
> "Okay!" she said, abruptly, gesturing for the screen to be turned away. She began sobbing. There were no tissues in the room, so her husband gave her a paper towel, which she crumpled to her face. The patient spent the rest of the procedure with her hospital

---

4. Saletan, "Sex," paragraph 9.

gown over her face, so she would not see any more of what was happening."[5]

No argument is needed in cases like this, because the mother already knows exactly what's happening; if she did not, then she would not have to hide from it. All that is necessary is someone to point out that the emperor has no clothes.

THE FETUS IS NOT INNOCENT

This argument sounds as silly as the first two, but nevertheless seems to see significant use, particularly in academic circles. It may be surprising that people who would likely be horrified at the idea of original sin would proclaim the guilt of an unborn child. Nevertheless, the idea of the fetus as an intruder is considered compelling by many.

There is, for example, the famous "violinist argument," which dates back to philosopher Judith Jarvis Thomson in 1971. There are many different versions of the argument, but according to the situation posed by Thomson:

> You wake up in the morning and find yourself back-to-back in bed with an unconscious violinist. A famous unconscious violinist. He has been found to have a fatal kidney ailment and the Society of Music Lovers has canvassed all the available medical records and found that you alone have the right blood type to help. They have therefore kidnapped you and last night the violinist's circulatory system was plugged into yours, so that your kidneys can be used to extract poisons from his blood as well as your own.... To unplug you would be to kill him. But ... it's only for nine months. By then he will have recovered from his ailment, and can safely be unplugged from you.[6]

The point of this analogy is that, just like one would be justified in unplugging the violinist from her body because his right to live does not extend to using her as an external kidney, one would be justified in aborting an unborn child who has no right to live by using her as a host. This kind of argument is particularly compelling to libertarians and others who place great value on personal autonomy.

---

5. Mundy, "Too Much," W17.
6. Thomson, "Defense," 282.

Because this is argument by analogy, the first task is to examine it for important (not pedantic) ways in which the parallel situation is not really parallel. An example of pedantry would be to point out that fetuses do not actually play the violin. It is a difference, but it is irrelevant to the moral situation. If analogies did not contain any differences at all, they would merely be repetition. One might point out differences in the manner of death (e.g. the fetus is brutally dismembered, not simply disconnected), but this too is largely irrelevant. Ultimately one could merely dream up an even more bizarre situation in which brutal dismemberment would be a necessity for disconnection. Other differences might have some relevance. In pregnancy, the fetus does not enter and latch onto a woman's body, but the mother's body itself manages the connection after what is usually a voluntary activity. Nevertheless, these differences do not go far enough. Rape would not involve voluntary action on the part of the host, and one might argue that failed contraception would not either.

The most damning difference is that the violinist argument and its offspring confuse the relationship between a mother and her child by replacing it with the relationship between two strangers. Strangers have a certain kind of responsibility towards each other, but it certainly does not include the kind of situation described in the violinist argument. Mothers, on the other hand, have a whole host of responsibilities toward their children, such as caring for, nourishing, and protecting them. When a mother rejects such responsibilities, we call it neglect or abandonment. As moral beings, we recognize such a rejection as wrong, and our laws are in agreement. Just as a mother does not have the freedom to choose to eject a toddler from her home as an intruder, she does not have the freedom to eject an even younger child from her womb—the only means[7] by which she can fulfill her responsibilities before birth.

The argument is clearly not valid, but it is also worth considering what could lead an intelligent person to mistake a mother and child for strangers in the first place. The stereotypical Puritan was supposedly a prude who was scandalized by the details of sexual activity. Sex was a necessary evil for the continuation of the human race, but otherwise it was dirty, unnatural, and ought to be done through a hole in the sheets. Ironically, many who mock those caricatured prudes have become prudes themselves. They certainly do not see sex acts as anything to ashamed

---

7. Means that are not extraordinary.

of, but they have nevertheless become so scandalized at the thought that it naturally results in offspring that it brings to mind an eight-year-old boy saying, "Babies come from *where*? Ew!" For example, abortionist Dr. Warren M. Hern concludes an article on his website by writing:

> The foregoing discussion should allow us to abandon the erroneous assumption that pregnancy is per sé a normal and desirable state, and to consider instead a more accurate view that human pregnancy is an episodic, moderately extended chronic condition with a definable morbidity and mortality risk to which females are uniquely though not uniformly susceptible.[8]

According to Hern, pregnancy thus becomes an illness that can be prevented through contraception, treated by "evacuation of the uterine contents," or may be tolerated for reproduction. The disgust with which the man views human nature is palpable. A "condition" in which every human being who has ever lived has participated is not normal "per sé"? From extreme examples like this, to everyday high school health classes which treat pregnancy as just another STD to protect oneself against, the thought of a human life growing inside a woman as a result of intercourse and being nourished directly by her body has become something from which people turn away in disgust. Like the stereotypical prude, if such people had been involved in human design, they would no doubt have come up with a more sterile and convenient means of reproduction.

Design is, in fact, the crux of it. Once one loses the idea of God deliberately designing the family to communicate something about Himself, one loses the idea that there is anything special about familial relationships. If humans happened to emerge through a completely undirected process, the relationship between a mother and a child is really just a chance occurrence. If life is random, there is little doubt that an intelligent human could improve on the "design"; fans of science fiction are no strangers to the idea of artificial wombs which are much safer, cleaner, and more convenient than the old-fashioned way. Nevertheless, such a perspective is a double-edged sword. If one accepts that the relationship between a mother and her child is sufficiently arbitrary or meaningless to preclude responsibilities, then the relationship between strangers necessarily loses such significance as well. Strangers are oriented to each other through no less chance than a mother and child. Even the violinist argu-

---

8. Hern, "Pregnancy," paragraph 42.

ment is founded on the idea that a woman has a right to treat a stranger in a particular way and that the violinist does not have a right to treat a stranger in a particular way. If the stranger-stranger relationship is as arbitrary as the mother-child relationship, then there is no basis for human rights at all. This seems like a high price to pay for the convenience of murdering our children.

THE FETUS IS NOT HUMAN

This category is perhaps the most popular rationalization given in our culture. Everyone knows that human life is a precious thing[9] that should not be subject to procedures like abortion, but if we can convince ourselves that the fetus is not human, than we no longer have to treat it as precious unless we choose to. A fetus may be precious because of the hopes that parents attach to it—that it will grow up and live a good life—but when there is no such hope, any value evaporates as well. The idea that the fetus is not human seems like a dicey proposition given that biology has long recognized that species reproduce after their own kind. Cats come from cats, fish from fish, etc. The idea that human offspring early in development are something other than humans is a little hard to swallow, but there are a number of tactics used to make it easier.

One tactic is to claim that a fetus is not a human per sé, but merely a potential human. One common attempt to explain such a difference is the acorn analogy. A fetus is not a human anymore than an acorn is an oak tree. It might turn into a human eventually, just like the acorn might turn into a tree, but it is just potentiality; one is under no obligation to act as though a fetus is a human while it is in the womb. Like the violinist argument, this is argument by analogy and so the first question to ask is whether there are any important differences between the two situations.

The difference appears in the content of the two terms: "oak tree" and "human." The former has implications concerning age and stage of development—specifically that the organism has been around and nourished long enough to grow from an acorn and continue beyond a sapling. "Human," on the other hand, does not necessarily imply anything about age or development. Children, teenagers, and adults can all legitimately

---

9. There are certainly those who have a very dim view of humanity, but behind this, there is nearly always a set of observations on how humans do not act as humans should. The reality falls short of the ideal. Nevertheless, if the ideal were not precious, there would be no cause for complaint.

be called human. If one wants the term to imply development, they need to make a case as to why (we will examine such cases a little later). A more accurate analogy might therefore read, "A fetus is not an adult anymore than an acorn is an oak tree. It might turn into a adult eventually, just like the acorn might turn into a tree, but one need not act as though it is an adult while it is in the womb."

This corrected analogy is certainly true; one does not treat fetuses as adults. Nevertheless, the analogy fails to show that the fetus is not a human life but merely that it is not an adult human life. This distinction, however, is not important in the case for abortion because babies are not adults, teenagers are not senior citizens, and toddlers are not tweens. All of these are human beings at different stages of development, just like an acorn, oak tree, and oak sapling are all oaks at different stages of development. Few believe that it is okay to kill a toddler simply because he is not an adult. If one does actually want to claim that the word "human" implies some level of development, then they need to make a case for that, not simply rely on an analogy that *suggests* the implication of development.

The more careful thinker may very well try and make such a case. This, of course, requires a redefinition of human that goes beyond species or, more precisely, another term to take the place of "human" in the common moral precept. Everyone knows that human life is precious, but many find the idea of human exceptionalism to be "speciesist." Why would an organism be valuable simply by arbitrary membership in one particular species among many? The logic then goes that if humans in general are to be considered precious it must then be due to some quality that humans have that other life forms could also theoretically have. One of the most common expressions of this idea is personhood. According to this notion, a being is more or less precious according to whether it is more or less a person. Consequently, the rights and privileges of the precious ones should take precedence over the rights and privileges of those who are not precious.

What makes somebody a person? The criteria are frequently tweaked, but they often include moral agency (making and carrying out moral choices), reason or rationality, language or the mental capacities for language (such as intentionality or self-consciousness), and the ability to enter into suitable relationships with other persons. It should be obvious, however that many humans who are not fetuses fail to meet one or more of these criteria. Babies, the developmentally disabled, humans suffering brain diseases (Alzheimer's), some physically handicapped people (i.e. those who cannot carry out their moral choices), and even people who are asleep come up short.

It must also be observed that such characteristics are not binary. It is not the case that people either have them or not—they are possessed in different degrees. If these are the things that make a human valuable, then those humans who possess these in greater quantities *must* be considered more valuable than others. Most proponents of abortion would find these conclusions unsettling, but this is exactly where their argument logically leads. Moreover, this is exactly what a society that adheres to this argument must eventually develop into. Even if the adults embrace incoherence,[10] those children who survive until their coming of age will begin to ask "why," and their parents will have no answers for them. If these survivors are like every other generation, they will then dismiss their parents' scruples as meaningless tradition that must be tossed aside for the sake of progress.

This type of argument is called *reductio ad absurdum*—reduction to the absurd. Such arguments work only as long as one finds the logical conclusion unacceptable. Could someone accept the logical conclusion that all these people are less than persons and the caste system that comes along with it? Perhaps, but if she does so in front of an audience, she has just lost the debate. Even without an audience, the argument still succeeds in holding up a mirror and presenting a reflection—a hideous reflection that, God-willing, she will never entirely forget.

SOMETIMES WRONG OUGHT TO BE DONE

This leads to the final option: sometimes wrong ought to be done. The idea is, of course, self-contradictory. That something ought not to be done is what "wrong" means. Nevertheless, this book has reported many common incoherent beliefs; the fact that many moderns believe such nonsense should come as no surprise. Indeed, many accept that the arguments given for abortion are inadequate to justify it but maintain that it should be allowed anyway. Why should we care more about abstractions like logic and argument when women and children are suffering and abortion could help them? This is the idea of the ends justifying the

---

10. Or as it is sometimes referred to, "becoming comfortable with ambiguity."

means, or "doing evil that good may result," as Paul put it.[11] This is a particularly common error once utilitarianism enters the philosophical mix. According to utilitarianism, the morality of an action depends solely on the amount of aggregate pleasure it brings vs. the amount of aggregate pain it causes. As such, any action is moral as long as it benefits people more than it hurts.

For example, in a commentary in the *Times of London*, "Abortion: why it's the ultimate motherly act," Caitlin Moran wrote about a reporter whose pro-choice views were challenged after having a child. The reporter found herself calling her unborn child a baby because she wanted it, while she would have called it a clump of cells if she had not. She was perceptive enough to realize this was both irrational and immoral, and while maintaining pro-choice views, became troubled about pro-life arguments concerning the humanity of the fetus. In response to this, Ms. Moran questions whether it is even relevant when human life begins, noting the supposed difficulty science and philosophy have pinpointing it. Instead, she raises the possibility that mothers, as those who have authority over bringing life into the world, might also have authority to end life. She goes on to argue that this authority would mean that abortion is a moral imperative because of all the benefits it provides. After describing how important it is for a child to be wanted by a "sane stable mother," she then comments on the ease with which she decided on her own abortion. She knew giving birth would reduce the time spent with her existing children and husband and did not believe she had the energy for another child. She eventually goes on to explain the necessity of preventing more "unbalanced, destructive people" from coming into the word:

> By whatever rationale you use, ending a pregnancy 12 weeks into gestation is incalculably more moral than bringing an unwanted child into this world. Or a child that, through no fault of its own, would be the destructor of a marriage, a family, a parent. It's fairly inarguable to say that unhappy children, who then grew into very angry adults, have caused the great majority of mankind's miseries. If psychoanalysis has, somewhat brutally, laid the responsibility for mental disorders at parents' doors, the least we can do is to tip our hats to women aware enough not to create those troubled people in the first place.[12]

---

11. Rom 3:8.
12. Moran, "Abortion," paragraph 10.

Her conclusion is that abortion ought to be considered a high point of mothering—an intelligent and compassionate action.

Ms. Moran's commentary implies the absence of a human being by her description of women "aware enough not to create those troubled people in the first place," not through contraception, but through abortion. Likewise, she writes about her "existing daughters" in contrast to the one she aborted. Despite comments that it does not matter when life begins, she does assume that the subject of an abortion does not yet exist. There is no question that there is an assumption of "the fetus is not human or not alive" in this article despite the declaration that such arguments are irrelevant. Nevertheless, another element is certainly present. If one gives the author the benefit of the doubt and sets aside the obviously self-serving assertions that mothers ought to have dominion over the deaths of their children for the sake of their careers and time commitments, then her argument basically goes this way: If a mother does not want her child, her parenting will end up having a severe and negative psychological impact on the child. The child will be hurt because he will not be provided with what he needs and will grow up unhappy and angry. Society will then also be hurt because it will have to deal with these unhappy, angry, and destructive individuals. Because of this, the compassionate choice—the choice that spares the child and society from suffering—is for the mother to kill the child.

The problem with this argument should be obvious. Who are the child and society actually in danger from in this picture? The poor parenting of the mother is clearly the culprit. The argument can be paraphrased thusly: "I have decided to treat this child so badly that he will be better off dead." Is it really merciful for the mother to kill children to save them and society from herself? The argument piles up all the "good" consequences of abortion and hopes the pile is large enough to hide what is actually going on. Society and the child are simply being held hostage by a mother who lists the child's death as one of her conditions for surrendering. As twisted as it is, one really ought not be surprised that such arguments are made. Humans are moral beings. When we have already given into a temptation, we try our best to make that temptation appear irresistible after the fact to avoid the shame that accompanies guilt.

COMPASSION

The supposed necessity of wrong reveals the motivation of a large part of the pro-abortion movement. Despite the popularity of other rationalizations, I believe this supposed necessity is the primary reason abortion is still legal. The pro-life movement has largely restricted itself to demonstrating that abortion is unjust—that it is intentionally killing an innocent human being which should not be allowed. There is, however, another element to the issue as a whole that must be dealt with but is addressed far too rarely by the pro-life side. What about compassion for the mother? We hear stories of back alleys and coat hangers, or young women who have their lives rearranged by unexpected children that happened to have been the result of one little mistake that any of us can make and many of us have. Abortion can shield women from such unfortunate consequences and is therefore considered by many to be the compassionate choice. The pro-life movement has done an excellent job of making it clear that the course of action being proposed as "compassionate" is unjust and should therefore be abandoned. Strictly speaking, that is a correct way to argue. However, to many of the pro-abortion people we try to convince, it sounds as if we are saying, "I am being just; therefore I do not have to worry about being compassionate." Meanwhile, they are likely thinking, "If I have to choose between justice and compassion, I am going to choose compassion because I feel badly for the woman pursuing the abortion and these mothers are more important than mere abstractions like justice."

The fourth chapter of this book argued that all good things are coherent with each other. Love is coherent with truth. Justice is coherent with mercy. We cannot simply call ourselves good because our actions reflect one aspect of goodness while violating all of the others. Consequently, if a person is contemplating "compassion" that violates justice, they are not contemplating true compassion, but a counterfeit. Nevertheless, this concept remains very abstract (which is a problem of communication, not truth), so it is important to be able to communicate it in concrete terms.

When I was in high school, I attended a free concert at Grant Park in Chicago over the Fourth of July weekend. During the event, I was greeted by name by a young woman my age who I did not recognize. Usually, in such situations, I try and act like I know the person, hoping that I can figure out their identity before the conversation ends. Unfortunately, she was perceptive enough to realize that I failed to recognize her, and I had to own up to it. She gave me her name and said she knew me from school, but I had to admit that the name did not sound familiar to me. She could have just given up at that point since I obviously did not remember her as well as she remembered me, but instead she tried again. The next thing she said was, "I'm the one who had the abortion." It ended up being something of a conversation killer. I immediately knew it was an odd response—after all, she might have instead said something along the lines of, "I sat next to you in Algebra 1 during first period freshman year." It was only in retrospect that I realized exactly what was odd about it.

First of all, anyone familiar with my high school would realize how silly it would be to think she was *the one* who had *the* abortion. There were over 3,000 students attending, and that kind of situation was not exactly unheard of. Secondly, while she obviously knew me (she told me both my first and last names without having to be reminded), we could not have known each other too well. To this day, I cannot remember knowing her prior to that concert. Abruptly bringing up something as personal as an abortion is very odd in casual conversation with a mere acquaintance. Finally, she was using her abortion as a way to identify herself when any number of other obvious things she could have told me would have done a much better job of it. She assumed that her own identification was how everyone else thought of her—as the one who had the abortion.

When I added this all up, I realized that she assumed people thought of her this way because this was how she thought of herself. She said it so freely because she assumed everyone knew it. It was one of the foremost things on her mind, it was something she considered unique to her, and she felt guilty enough over it to confess it to anyone. She knew exactly what she had done, and she was suffering for it. I do not know the circumstances around it. I do not know who drove her to the appointment or who paid for the procedure—maybe the boyfriend, maybe the parents—but it is probably a safe assumption that they did so out of an attempt to be compassionate toward her. They wanted to save her from a bad situation. They might have thought they were helping her out or solving her problem, just like those who vote and campaign to keep abortion legal think they are helping young women, but all they do is take away a difficult burden that she could have borne and replace it with one she could not possibly bear. I have known single mothers, both teen and adult, and life is not easy for them. Nevertheless, they strive and work and succeed. How does one succeed at bearing the burden of having murdered one's own child when the accusation comes from the law written on her own heart? Does she forget? Pretend that it does not matter? Forgive herself as though she were accountable to no one else? How are these options anything but abject failures at being human? We simply cannot bear the weight of our own sins; only Christ can do that for us.

This is one of the greatest confusions of modern America. Despite the claims, offering abortion as a solution is not compassion, but sentimentalism. What is the distinction between the two? Compassion is a virtue: a disposition towards making right choices and avoiding wrong ones.[13] Specifically, it is oriented towards rightly choosing how to help people who are suffering. Sentimentalism, on the other hand, masquerades as compassion, but as the name implies it is oriented around sentiment—emotion. Because of this, sentimentalism drives a person to seek out pleasant emotions and avoid unpleasant ones. It is entirely appropriate to feel pity for those who suffer, but because pity is an unpleasant emotion, sentimentalism seeks to avoid it. While the goal of compassion is to help the suffering, sentimentalism merely tries to make the feelings of pity go away. While this *can* be achieved by actually helping the suffering (which is what makes it a believable counterfeit), it is usually far easier to make symbolic gestures that make a person feel better or to turn one's eyes away from the unpleasant sight altogether. For example, where a compassionate person would feed the hungry, a sentimentalist may simply complain about hunger on his blog and call it a day. Like beating the dashboard of a car that will not start, it feels better to have done something even if it was not what was actually needed. In the case of abortion, the procedure places an even greater burden on the mother than the child ever could have been, but it is a burden that the sentimentalist does not have to experience, and so the path of least resistance is taken.

OTHER LIFE ISSUES

The topic of this chapter has been abortion, but because of our common moral precepts, every other "life" issue comes down to the same types of arguments. Do we want to kill our old and our disabled? Perhaps we manufacture their guilt and tell ourselves that they are useless eaters who deserve to die because they can no longer contribute to society. Perhaps we want to sate our pity by removing them from our sight. Do we want to

---

13. The nature of virtues will be covered at greater length in chapter 13.

harvest our young for their stem cells or organs? Perhaps we deny their humanity or congratulate ourselves on how many diseases will be cured and how much suffering will be relieved. Whatever the specific topic, if one is dealing with the unjust taking of human life, then the same issues remain. If we want to make our victims guilty, then we must take some element of human nature and reinvent it as a perversion. If we want to dehumanize them, we must redefine what it means to be human. If we want to stop feeling pity, we must call our sentimentalism compassion and use it as an excuse to take the easy way out. The details and applications may change, but the point always remains the same. We are, from conception, made in the image of God and are valuable because he loves us. Any other foundation will ultimately fail. Whatever the details, the ethical responsibility of Christians remains to remind opponents of these facts and take away their favorite hiding places.

But this is not the end of our task. According to a 2007 Fox News report, one in five pregnancies worldwide ends in abortion.[14] With such prevalence, more and more women will have had abortions, more and more doctors will have performed them, and more and more friends and family will have enabled them. On some level, every one of these people understands what she has done. In this sense, abortion is no different than any other sin. We have all sinned, we have all fallen short, and we are all guilty. As important as arguments are to working toward preventing more abortions, they cannot solve the problems or relieve the burdens of those performed in the past; arguments can only identify them. We need Christ. As much as Christians ought to argue against abortion, we also need to proclaim the Gospel. Preventing abortion might and should be achieved through social or legal means, but healing can only come through faith in Christ Jesus.

---

14. "1 in 5," paragraph 1.

11

Biblical Sexuality: Not So Strange

INTRODUCTION

G.K. Chesterton once wrote:

> You cannot evade the issue of God, whether you talk about pigs or the binomial theory, you are still talking about Him. Now, if Christianity... be a fragment of metaphysical nonsense invented by a few people, then, of course, defending it will simply mean talking that metaphysical nonsense over and over. But if Christianity should happen to be true—then defending it may mean talking about anything or everything. Things can be irrelevant to the proposition that Christianity is false, but nothing can be irrelevant to the proposition that Christianity is true.[1]

Sexual morality is one of those topics that may seem irrelevant to the overall issue of Christianity but still comes up with surprising regularity in objections to it. Like abortion, it is a moral issue, and consequently there is nothing uniquely Christian about it—all civilizations have valued chastity to various degrees and in various ways. Nevertheless, in the West, rhetorical attacks on religion in general and Christianity in particular often involve explicit rejection of Christian teachings on sexuality. Rejecting the moral principles described in the Bible has long been seen as a means of leaving the benighted past behind and moving into a brave and enlightened new world. The idea that sex is wrong outside of marriage is typically considered a quaint and antiquated relic of the past.

A prime example of this is the second Humanist Manifesto. Its sixth point expresses a sexual ethic that has much in common with the typical view among Americans today: "orthodox religions and puritanical cul-

1. Chesterton, *Orthodoxy*, 8.

tures" are repressive. In their place, it advocates a relatively libertine approach in which all sexual expressions are acceptable as long as they are consensual and do not harm others.[2] The same point appears in Richard Dawkins' *The God Delusion*, in which he replaces the usual commandments with some of his own. Among them is, "Enjoy your own sex life (so long as it damages nobody else) and leave others to enjoy theirs in private whatever their inclinations, which are none of your business."[3] This view stands in stark contrast to the Christian ethic that sex belongs only between a husband and wife.

In addition to being the topic of many overt attacks from non-Christians, attention to sexual morality is warranted because many Christians underestimate it as one of the causes of so many Christian youth wandering from the faith in the high school and college years. Viewing sex as mere recreation is typical of modern Americans, but this is at extreme odds with Biblical teaching. This tension naturally leads a person to eventually arrive at one or the other. One can only live in contradiction for so long. Many, unfortunately, choose to reject their faith—not dropping it all at once, but gradually increasing the distance between themselves and any reminders that they are sinning. The problem is *not* that sexual sins are so horrible that the Atonement does not adequately cover them or that God will reject people from His Church as long as they commit them. The problem with sexual sin is that it provides one with a powerful incentive to begin intentionally doubting those unseen things which stand in the way of something enjoyable. Because faith is the certainty of things unseen, sexual sin can lead one to set his faith further and further aside in its pursuit.

INADEQUATE WAYS OF ADDRESSING SEXUAL SIN

Evangelical Christians give a great deal of attention to this topic, but unfortunately their approaches to convincing others of the validity of Christian morality are often grossly off the mark. One common approach is to argue that sex is just better when one waits until marriage. A particularly crass example of this can be found in the documentary, "Friends of God: A Road Trip with Alexandra Pelosi." In it, there is a scene in which Ted Haggard, a prominent megachurch pastor who later admitted to ho-

---

2. Kurtz and Wilson, "Humanist Manifesto II."
3. Mohler, "The Dawkins Delusion," para. 20.

mosexual conduct and drug use, mentions a survey that says Evangelicals have better sex lives than other groups. He then asks two young men with him to tell the camera how often they sleep with their wives and even what percentage of the time their wives climax, to which the men of course give exceptionally favorable responses.[4] Admittedly, the case certainly can and has been made in less degrading ways. Even when that is true, however, it still completely misses the primary challenge. Basing the case for abstinence on delayed gratification leaves the erroneous idea that sexuality is all about being gratified completely untouched. As such, sexual morality merely becomes a personal preference that only encompasses personal gratification. It becomes as trivial as whether one prefers to receive his lottery winnings in monthly installments over the next thirty years or in a lump sum.

Another common means of addressing the topic is to make an appeal to self-interest—abstinence-only sexual education programs in schools often take this approach. There are, after all, many risks associated with premarital sex. There are diseases that can be contracted, unexpected pregnancies, higher risks of suicide, emotional distress, and so on. Such risks are real and should not be trivialized. At the same time, the fact that such consequences are natural results of violating the moral law does serve as a reminder of that moral law. Nevertheless, there remains a very serious flaw in this approach: a full human life is one that involves taking calculated risks. One cannot live life well by hiding from anything that might have negative consequences. What is more, many of these risks can be mitigated to some degree by various techniques and equipment.[5] The message becomes "be careful" rather than "be chaste." A reasonable person could conclude that premarital sex is worth the risk as long as she takes sufficient precautions, and many do exactly that. As a result, this line of reasoning is relatively unconvincing. However, a worse consequence becomes apparent when a person actually is convinced because at that point, he begins to make a virtue out of timidity. Those who abstain solely due to the danger no longer practice the virtue of chastity but are merely immobilized with fear. When timidity is treated as a virtue, it fosters the idea that "nice guys" and "good girls" are sedentary when it comes to sex. Consequently, people do not pursue appropriate use of their sexuality by

---

4. Linton, "Friends of God," para. 11.

5. The effectiveness of these techniques is often oversold, but they remain at least somewhat preventative.

intentionally seeking out marriage—both through acquiring the traits that make someone a good husband or wife and by searching for those traits in potential partners. What is more, abstinence is frequently abandoned anyway if a relatively safe prospect happens to fall in their laps.

MISSING THE POINT

The fundamental flaw in all of these approaches is that they never properly address the purpose of sex—they merely assume along with the culture that it is entirely about good feelings. In short, they accept the basic sexual philosophy of the culture and then try to add Biblical ethics to it. It is no wonder that the Biblical rules seem so bizarre in such a context. However, it can be easily shown that the philosophical context itself is bizarre. One might imagine a society like the one in *Brave New World* in which sex is available at all ages and women are sterile and pneumatic. Such a complex system of drugs and conditioning may remove all risk and create a situation where gratification no longer needs to be delayed and sexual pleasure can be maximized. However, readers still intuitively recognize that such a society does not represent how things ought to be. If sexuality is all about one's own well-being, then sexuality ends up being entirely self-centered—a very odd idea when applied to an activity that typically requires more than one participant.

It is likewise odd that sex be only about pleasure. If it were, then the ethic proposed by the Humanist Manifesto is a sensible one. As long as enjoyment is had and no one is hurt, then any pleasure-centered activity is acceptable. Nevertheless, real incidents show the ethic itself to be absurd. There is, for example, a case reported by the *LA Times* in which a doctor allegedly put his patient under anesthetic before raping her. As Gregory Koukl pointed out while considering the case, the victim would not have experienced pain while anesthetized, and the doctor presumably had a great time. If sex is all about pleasure, and this act generated pleasure without pain, then it would necessarily be morally acceptable.[6] Nevertheless, nearly anyone would recognize that it is actually abhorrent. An ethic based purely on enjoyment would mean that rape is a bad thing only inasmuch as impotence is a bad thing—it merely means that sex is not as much fun as it otherwise would be. The wrong of rape goes deeper than mere pain, and so the right of sex must be deeper than mere pleasure.

---

6. Koukl, "Minimalist Ethic—Too Minimal," para. 14.

It must also be deeper than mere autonomy. Rape is categorically different than wearing a roommate's favorite shirt even after being told not to.

If our culture's view on the point of sex needs to be addressed and the ways modern Christians typically engage the issue are inadequate, then another approach must be found. One could attempt to construct a competing philosophy on the purpose of sex using only the Bible as a source.[7] Even if possible, however, this would be of no apologetic value; an effective argument depends on common ground. As chapter 3 argued, the common ground for moral questions is the law written on our hearts. Different people try to hide different parts of the law and consequently end up acting upon different details, but they are all defacing the same picture. People repress what they know about sexual morality, but everybody knows some things about it. As C.S. Lewis noted in *Mere Christianity*, "Men have differed as to whether you should have one wife or four. But they have always agreed that you must not simply have any woman you liked."[8] Although Christians often complain that in our corrupt and libertine society there are absolutely no rules anymore when it comes to sex, this is not actually the case. While our society is corrupt, and one is unlikely to find the virtue of chastity in ample supply, it is easy to find inclinations towards it if one looks closely enough.

THE WRECKAGE OF SEXUAL MORALITY.

Christians often fail to notice society's rules for sexuality because these rules fall so far short of the Biblical rule: no sex outside of marriage. Nevertheless, even casual observation reveals a surprisingly long list of common moral precepts. What criteria qualify a moral precept as "common?" A common precept is not one that every last person agrees with; if humans willfully ignore what they know about morality, then no rule could ever meet such a criteria. Also, a common precept need not be a stark "this action is absolutely forbidden." Just as there are varying degrees of punishment for breaking different laws, reactions against the violation of moral precepts can range from severe punishment to simple condescension. A common moral precept is therefore a frequently oc-

---

7. It should be noted, however, that because the Bible is not primarily a guide for right living, one makes surprisingly little progress if he is consistent in using no source of the knowledge but the Bible.

8. Lewis, *Mere Christianity*, 6.

curring belief that expresses some degree of approval or disapproval. The end result should not be a list on which every person agrees with every item; it need only be that most people would agree with most items. If the list reveals anything about the contents on the natural law, these contents should not hinge on any single item.

There are certainly sexual behaviors that are commonly condemned in our society whether or not there is an associated legal condemnation. The first and most obvious behavior has already been mentioned: rape. Most people understand that mutual consent is essential to sex thus rape is considered a dire wrong.[9] Likewise, sex with children and relatives is clearly abhorrent to nearly everyone. There may be organizations that advocate pedophilia, but such organizations are strongly condemned even by others who seek to walk away from traditional sexual morals. Cheating (and adultery in particular) is also largely seen as reprehensible. It may happen frequently, but it is also a common cause for ending a relationship when it is discovered. Cheating is not usually ignored, and where it is, most people think there is something wrong with the person ignoring it. Such condemnation is not merely for the practical reason of safety from disease either—if a husband is confronted over his affair, "don't worry honey, I was wearing a condom the whole time" is unlikely to set things right. Finally, there is the exhortation to practice "safe sex." Schools, parents, the government, and the media frequently warn people to use protection and condemn those who do not as irresponsible.

In addition to such issues that are considered relatively black and white, there are a host of behaviors that fall under the category of condescension rather than condemnation. Casual shack-ups, for example, are generally looked down upon once actual relationships are being considered. As was mentioned in the third chapter, studies show that women who believe they are hooked up to a polygraph machine report a substantially higher number of partners that those who do not—they lie to minimize their number of partners when they believe they can get away with it. Likewise, while a man is unlikely to care how many one-night-stands his one-night-stand has been involved in,[10] he will certainly care how many his fiancée has had. In the same vein, it is typically believed that one ought to love or at least "care" about one's partner before having

---

9. One could argue about how one measures consent, but that is beyond the scope of this book.

10. As long as he is using protection, anyway.

sex. There is also condescension toward those who are unable to effectively please their partners, indicating that sex ought to be pleasurable for everyone involved. Masturbation is certainly the butt of plenty of jokes in popular media, and most recognize that there is something pathetic about it in comparison to the real thing with another person.[11] There is even condescension towards sexual inhibitions that ironically come from the very quarters that reject the application of rules to sexuality. It is a common belief that sexual encounters ought to be unbridled and free. Like impotence, frigidity is not held up as the sexual ideal.

If one connects the dots, a number of patterns begin to emerge. The patterns, however, do not amount to "do whatever you want as long as you hurt no one else." First, the ideas about the absolute necessity of consent and the condescension with which self-service is viewed indicate that sex ought not to simply be taken, but to be mutually given from one to another. Secondly, the ideas about mutual pleasure and the importance of protection indicate that it ought to involve the good of the other person. Thirdly, one can see from ideas about cheating and promiscuity that sex ought to involve an exclusive commitment between the people involved. Fourthly, the ideas about inhibitions show that this commitment ought to result in a very intimate union. Fifthly, one can recognize that a relationship ought to involve only certain kinds of complementary people. When it comes to sex, children do not complement adults, animals do not complement humans, and family members do not complement each other.

If one were to compile these five insights into their most idealized form, he would basically end up with the idea that sex ought to be an intimate union of mutual self-giving between two complementary people founded in a permanent and exclusive commitment to each other's good. Despite the fact that these insights did not come from "orthodox religion or puritanical cultures," they sound suspiciously like the traditional idea that sex only ought to be practiced within marriage. As it turns out, the Biblical ethic is not nearly so foreign to modern Americans as is typically believed. One can also begin to discern purpose from this idea. Commitment involves our wills, intimacy and self-giving involve our hearts and minds, and so on. The purpose of sex, then, is to bind a man and a woman's minds, bodies, hearts, and wills together in just

11. Consider, for example, the masturbatory event in *American Pie* that gave the movie its title. Nobody considers it to be the character's proudest moment in the film.

such a marital relationship—to become "one flesh" as the Bible describes it.[12] This also has an obvious connection to the biological purpose of sex. New life emerges from and is subsequently cherished through this love and unity. Such a reality goes far deeper than simply having a good time and even matches popular moral precepts about sex much better than the humanist ethic.

DISTORTIONS

This basic picture of sexuality gets distorted in different ways depending on which of these five factors are exaggerated and which are suppressed. For example, the common practice of serial monogamy[13] is generally accepted because it does not deny or invent new moral knowledge; it merely obscures and reshapes that which is already known. It acknowledges the need for committed relationships based on mutual self-giving, turns up the volume on ideas about pleasure and romance until these factors become paramount, and then softens the idea of exclusivity until it goes from "one" to merely "one at a time." Nevertheless, there is clearly something dishonest about this softening. When long-term relationships are on the table, the number of other partners one's partner has had suddenly becomes more important. As was mentioned, a man who says it makes no difference whether a girlfriend he takes to meet his parents has been with zero or a hundred other men is usually lying. It is not even honest with respect to romance. "You're the one for me" is romantic. "You're the one for me at the moment until I meet someone else" is not.

The damage to exclusivity, however, is not the end of the story. As it turns out, sexuality is too complete a tapestry to pluck out one thread without causing the rest to begin unraveling. Serial monogamy cannot succeed in watering down one aspect of sexuality while leaving all of the others intact. This becomes painfully obvious when it comes to the criteria of commitment. Commitments between people are made by means of promises. In serial monogamy, the sad fact is that the only promise made is to make sure one says goodbye to his current partner before sleeping with the next one. The obvious thinness of this promise perhaps explains why it very often turns into a commitment to merely say goodbye after sleeping with somebody else if one plans to continue doing so. Intimacy

---

12. Gen. 2:24, Matt. 19:5, and Eph. 5:31.
13. Or "successive polygamy," as it is sometimes called.

also disappears as inhibitions arise because partners begin holding themselves back. They learn not to invest too deeply in someone they will likely end up in a painful breakup with. Finally, self-giving breaks down because people realize that they are only offering loans. People expect their partners to act as though they are married—as though they are devoted only to them—but seldom hold themselves to the same standard. Their partners, of course, do the same thing, and the relationship is set up for inevitable disappointment.

People often try to work around this problem by changing the expectations of relationships. Marriage vows are changed from "till death do us part" to sentiments such as "as long as we both grow" or by holding moving in ceremonies with similarly pleasant but vapid rituals. There is also the workaround that was used in *Eternal Sunshine of the Spotless Mind*. In this movie, Jim Carey and Kate Winslet are in a relationship and become so sick of each other that they have their memories of each other erased. They end up "meeting" again and begin another romance when they discover what happened. Kate Winslet is about to call the whole thing off because they now know for sure that they will just end up hating each other. Jim Carey responds simply by saying, "OK." He is willing to accept the nasty break-up if it means they can have a happy relationship for a short time. The movie intends this resolution to be hopeful, but the idea that the best one can hope for is a few happy memories before moving on to the next relationship is exceptionally dismal. People can try to rearrange their expectations for relationships, but ultimately it cannot work. The expectations are not forced on us by tradition, but already exist within the framework of our minds. We can escape them only by ceasing to be human.

RATIONALIZATIONS

While serial monogamy is clearly a distortion of what sexuality ought to be, the fact that many of the practices involved are enjoyable provides a powerful incentive to continue those practices regardless of any sense of morality. As in the case of any violation of the natural law, people know to some extent that a behavior is wrong, but if they want to continue it, they have a need to make it seem right—to rationalize it.[14] While a person may, to some extent, know that sex belongs with marriage, one can still

---

14. See chapter 3 for more on this subject.

attempt to avoid concluding that one therefore ought not to engage in it outside of marriage.

For example, many claim that premarital sex is a practical necessity towards achieving marriage, and so acknowledge the ideal but abandon the particulars. Some argue that while sex belongs with marriage, partners need to have sex beforehand to figure out whether a marriage will work. There are as many variations on this theme as there are definitions of "work." A crasser variation is the idea of the "test drive." Not only does this clearly objectify one's partner, it is also dishonest. Few people immediately either stop "testing" or get married if their test drive goes well. If it goes poorly, few people actually tell their partner, "you know, I really like you, but that just was not as good as I had hoped; we should break up so I can find a better model," even if that is exactly how they feel. Likewise, rather than considering them a practical necessity, most people would still be concerned with how many "test drives" their partner has been taken on. If this begins to sound like the offensive notion of "damaged goods," one should recall that such a notion is only natural after treating a potential spouse as merchandise in the first place

Another increasingly accepted variation is cohabitation. Many people believe that living together is like practicing being married. However, while less repugnant than a test drive, it is no less of a rationalization. Marriage is founded on a permanent commitment—something that is absent in cohabitation. Learning to live together without a permanent commitment is inherently different than living with one. It is, for example, easier to put up with hurt and annoyances when one perceives that it is only temporary. When one believes these things to be permanent, one is tempted to fear and despair. If the idea that "at least I can get out if necessary" becomes an unconscious crutch, this crutch is easily carried into marriage as a greater willingness to divorce. This is perhaps part of the reason why, depending on which studies one looks at, people who have cohabited before marriage are between 33 and 151 percent more likely to divorce.[15]

Another common rationalization is that while one believes that sex belongs with marriage, a piece of paper and a public ceremony are irrelevant to the situation. Couples often consider themselves married in their hearts because they deeply love each other—standing in front of a priest

---

15. Wilcox, "Abstinence," 7.

or judge and reciting some words cannot make them more married. This is typically arrived at by defining love as a particular variety of romantic feelings instead of a commitment to the good of one's partner. While this may appear to work initially, it is ultimately naïve. Feelings mature and change over the decades, and basing one's relationship on them is shortsighted. What is more, if one only treats her partner the way she feels like treating him, it will become less likely to look like actual love the longer they are together. Even when both partners have a commitment in mind, however, it is a weaker one if it cannot be spoken aloud in front of witnesses as a matter of public record. First, a refusal to make a public promise robs a couple of one of the purposes of having witnesses: so that the witnesses may help the couple to live up to that promise. Secondly, even if one has no initial intention of leaving his partner, it remains much easier when it is not common knowledge that he has solemnly promised to be with only her. Thirdly, the lack of such a promise makes it more difficult for each partner to see and know the other's commitment when times get tough. If the basis for a couple's commitment is day-to-day feelings and behavior, what is one to think during those months or even years when an important issue is coming between them? In still other cases, of course, it is not both partners who have a commitment in mind. Children in grade school and junior high will sometimes say that they will be another child's boyfriend or girlfriend as long as the other promises not to tell anyone. It is clear that someone is being taken advantage of in such situations. This can also be the case in unspoken so-called marriages when one partner lies about his hidden commitment. In *Don Quixote*, there is a subplot about a man who sneaks into a woman's bed-chamber and convinces her to marry him right then and there with no one around. It is no surprise to the reader that he disappears and tries to marry another woman soon afterwards. In the end, marriage-like relationships without promises are often just another gateway into serial monogamy.

Others may claim that while their sexual practices are disconnected from marriage, they certainly do not get in the way of the ideal. One can use sex merely for pleasure now, but still use it according to its purpose at some unspecified time in the future. In "Sex at the Edge of Night," J. Budziszewski explodes this rationalization using duct tape as an analogy. As this chapter has already argued, sex is intended to bind a couple together—like tape, it acts as an adhesive. If one puts a piece of duct tape on a person's arm, it is going to stick whether one wants it to or not—that is its function. Accordingly, it will hurt when it gets pulled off. If one continues to attach and detach a piece of tape, however, it eventually will cease to stick (or hurt) at all. Budziszewski argues that sexuality works in a similar way; continually binding one's self to and leaving different partners eventually makes sex meaningless as a source of unity between two people. Ultimately, one cannot be promiscuous without damaging one's ability to be intimate.[16] One could, of course, say that he has no interest in marriage and so that this entire line of reasoning is irrelevant to him. At this point, however, even the pretext of not hurting people is lost. Even if one has no interest in marriage, one's partners might. Even if they do not at the moment, they may later on. Even if they consent to be harmed, the harm still occurs. The already insufficient ethic of "I can do whatever I want as long as I do not hurt anyone else" is revealed to merely be, "I do not care if I hurt anyone else as long as I have permission."

In the end, all of these practices are not merely adaptations to imperfect circumstances—they actively destroy what they are supposedly pursuing. They make use of sexuality in a way that is contrary to its purpose. Even if they somehow manage to "work" in a particular situation, they remain a perversion of sexuality just as binging and purging is a perversion of eating. One may manage to achieve some nutrition despite the behavior, but it remains a disgusting abuse of one's ability to eat. The fact that sex is enjoyable makes it more tempting to accept these rationalizations, but they remain just that.

HOMOSEXUALITY

Homosexuality is another distortion of sexuality that is highly visible in our society (even if it is not necessarily as common as the visibility would suggest). Just as with serial monogamy, the modern embrace of homosexuality as one among many beautiful sexual expressions typically exaggerates the romantic and pleasurable aspects of sexuality. This time, however, it is the part about complementarity that is distorted—the idea that sexual unions only ought to involve people who are right for each other. Depending on the individual, this may be in addition to obscuring other points like exclusivity and commitment. However, in some respects, that is no different from modern heterosexual practices.[17]

---

16. Budziszewski, "Sex at the Edge of Night," paras. 92–110.

17. There is, perhaps, good reason to believe that exclusive and committed relation-

Whatever the reality for each individual, though, the current rhetoric of homosexual advocacy does not focus on promiscuous sex but on the idea of gay marriage—a loving and permanent commitment that just happens to be between people of the same gender. Ideas of complementarity are therefore detached from the complementary differences of males and females. People of the same gender can, of course, be complementary in non-sexual ways. People with different talents and gifts are necessary for any kind of teamwork at all. The relevant question, however, is whether men and men or women and women can be complementary in a sexual way. Not every relationship is sexually complementary. A man and his dog, for example, might have a complementary relationship, but it would not be consummated by sex.

As was previously established, the purpose of sexuality is to bind a couple's minds, bodies, hearts, and wills together. It was also noted that this has clear ties to the biological purpose of sex (procreation) because such a bond is ideal for loving the new life that is created. Male and female complementarity is essential to this. In terms of simple biology, the complementarity is obvious; certain body parts have certain functions. Misappropriating these parts for other functions (as happens in homosexual relationships) can be very damaging to health. A full analysis of the dangers cannot be done in this space, but it is worth noting a couple of examples. Physical damage to the rectum is a typical consequence of repeatedly forcing something into an orifice designed for output.[18] Sexually transmitted diseases also remain disproportionately high among men who have sex with men. According to the CDC, this demographic represents 68 percent of men with HIV despite only representing 7 percent or less of men in the United States.[19] Ultimately, homosexuality is not healthy for the people involved. I once observed someone without a chisel attempt to use a screwdriver in its place. By the time he was finished, that screwdriver was too damaged to be used for its intended purpose. The human body often fares no better when it is forced to act contrary to its design.

---

ships are significantly rarer among homosexuals than the political rhetoric indicates. However, this line of argument will not be taken up in this book. Even if there is a statistical difference in the number of partners, the rationalizations (which are the main concern of this chapter) are presumably similar to those used by heterosexuals.

18. Klamecki, "Medical Perspective," 117.
19. CDC, "HIV/AIDS."

What is also clear, but often forgotten in the modern world, is that there are also complementary male and female traits that go beyond biology. The next chapter will examine the subject in greater detail, but put simply, being a man and being a woman are two different things. This difference is as essential to the sexual unity of spouses as sexual biology. Deviating from this design means that sexual unions do not produce the self-giving unity they ought to. In *What We Can't Not Know*, J. Budziszewski describes it this way:

> The difference between the spouses is crucial to the power of their union to take each out of Self for the Other. Sodomy resists that liberation; it is merely self-love with another body . . . A husband and wife can balance and complete each other, but the sexual reinforcement of identicals merely unhinges them; it makes them not less extreme, but more. The same dynamic of reinforcement takes place in the explosive promiscuity of men who mate men, and in the implosive dependency of women who mate women.[20]

Sexually binding the hearts, minds, and wills of two people who are sexually the same is not the same as a union of two who are sexually different because neither one ever needs to understand and cherish someone fundamentally different from themselves.

When such facts are considered, the rationalizations for embracing homosexuality ultimately fall apart. It is sometimes claimed that same-sex couples love each other just as well as opposite sex couples. If love is merely thought of as a feeling, this might very well be true.[21] However, love in the sense of a commitment to the good of another person does not involve actions that damage that person. Putting one's partner at high risk of emotional and physical damage is not for her good. Driving one's partner to extremes is not in his best interest. Love certainly has a subjective side to it. Each person is a unique individual and therefore every couple will also be unique. No marriage works exactly the same as another. Nevertheless, love has an objective side as well. No person is so unique that he is not a human. No human is so unique that he or she is not either a man or a woman. Therefore, no genuine marriage is so unique that its workings have nothing in common with every other mar-

---

20. Budziszewski, *What we Can't Not Know*, 100.
21. Although virtually impossible to either verify or falsify.

riage. A love that cuts itself off from the objective good of another can no longer be accurately called love.

CONCLUSION

There are, of course, any number of other corruptions of sexuality, but there is no need to go into them all. Each one will acknowledge some parts of the purpose of sex while denying others. The task of the apologist remains the same: discover what remains of the natural law within the distortion and then connect the dots to the parts that are being suppressed. Despite the claims of skeptics, one need not fall back on traditions or religious dogma to establish sexual morality. It is not imposed by society; it is inherent in human design. Different cultures may arrange their relationships in different ways, but marriage is recognized in all of them. Even when other arrangements are allowed or encouraged, marriage is still set higher than the others.[22] As long as people remain human, the sexual revolution will never succeed in its goals.

Modern Americans have the odd idea that good is "good," but that it is also boring. As the saying goes, "God created food, but the Devil created spice." The church has unfortunately had a large hand in the development of this erroneous idea. Christians often think of sexual morality as merely a list of thou-shalt-not's. While it is entirely right and proper to proclaim certain behaviors as wrong, such proclamations should not be allowed to exclude a positive approach to the subject. Explaining what sexuality should not be is not the same as explaining what it should be. Abstinence in and of itself is not what sexuality is made for. In the absence of any teaching on God's purpose, other purposes will fill the void. For the unreflective, pleasure will be the first thing that comes to mind. At that point, any rules will seem like a small box in which something wonderful is being imprisoned. However, when the purpose of sexuality is acknowledged—when it is proclaimed as a means of creating a deep and permanent bond between a man and a woman—the rules cease to be a prison and instead become a guide by which sexuality can flourish. As with any other gift of God, appropriately using sexuality is not boring as long as one acts according to its purpose.

---

22. Budziszewski, *What We Can't Not Know*, 36.

12

Christianity and Feminism

INTRODUCTION

THE CLAIM IS OFTEN made that orthodox Christianity is misogynistic—that it is anti-woman. For some, this alleged misogyny takes the form of a handful of old customs and teachings that really need to be set aside in more enlightened times. For others, Christianity is not merely a little old-fashioned, but downright sinister. As a more extreme interpretation sometimes goes, women have been oppressed by men for almost all of human history, and it is only in the past century or so that they have finally been able to wear shoes and step outside the kitchen. Hampering this progress is Christianity. As a relic of the past, its teachings are necessarily steeped in this historical oppression. This is perhaps most clearly seen in the writings of the Apostle Paul, who had a deep-seated hatred for women. Within these writings are statements that women are not allowed to teach and have authority over men in the church[1] and that they ought to submit to their husbands as to Christ.[2] Of course, the Old Testament is even more obviously anti-woman due to the rampant polygamy and many other examples of poor treatment of women. Whether one's interpretations lean toward old-fashioned or sinister, the presence of such things in the Bible can be a very sore spot for many who believe them to be harmful to women.

While it is unfortunate that so many non-Christians believe that the Bible is misogynistic, the sad fact is that most Christians seem to believe it as well. While not putting it in so many words, the tendency towards the difficult passages on this subject is to dismiss rather than defend. A com-

---

1. 1 Tim 2:12.
2. Eph 5:22.

mon contention even among Christians is that the New Testament simply reflected the mindset of the benighted time in which it was written, and if Paul lived today, he would have taken a more mature approach to gender issues. Others suggest that the Bible is just exceptionally difficult to read, and while those verses mean something, they certainly do not mean what they say. The next step is to quote parts of the Bible that seem to support feminism, the "belief in the social, political, and economic equality of the sexes."[3] Perhaps one talks about Deborah, a prophetess and leader of Israel before the monarchy.[4] Perhaps one mentions Paul's comment that in Christ there is no male or female.[5] What more could a feminist ask for?

While these considerations are certainly necessary for understanding the whole picture, making them the entirety of the response misses the point of the critique. It is true that both the Old and the New Testaments prescribe a treatment of women that is far superior to and closer to feminism than what was normal in the cultures in which the documents were written. While this should not be dismissed, the problem with solely taking this approach is that it does not really address the parts of the Bible that contradict feminism. It only makes the Bible either schizophrenic or incomprehensible. If either of these are true, then the Christian's only real option is to accept the parts of the Bible that can be used as stepping stones to progress and leave the rest to the past. On the other hand, if the Bible is the Word of God, as previous chapters contended, then this "progressive" approach is not an acceptable option.

In short, "it's not what it looks like" followed by redirection is the common response to uncomfortable verses, but a faithful defense requires an attempt to demonstrate that God knew what He was authoring even in the uncomfortable parts. In light of the situation, a defense must be made among Christians as well as among those who reject Christianity on these grounds. Accordingly, this chapter will make more use of the Bible than other chapters in this final section of the book. It may not be common ground between Christians and unbelievers, but it is relevant when making a case to Christians. While this chapter will not be addressing every

---

3. Academics can understand feminism in a wide variety of ways. This chapter, however, will use this basic definition provided in the *American Heritage Dictionary*.
4. Judg 4 and 5.
5. Gal 3:28.

verse that a feminist could object to, it will take a sample of different kinds of verses to deal with the most common kinds of objections.

THE OLD TESTAMENT

The events recorded in the Old Testament are often brutal. Because of this, examples of cruelty and misogyny within it are frequently brought up as evidence that if God is real, He surely hates women.[6] One example of this is in Numbers 31:17–18. In the aftermath of a war commanded by God between the Israelites and the Midianites, Moses tells his commanders, "Now kill all the boys. And kill every woman who has slept with a man, but save for yourselves every girl who has never slept with a man." What kind of god would command his people to not only kill all these people, but to keep the virgin prisoners as their sexual playthings? As is typical for such difficult passages, one must look at the context in which this command is given in order to understand. This war was in response to events recorded in Numbers 25. The Midianites were involved in an affair in which Israelite men were committing debauchery with pagan women of a neighboring tribe. This fornication was being used as a means to encourage the Israelites to worship the pagan gods instead of the One who brought them out of Egypt. The war was God's retribution for those events.[7] This command, however, was not part of God's original instructions, but a command given by Moses in anger.[8] His anger was only natural upon finding that his troops returned with the Midianite women as spoils of war; these were the very women who were amongst those leading the Israelites astray in the first place.

Under such circumstances, Moses' command of "save them for yourselves" cannot be justifiably interpreted to mean "make them your sex slaves." Fornication and debauchery were the problems that caused the situation in the first place. Moses' command is more likely an instruction that they be taken as wives instead of being used as slaves. The specification that only virgins be taken eliminates the possibility that the women involved in the original affair would end up married to the Israelite men. The society of that time and place was not one in which a woman with-

---

6. Some would claim the Old Testament shows that God hates humanity in general, but this chapter's scope is the issue of misogyny.

7. Num 31:1–2.

8. Num 31:14.

out a family could provide for herself. Marriage was the only available protection for a lone woman, and Moses provided it. Even the idea of "taking" wives, however, grates on modern ears. While the temptation is to judge all other cultures using our own as the gold standard, it must be remembered that arranged marriages have been common throughout human history. They still are in many cultures. Evaluating the merits of different marriage customs is beyond the scope of this chapter, and Moses' arrangement of these particular marriages is in no way, shape, or form the ideal for arranged marriages. Nevertheless, one should at least note that while being captured in warfare is never a good thing, marrying a stranger due to external circumstances rather than one's own choice was normal at that time and place. While many arranged marriages are no doubt unhappy (just as many marriages in our own culture are unhappy), it is difficult to maintain the claim that becoming a wife due to another's choice is essentially slavery. Of the few people I have met whose marriages were arranged, none of them equated their marriage to the relationship of master and slave. The situation of the Midianite women was tragic, but it was not God-ordained sexual slavery.

Most importantly, it should be noted that while God commanded the war in the first place, there is no indication within the text that the command about the captured women is anything other than Moses' own initiative. The Bible records many events that it does not condone. It is rare for the Israelites to ultimately be held up as fine moral examples, and this event is no exception. To be fair, there are other instances in the Old Testament in which God does specifically instruct the Israelites to kill every living thing when they go to war against nations in Canaan. It must be remembered that these accounts are not the glorious exploits of the brave Israelites as they take back what is rightfully theirs. These are accounts of God punishing reprehensibly wicked nations using the Israelites as a means while simultaneously establishing them as a nation from which the Messiah would come. They have nothing to say about the ethics of warfare—neither ancient nor modern. When reading the Old Testament, one must be very careful to discern exactly what is happening, what kind of people are involved, and what God is actually commanding in various instances. This same rule must be observed on the issue of polygamy. The patriarchs' propensity for taking multiple wives and concubines is not an endorsement of that practice by God. It is something He tolerated rather than ordained. After all, from the very beginning, man was intended to "leave his father and mother and be united to his wife."⁹ As Jesus points out, these words clearly imply a one-time event.¹⁰ The patriarchs needed forgiveness for their sins as much as we do for our own. Not every Bible story is a story of faith and heroism.

THE OFFICE OF THE MINISTRY

Another common complaint among feminists is the restriction of the office of the ministry to men alone. When one observes women successfully entering all sorts of careers in modern times, the job of pastor can appear to be the last holdout that must inevitably be opened up to women. In light of this, the main objection to this restriction is that women are just as capable of acting in the office of pastor as men, and therefore women should have just as much representation among pastors as men. Examples of successful female pastors are frequently given in support of this contention.

There are counter-arguments that support an all-male clergy based on an idea that men in general are better equipped for ministry than women in general. Some of these arguments may have merit while others do not. Either way, however, they are largely irrelevant because such a discussion misses the point altogether. If one begins by speaking of ability or results, he has put the cart before the horse. Although any Christian will confess that God is omnipotent, we often forget certain consequences of this fact. Most notably, we forget that God does not need to find people with ability in His church to make it run; He chooses to create people with ability and then puts them in His church to make it run. He could raise pastors out of the dust of the ground who would shepherd His flock better than any sinful Christian. The fact that God allows a Christian to act in any capacity in His kingdom is a profound act of grace. The fact that He calls people to work that actually has eternal consequences is even more amazing. Any place in His kingdom at all is therefore a privilege given by Him according to His will. The logical consequence of this is that nobody can, for any reason, claim the right to any position in the church on the basis of ability.¹¹ This includes women claiming their rights to be pastors

---

9. Gen 2:24.

10. Matt 19:9.

11. The converse, on the other hand, is not true. Incompetence can rightfully disqualify a person from office.

on the basis of ability. The objection is a non-starter. God gave us our abilities in the first place, so their existence can hardly merit any status before him. Social justice and rights are simply not relevant to this issue.

Calling is the crux of the matter. Our abilities do have some bearing on giving us clues to our calling. For example, if one loves the idea of being a writer but after years and years of practice cannot put together a coherent sentence, he probably is not called to be a writer. However, abilities are not the whole or even the start of it. While discerning God's calling can be complicated in some respects, other respects are crystal clear: God does not contradict Himself. He does not say one thing in the Bible and a different thing by the Holy Spirit or by circumstance. God could never call a person to divorce a faithful spouse because He has already made it clear in His Word that one is never to divorce a faithful spouse.[12] Likewise, He could never call a woman into the office of the ministry even if she has wonderful understanding of Scripture, great leadership and speaking skills, and a servant's heart, because God has already made it clear that He does not permit a woman to teach and have authority over a man in the church.[13] She is no doubt called to another office that involves such wonderful gifts, but not to this particular office that involves such gifts. If one imagines she is being called to something to which God has already said no, she is wrong—it is as simple as that. It does not matter if it ends up "working out" or if it brings about any great things. As C.S. Lewis noted in his novel, *Perelandra*, God is in the business of bringing about good—humans cannot stymie Him. He makes good out of what whatever we do, but it will not be the same good as if we had not sinned.[14] Unlike God, Christians are not in the business of bringing about anything, but rather are in the business of loving God with all our hearts, minds, and souls regardless of the consequences. One cannot love Him with all her mind if she uses her mind to ignore or explain away what He has told her.

This approach, of course, is incomplete because it does not venture to explain why God only calls men to be pastors. The question of why will be considered later in this chapter. Nevertheless, understanding the "why" is not a prerequisite for obedience as though one needs to check up

12. Matt 19:9.
13. 1 Tim 2:12.
14. Lewis, *Perelandra*, 104.

on God and make sure He is doing the right thing before acting. As Plato pointed out, right opinion is a mean between ignorance and wisdom.[15] Wisdom is the goal, but one should not simply disregard right opinion until he has wisdom to go along with it; one instead seeks to understand that right opinion and thereby attain wisdom. Before addressing the question of why, however, it is necessary to address the issue of submission in marriage.

SUBMISSION TO HUSBANDS

In Ephesians 5, Paul begins talking about living lives that are consistent with the Gospel. In verses 22–24, he writes, "Wives, submit to your husbands as to the Lord. For the husband is the head of the wife as Christ is the head of the church, his body, of which he is the Savior. Now as the church submits to Christ, so also wives should submit to their husbands in everything." This is not an isolated teaching. In the third chapter of his first letter, Peter puts it in even stronger terms.

> Wives, in the same way be submissive to your husbands so that, if any of them do not believe the word, they may be won over without words by the behavior of their wives, when they see the purity and reverence of your lives. Your beauty should not come from outward adornment, such as braided hair and the wearing of gold jewelry and fine clothes. Instead it should be that of your inner self, the unfading beauty of a gentle and quiet spirit, which is of great worth in God's sight. For this is the way the holy women of the past who put hope in God used to make themselves beautiful. They were submissive to their own husbands, like Sarah, who obeyed Abraham and called him her master. You are her daughters if you do what is right and do not give way to fear.[16]

This view of marriage by which wives obey their husbands is obviously contrary to the modern view in which wives and husbands ought to be completely equal, with no authority of one over the other. According to such a view, equally sharing chores, child-rearing, decision-making, bread-winning, and everything else right down the middle is the only fair way to manage a marriage. Otherwise, women end up being crushed and oppressed by their families—unable to grow into the complete people

---

15. Plato, *Symposium*, 26.
16. 1 Pet 3:1–6.

they ought to be. While one ought to agree that everyone should grow into their full potential, one need not agree that submission to husbands stymies the potential of wives. There are a number of allegedly oppressive elements in the Biblical vision of marriage that are not inherently harmful.

One common objection is that submission stunts a woman intellectually because her husband ends up doing all her thinking for her and she never makes any decisions. Because women are clearly capable of and equipped for thinking and making decisions, submission therefore makes her less than she is. But is this truly the case? Paul draws the analogy between a wife's submission to her husband and the church's submission to Christ, and so it makes sense to examine the latter first. Not everyone has been or will be a wife, but all Christians should have some experience submitting to Christ. Of course, the reality is that submission to Christ does not mean failing to think, act, or make decisions. On the contrary, submission to Christ means using one's gifts and talents to their fullest. In Jesus' parable of the talents, for example, the master leaves his servants in charge of some of his property. When he returns, he rewards the ones who stewarded it well by thoughtfully taking charge and investing it. On the contrary, he punished the servant who thoughtlessly buried the property in the backyard for safekeeping out of fear of what his master would do if he lost it.[17] God expects us to take appropriate risks with the gifts He has given us; He wants us to be active, even in submission. The task of submitting to Christ is ultimately a thoughtful one because Christ does not micromanage. He gives people the opportunity to use their minds, wills, and all their other gifts in His service. The Bible is not a flowchart for living, and does not in any way contain enough rules and advice to substitute for a person's brain.

Life is complex. Even where Biblical commands are given, it still falls on the Christian to consider how they are to be carried out. Even where the Bible declares some things to be good and others evil, one must consider how to pursue the former while avoiding the latter. Ultimately, one finds that submission to Christ requires more thought that merely going his own way. According to the latter, if one wants to do something, he need only ask "Do I want to?" and "Am I able to?" Submitting to Christ adds entirely new dimensions to one's considerations. One could draw an

---

17. Matt 25:14–30.

analogy to brain-teasers. Far from being thoughtless because of the given criteria, figuring out the solution is difficult *because* of them. Likewise, submission to a husband does not mean sitting and watching the grass grow until there is a command. It does not mean fearing to act lest one make a mistake. It means loving one's husband by seeking after what he seeks after and working towards his ends using her gifts. Any wife who has attempted this knows it is far from simple, thoughtless, or passive. A husband can certainly disrupt this arrangement through micromanaging or domineering, but there is nothing inherently destructive about it.

FREE WILL

Another objection against submission is not an objection to the function of it (for example, that it stifles women in day to day life) but to the principle of it. Like men, women have free will and some claim that to put a wife under the authority of her husband is to imprison what would otherwise be free. This supposedly violates the very essence of a free will and thereby the very nature of a woman as a free human being. This is often expressed by saying that a woman's (or indeed any person's) choice is valuable simply because it is her choice. Making some choices off-limits would therefore deprive her of her options and is therefore inhibiting her free will.

One should immediately recognize that this argument does not work because it proves too much. If it were true, the argument would not only apply to a wife's submission to her husband, but to anyone's submission to anyone else: a child to his parents, a citizen to her government, or even a human's to God. Even submission to ideas of equality would be excluded by this argument. Knowing *why* the argument does not work is another matter. In *Orthodoxy*, G.K. Chesterton points out its problem:

> You can praise an action by saying that it is calculated to bring pleasure or pain, to discover truth or to save the soul. But you cannot praise an action because it shows will; for to say that is merely to say that it is an action. By this praise of will, you cannot really choose one course as better than another. And yet, choosing one course as better than another is the very definition of the will you are praising. The worship of the will is the negation of the will. To admire mere choice is to refuse to choose.... All the will-worshipers, from Nietzsche to [John] Davidson, are really quite empty of volition. They cannot will, they can hardly wish. And if anyone

wants a proof of this, it can be found quite easily. It can be found in this fact: that they always talk of will as something that expands and breaks out. But it is quite the opposite. Every act of will is an act of self-limitation. To desire action is to desire limitation. In that sense, every act is an act of self-sacrifice. When you choose anything, you reject everything else.[18]

This principle of "opportunity cost" is the source of the saying in economics, "There's no such thing as a free lunch." Simply by spending time eating the lunch one gives up whatever else she might have done with her time or whatever other lunch she might have eaten. In the same way, there is no such thing as a "free" will to the extent that people making this objection take it. Yes, one can freely choose between different options, between good and evil,[19] and so forth. However, a human being's will is not so free that it can say "as I will it, so shall it be." A man cannot choose to be a cheeseburger on the simple basis that the world does not allow it. A man can choose to murder, but he cannot choose to righteously murder. Such a choice can be rightly condemned as evil and as one that ought never to have been made.

To put it succinctly, our wills do not operate in a vacuum, but in a world created by someone else. Both physical and spiritual realities direct the will in particular directions. Authority and appropriate submission to that authority are a part of how the world was created. It is a reality found even within God himself, for the Son is in a relationship of submission to the Father despite being coequal in power and majesty.[20] Even God's will is not utterly separated from what and who He is. The human will is purposed for love—for making a free commitment to another. Far from freeing it, separating the will from love ruins it by depriving it of its purpose. People have the erroneous idea that if a free will has any standard of judgment attached to it, it is not really free. On the contrary, if it has no such standard, it is not really a will.

---

18. Chesterton, *Orthodoxy*, 66.

19. To an extent at least. Human wills are damaged by sin; our freedom is not really as wide as many believe. Nevertheless, broken wills remain wills, and the limited options remain chosen.

20. Phil 2:5–8.

WHY SUBMISSION?

While this does undercut several objections, it does not explain why submission is a good thing. Even if submission is not as stifling as many claim, why apply it to wives at all? Part of the difficulty comes from the place given to equality in our culture that submission seems to undermine. It would be very difficult to argue against the proposition that much of the freedom and prosperity that has been enjoyed in the past few centuries was a result of embracing equality. The equality of slaves with masters and peasants with royalty has brought about considerable good. Should it not therefore be extended to all facets of society including marriage?

C.S. Lewis addresses this notion in his novel *That Hideous Strength* by means of a conversation between Ransom and Jane, a young woman in a difficult marriage. When she suggests that marital love depends on equality, Ransom suggests an alternative view. He acknowledges that equality has value as a mechanism of government. In a fallen world, equal rights can be an effective means of protecting people from each other. However, this equality is not the deepest reality between people. Ransom describes it as "medicine" rather than "food"—it can treat certain problems, but it is not itself something on which people thrive. This is especially true in marriage, which Ransom says is "just where [equality] ought not to be." Obedience, he says, is an "erotic necessity."[21] The previous chapter argued that the purpose of sexuality was to facilitate a permanent "one flesh" union between a man and a woman. It also suggested that such a union functioned because men and women are different but complementary by nature rather than equal and interchangeable. Because sex is so closely tied to marriage, the nature of sexuality as a means of creating such a union ought to give us an insight into the workings of marriage itself. After all, it is not by accident that they are so joined. Like sexuality, marriage works because men and women are different but complementary. Submission is a part of this. Lewis goes on to give a more lighthearted example of obedience making a complementary relationship work. Ransom spills some crumbs on the floor and blows a small whistle. Mice come out and clean up the crumbs then return. He notes that humans want their crumbs cleaned up and that mice are eager to do so. With the introduction of obedience, they get along well. Without it, they become enemies and both are worse off. While this simple "drill" illustrates his point, Ransom

21. Lewis, *That Hideous Strength*, 147.

likens the far more complicated relationship between husband and wife to a dance.[22] In light of this, it is worth examining a few ways in which submission makes the steps of this dance work.

ROMANCE

Romance within a marriage is one facet of the relationship that hinges on submission. Lewis went so far as to call it an "erotic necessity." Why this is the case should become clear upon examining the nature of romance. While different people can have very different ideas on what kinds of things are romantic, there are some common metaphors for romance that have almost become cliché. People speak in terms such as "being swept off your feet" or "falling head over heels in love." Both of these common metaphors imply a giving in to something, and neither leaves much room for insistence on equality. If someone is giving his wife a surprise gift and asks her to close her eyes, nothing would kill the romance faster than to refuse until a suitable explanation was given. The romance of being literally swept off one's feet would likewise be ruined by saying "Put me down! You might drop me!" At the same time, asking permission before doing any of these things would be similarly unromantic. There is no romance without a willingness to place oneself in the hands of another without guarantees.

This reveals another side of romance—the necessity of trust. If a man were too untrustworthy to submit to, it would also kill romance eventually. A woman who has been dropped is not too keen on being swept off her feet again. This is why Paul pairs his words to wives about submission with words to husbands about loving their wives as Christ loved the church—even to the point of sacrificing his life for her.[23] Without such a commitment, submission would be an invitation to harm. This other side of Paul's instruction is largely sidelined in this book not because it is unimportant, but because nobody in modern culture really objects to it. Husbands may not actually love their wives in this way, but unlike the Bible's teachings on submission, few object to the idea that husbands ought to so love. A husband places his well-being in his wife's hands when he puts her before himself. It is not as though he gets a pass if it is her own fault that a sacrifice is necessary. When Eve disobeyed God's command in

---

22. Lewis, 147.
23. Eph 5:25.

the Garden, for example, Adam's response should have been to bring her before God and offer Him his own life in place of his wife's—not to follow her into sin. This is the love Christ shows to His Church. A husband ought to be willing to sacrifice his life, health, property, and happiness on behalf of his wife. Likewise, a wife places her entire well-being in her husband's hands when she submits to him. She also does not get a free pass if her husband leads poorly.

Unlike the husband, however, the wife does have a mitigation on this responsibility. If her husband leads her to sin, she is to obey God rather than man.[24] Additionally, as this book has frequently pointed out, it is not loving to pretend a person's sins are not really sins. In such cases, submission to her husband as a man made in the image of God necessarily involves appropriately addressing the sin for her husband's sake. For example, if a husband is struggling with pornography, a wife should not submit by turning a blind eye to the telltale magazines and internet histories; she should confront him and actively find ways to help him win the struggle. Submission does not involve the rejection of truth or passivity in the face of sin, but it nevertheless ought to remain even when the husband is a sinner. Submission and trust are the two sides of a life-long romance, and they are clearly a dangerous business. Romance is never safe, but it only avoids destruction when it involves actual love—a mutual commitment to the good of the other.

One can see the corruption of this relationship in the popular "bad boy" and "nice guy" dichotomy. Nice guys are the ones who care about women and would never want to upset or harm them in any way. Bad boys, on the other hand, typically care about women only as a means to their own pleasure and are unashamed about it. Nice guys usually complain about the fact that women tend to be more attracted to the bad boys despite not having their best interests at heart. Women who are inclined towards the bad boys sometimes make this same complaint about their own inclinations as they wonder why they always end up hurt. The riddle is not that difficult to figure out. Nice guys are focused on passively avoiding conflict or causing offense; this is more akin to fear and weakness rather than confidence and strength. The bad boys, of course, have sufficient confidence and strength to buck authority even if they only use them for their own good. Although simple to understand, the dichotomy

---

24. Acts 5:29.

is hard to solve in practice because both sides are deficient. There is nothing attractive about a man who never makes waves and there is nothing trustworthy about a man who cares mainly for himself. If a man's leadership and a wife's submission are consciously excluded as factors in relationships, there is no way to solve the dichotomy.

DECISION MAKING

Although both wives and husbands make decisions in a marriage, there are also many times in which a single decision must be made as a couple. Ideally, of course, spouses will be able to discuss and come to a mutually satisfactory decision by learning from each others' insights. In practice, however, this is not always the case. Disagreements are possible even when both spouses are acting in good-will, and good-will is not exactly a constant in sinful men and women. Between two people, is there a way in which decision-making in such instances is equally divided and each person has exactly equal representation with the other?

Although political equality has frequently led to more democratic forms of government, voting does not work in a two-person system. There is only a majority when there are no disagreements; it provides no help when disagreements exist. Attempting to indefinitely extend the discussion phase of the decision-making process until agreement is reached is likewise impractical. Most decisions come with a time-limit. A decision on whether to accept a job offer in a different part of the country is limited by the amount of time the offer is open. A decision on how a child is to be schooled is limited by enrollment deadlines. To continue discussion indefinitely merely means that the most obstinate person gets their way. Neither can two people take turns in making the important decisions, for this assumes perpetual agreement on which things are important—a very unrealistic assumption. Disagreements cannot be resolved by still other disagreements. Two people cannot even depend on an intention that each decision be made by the most qualified person for that decision. It is sometimes clear which spouse is more qualified for a topic, but it is by no means always clear. Like importance, each spouse will likely have different views about who is more qualified in different cases. Even if one were able to create a system in which importance and qualification could be given mathematical values and there was a flowchart to follow which would ensure exactly equal representation, this would no longer describe a marriage. It would be a relationship between two computers rather than two people.

There are times when a husband and wife must act as one. If a couple decides to send their children to a private school, one parent ought never to scale his involvement according to how much he agreed with the decision. If a couple decides to move to a new city, one spouse ought never scale her assistance and support in their new home according to how many misgivings she had. When a decision is made and cannot be reevaluated, both spouses must do their parts to make the best of things. Ultimately, if two people must act as one but are in disagreement, there is no way that both can equally get their way. Headship is therefore a practical necessity for two different people to work together as one flesh. This is particularly true when two complementary people are designed to be more inclined towards and invested in different areas of life as are men and women. With the addition of headship, it becomes possible for these two different outlooks to be united in a single direction.

But if headship is a necessity, why should the man be the head? Lewis addresses this suggestion in *Mere Christianity*:

> Is there any very serious wish that it should be the woman? As I have said, I am not married myself, but as far as I can see, even a woman who wants to be the head of her own house does not usually admire the same state of things when she finds it going on next door. She is much more likely to say, 'Poor Mr X! Why he allows that appalling woman to boss him about the way she does is more than I can imagine.' I do not think she is even very flattered if anyone mentions the fact of her own 'headship.' There must be something unnatural about the rule of wives over husbands, because the wives themselves are half ashamed of it and despise the husbands whom they rule.[25]

Lewis' observations still seem to hold today. It appears that the most common response from a wife who is confronted about her headship is along the lines of, "of course I'm in charge, my husband is a nitwit" accompanied by a list of his deficiencies. This is hardly a declaration that all is well in a marriage. Even when a wife does intentionally claim headship, it seems to be because something is wrong, not because something is right.

If a wife despises her husband for being unable to lead, it is probably because she expects him to be leading. After all, nobody despises a

---

25. Lewis, *Mere Christianity*, 113.

Christianity and Feminism

baby for being unable to read a book. When design inclines a woman to expect her husband to lead but she is simultaneously taught by her culture that she ought to take offense at the very thought of being led, all sorts of destructive behaviors begin to emerge from the contradiction. One common example can be seen when a wife expects her husband to lead, but only in exactly the way she thinks she should be led. This, of course, is an illusion of submission, not the real thing because she remains the sole source of her own direction. To make the illusion more convincing a wife may even stop giving her own input on matters because her husband "ought to be figuring it out on his own." Such a burden is, of course, an impossible one. The husband's perpetual failure to carry it increases the wife's dissatisfaction with him and very likely his own dissatisfaction with himself. There is little joy or romance coming from such a circumstance.

Of course, a husband can sin by dominating or micromanaging his wife and confound this kind of union no less than a wife can confound it by refusing to submit at all. It has already been established that marriage requires two people to function, so it only makes sense that either person can stymie it. Nevertheless, a person can only be responsible for his or her own actions and do his or her own part. This is very likely the reason why Paul does not make his instructions contingent by saying "wives submit to your husbands *if* they love you as Christ loves church" and "husbands, love your wives *if* they submit to you as unto Christ." In the end, one is only responsible for his or her own part in the dance. One cannot be responsible for a partner's steps.

BEAUTY

Beauty is a third area in which submission is of functional importance. This should not be altogether surprising considering the relatively clear complementarity of men and women in this area. Men are attracted to appearances in a way that women are not, and women care about their appearances in a way that men do not.[26] It is also another area in which our society is in deep distress. It has become almost a cliché that modern women look on their own bodies with disappointment—they pursue

26. This is not to say that women are not or should not be attracted by men's appearances, nor that men are not or should not be concerned with their own appearances. It is merely to assert the existence of a qualitative difference between men and women in this regard—a difference that should be obvious to anyone who looks up from theory long enough to make actual observations.

beauty but are seldom satisfied by what beauty they have. It is hardly uncommon for women to lament over hair, weight, shape, and so on. Such a mindset even has a clinical name now: "negative body image." The blame is usually laid at the feet of the media for its consistently unrealistic portrayal of women. Women are then consistently unsatisfied by their own appearances because they cannot meet the unattainable standards set by models and actresses. While the media does act in a reprehensible fashion, this cannot be the root cause of the problem. Nobody condemns the makers of *Lord of the Rings*, or *Spider-Man* for setting unrealistic standards for courage. Nobody condemns professional athletes for setting unrealistic standards for physical prowess. Nobody condemns museums for setting unrealistic standards for artistic talent. If somebody were to condemn such things, the condemnation would be instantly recognized for what it is. Envy is the name for looking at the good fortune of another and complaining that one does not share it.

The wrinkle this adds to the situation is that envy has long been considered a sin. If there is any truth to this, it becomes difficult to blame it on external circumstances. The world may tempt a person to sin, but it does not force a person to sin. As Jesus taught, "Nothing outside a man can make him 'unclean' by going into him. Rather, it is what comes out of a man that makes him 'unclean.'"[27] In our culture, women have to deal with unprecedented temptations towards envy much as men have to deal with an unprecedented temptation towards lust. This is not to deny the guilt of certain media for causing the temptation. They can rightfully be considered guilty for their own sins. Nevertheless, a temptation, no matter how strong, does not create sin.

So what are the roots of envy? It arises when one corrupts the purpose of a thing so that it is bent towards himself. For example, one begins to envy another's wealth when wealth ceases to be something of God's of which he is a steward and becomes a means to his own pleasures. One envies another's wisdom when it ceases to be something with which she serves others and becomes something to provide her with admiration. This self-ward focus creates a perceived deprivation when one encounters another who is more blessed in a particular gift than herself. In this same way, a woman would envy the physical feminine beauty of another when

---

27. Mark 7:15.

such beauty ceases to serve God's purpose, but instead serves a purpose of her own.

There are plenty of ways the purpose of beauty can be bent. For example, one can make a side-effect of beauty such as admiration into the purpose. There is, of course, nothing wrong with wanting to be admired, but when one makes herself beautiful in order to be admired by others, then envy and resentment begin to arise. The envy could be towards others who seem to be hogging the coveted admiration. The resentment could be towards the parent from whom one inherited a particular unpleasant feature. Another side-effect that can be perverted into a purpose is satisfaction with one's own appearance. When self-satisfaction becomes a goal, it is likewise very easy to begin comparing oneself to others and coming up short.

But what does this have to do with submission? Peter ties the two concepts together in the verses given earlier. Like everything else, the ultimate purpose of beauty is to glorify God. However, the other thing Peter does in those verses is to direct a wife's inclination to make herself beautiful towards her husband through submission. When this occurs, envy is bypassed altogether. The impossible task of seeking everyone's admiration is replaced with the possible task of seeking only one person's admiration (with the bonus that it happens to be the one person who can appreciate it more than anyone else). The need to compare one's self to other women disappears as a wife is ideally without competition in her husband's eyes.[28] What is more, in a world that is now ruled by decay, such submission provides the only option for lasting beauty. A seventy-year-old woman is unlikely to arouse aesthetic appreciation in a twenty-year-old man as he passes her on the street, but she certainly can in her seventy-year-old husband's eyes because he sees her as she has been throughout their many years together. In a marriage where physical beauty was inseparable from that "gentle and quiet spirit", the persisting spirit will always bring to her husband's mind the physical beauty of her youth. Even when the physical beauty has faded to the world, it remains inseparable from that spirit as long as the spirit lasts.

---

28. Of course, this is not always the case, but the previous chapter covered that particular sin.

IMPOSED BY SOCIETY?

The obvious rejoinder to these observations is that this supposed complementarity between men and women is merely imposed by society. After all, Western society was heavily influenced by Christianity sometime in the past, so one might therefore claim that it is only natural that men and women still tend to act in some ways that reflect that history. Most modern Westerners are taught that the more enlightened perspective is to see the differences between men and women as only skin deep—which is to say that except for biology, men and women are really identical. Any substantial differences in behavior are therefore unjust teachings of an archaic culture. While there certainly are gender-specific behaviors and inclinations that are taught by culture, the first question pertaining to complementarity is whether all gender differences other than biology are taught by culture.

The "except for biology" part of such a view is the key to its dubious nature. One would have to ignore objective reality completely in order to argue that there are no physical differences between men and women.[29] There are certainly more similarities than differences. After all, men and women have the same number of digits and limbs, the same senses, similar skeletons, muscles, etc. Nevertheless, there remain clear differences between the sexes that tend to fall into three categories. First, there are the fairly broad generalizations. For example, men tend to be taller and stronger than women. Most women are taller or stronger than at least some men, and it is not exactly uncommon for a woman to be taller or stronger than the average man. Nevertheless, the tendencies are undeniable. So while the differences are certainly not absolute, there are clear differences in tendencies between the sexes. Second, there are differences that fall within the realm of normalcy, which describes most secondary sex characteristics. For example, one could observe that women have larger breasts than men or that men have more facial hair than women. There are still exceptions to characteristics in this categories, but they are not typical or by design. Men who are overweight or heavy marijuana users may have larger breasts than some women. Occasionally a woman will have more facial hair than some men. Such scenarios do exist, but it is clear that they exist because something is not quite right—perhaps poor

---

29. As Hollywood action movies often do in their scenes of women trading punches with men and taking them just as well.

Christianity and Feminism 221

nutrition, hormonal imbalances, genetic differences, or the like. Finally, there are primary sexual characteristics. These are mostly along the lines of differences in the reproductive system—the kind of differences upon which the continuation of humanity depends. Even in this category, there are exceptions, but only in the most extreme of circumstances. For example, like a man, a woman might not have a uterus, but that would only be because of either some kind of severe birth defect or through surgical intervention. A man might have genitalia that resembles a woman's, but it is only through the most severe deformity or mutilation that such a thing occurs.[30] Such circumstances exist only when something has gone very wrong.

These observations are nothing new, but they do provoke a very important question. Do people's bodies have anything to do with the rest of them, the parts that are non-physical? A materialist might object to the question itself and claim that bodies are all that humans are and that there are no non-physical aspects. A materialist of this kind, however, would have nothing more to say on the matter at hand. If all humans are just bodies, then one needs no more observations than those that have already been made in order to say that men and women are different and complimentary. A more astute materialist might admit that there are non-physical parts of humans in some sense but would call upon emergent behavior as an explanation. Things like the mind might be non-physical per sé, but they somehow arise out of the complexity of biology. In this case, there is more to talk about than just the body, but because non-physical aspects arise out of it, there is a very clear connection between the two. As a result of this connection, one should expect to see the same categories of difference in people's non-physical aspects as one does in their bodies. Even the society that allegedly imposes the differences would have ultimately arisen out of these same bodily differences. If one still wishes to complain about differences between men and women under such situations, all he can do is shake his fist at the impersonal cosmos because women are so cursed by their biology. However, I cannot think of a more misogynistic lament.

Of course, there is also the idea that people's bodies and "the rest of them" were designed and created together by God. In this case, there should also be a profound connection between our bodies and any non-

30. Surgery that brings this about would typically fall under the category of mutilation.

physical aspects. A good God would hardly give people natures that are at war with themselves. When Paul does describe such inner conflict, it is not the God-given nature fighting itself, but the God-given nature fighting a sinful nature that humankind "achieved" on its own. So when one considers that God designed the female body with unique features like breasts whose purpose is to nurture young life, it only makes sense that women would typically be given a nature that makes them more inclined towards nurturing. When one considers that God designed men as generally larger and stronger, it only makes sense that He would give them natures that would be more inclined towards offering physical protection when necessary. Of course, like male and female nature, being nurturing and being protective are very similar things, but they are also very different things. If one were interested in spending time reflecting on and enumerating all the differences, she would likely see them falling into the same categories as before. There will always be exceptions in the real world, but the exceptions will exist because some differences are just generalizations, because something went slightly off track, or because something is very wrong.

This can all be brought back to the notion of society imposing gender differences. If people are designed with certain differences, then the culture is providing either rituals and customs that facilitate the operation of these designed differences or rituals and customs that obscure real differences and artificially create fake differences. If such customs are contradictory to human nature, one would expect to see everything begin to break down when they come into play. However, as was demonstrated concerning submission, it is in fact quite the opposite. Things break down when submission is removed from the mix, not when it is added. It is fair to conclude, then, that submission is given to humankind by nature, not imposed by society.

WHY MALE AND FEMALE?

All of these considerations have left one more question unanswered. What is the point of the inborn differences between men and women, the necessity of submission, and so forth? God could have made humans to function in any way at all, so what significance does this particular way have? Answering this question first means looking at the purpose of creation in general: to glorify God. According to Psalm 19, "The heavens declare the glory of God; the skies proclaim the work of his hands. Day after day they pour forth speech; night after night they display knowledge. There is no speech or language where their voice is not heard. Their voice goes out into all the earth, their words to the ends of the world."[31] This is entirely consistent with what chapter 4 of this book established concerning God and creation—that God Himself is Goodness, and a created thing is only good inasmuch as it reflects God. Humankind, as a creation of God, shares that same purpose and is likewise only good inasmuch as it reflects God.

Of course, humans are fundamentally different than anything else in the visible creation. Humankind was intended to glorify God by reflecting His goodness in a special and personal way—by symbolizing God in a way that the rest of creation does not. As Genesis says, "God created man in his own image, in the image of God he created him; male and female he created them."[32] This "image of God" ties in with everything this chapter has considered concerning men and women. Men and women are different in many ways—they have different callings and relationships within the church and the family, they are all distinct and individual persons, and so on. At the same time, men and women are the same in many ways. There are only male humans or female humans, but all of them are humans. Both man's and woman's existences are dependent on each other—women cannot be conceived without men, nor can men be conceived without women. Finally, men and women were created from the beginning to share in a one flesh union. In a sense, men and women are therefore simultaneously one in their substance and existence and yet distinct in their persons and relationships. This ought to sound very familiar to Christians.

In his article, "Man as Male and Female: Created in the Image of God," Nathan Jastram considers at length what is meant by humans being made in the image of God. He argues that the unity and diversity in humankind is meant to reflect the unity and diversity in God Himself—the three distinct persons who share one substance. Man and woman together are therefore meant to represent God to the rest of creation. Jastram makes the helpful distinction, however, that while man and woman are to be united in their relationship to creation, they are diverse in their rela-

---

31. Ps 19:1–4.
32. Gen 1:27.

tionship to each other.[33] Though man and woman reflect God to the rest of creation, the husband represents God to his wife while she represents the creation to him—submission is how God painted this picture. This same work of art is ultimately the reason for the office of the ministry being given only to men. A pastor's job is to represent God to his congregation by announcing His word and administering His sacraments. A husband or a pastor is not actually God, but he is the symbol painted onto the canvas of creation itself. It is usually suggested that when people call God "Father," it is merely an imperfect analogy created by humans to explain God to each other. On the contrary, fathers are the analogy created by God to explain Himself to humans. A wife's submission to her husband is then a mirror of the loving response of the creation to the love of its Creator. Submission is a profound and beautiful act of worshiping God Himself. It glorifies Him, just as all of creation is meant to do.

CONCLUSION

The mutual love between a man and a woman, expressed in authority and submission, is meant to reflect the love by which the Father, Son, and Holy Spirit are given to each other so completely that they are indeed only One. There is therefore nothing arbitrary or terrible about the differences between man and woman. On the contrary, it is the most glorious thing imaginable short of The One whose glory it is meant to declare. Sin corrupts these natures and relationships, and neither men nor women live up to that which they symbolize. This has often meant great suffering for women, as it has for all people everywhere. Feminism is intended to help such women, using political, economic, and social equality as the means. Equality in politics and the economy may have a place.[34] Social equality, however, is different. If attempting this kind of equality obscures what God has created in the family, then it is no real solution. It is sin that needs to be remedied, not God's work of art in creation. There is no liberation to be had in throwing this away. As G.K. Chesterton put it, "Do not go about as a demagogue, encouraging triangles to break out of the prison of their three sides. If a triangle breaks out of its three sides, its life comes to a lamentable end. Somebody wrote a work called The Loves

---

33. Jastram, "Male and Female," 63.

34. The political angle has already been briefly considered, and the economic angle is well outside the scope of this book.

of the Triangles; I never read it, but I am sure that if triangles ever were loved, they were loved for being triangular."[35] One cannot cure the very real sins against women by destroying the natures of man and woman. This would be akin to curing a disease by killing the patient. Our cure for sin is given in the work of Christ, not in social re-engineering.

At the church I grew up in, a visiting student pastor once gave a sermon that touched on this topic.[36] He opened by citing a meeting of denominational leaders where the ordination of women was discussed. He described it in the most condescending tone possible as "deciding whether we would finally join the 20th century." In his view, allowing women to be pastors was in step with the inevitable drumbeat of progress. Feminism is often seen as an irrevocable advancement that consequently makes Christians very uncomfortable when contradicting it. Even those who hold to Biblical ideas on gender can fall victim to this mindset. They may be willing to live in the past if God commands it—to be the last ones standing—but they often cannot shake the idea that rejecting feminism is also rejecting progress.

Defacing the portrait painted by God in creation, however, is not progress, and it will not ultimately stand. Humanity is not constructed in such a way that such things can endure. A society that insists on social gender equality that supersedes the differences between men and women does not possess sound prospects for survival because procreation depends on such differences. Christians should not fall into the chronological snobbery that says our own era is superior to all others and that our culture's ways will persist forever. It is worth noticing that the young pastor's phrase, "joining the 20th century," already sounds very odd now that the 21st century has begun. The Church has persisted through many more centuries than the one to which people attempt to tie it, and unless Christ returns first, it will persist through many more. Ideas come and go, then come again. Empires rise and fall. Cultures flourish and die out. Our culture and its ideas will be no different. God's Word, however, endures forever. Christians may be confident, therefore, not only that Christianity embraces women as women, but that asserting this truth is not a hopeless task.

---

35. Chesterton, 67.
36. One that offended many in the congregation.

13

The Nature of Tolerance

INTRODUCTION

IF ONE WERE TO judge solely by the frequent demands for it, tolerance is very highly valued in our society. Many consider attempts to suppress ideas and behaviors of which some do not approve to be a primary source of human conflict. Tolerance is consequently held up as a fundamental necessity in solving such conflict. According to UNESCO's "Declaration on the Principles of Tolerance," "Tolerance is respect, acceptance and appreciation of the rich diversity of our world's cultures, our forms of expression and ways of being human. Tolerance is harmony in difference. It is not only a moral duty, it is also a political and legal requirement. Tolerance, the virtue that makes peace possible, contributes to the replacement of the culture of war by a culture of peace."[1] In that same vein, the website Tolerance.org has a "Declaration of Tolerance" by which users pledge, among other things, that "For all our differences, we share one world. To be tolerant is to welcome the differences and delight in the sharing." In a diverse world, tolerance is given as our only hope for finally getting along—the means by which we replace conflict with celebration.

While it is difficult to argue against peace, harmony, and delight, the advocates of tolerance indicate that not everyone is cooperating. People in general who consider their religion to be true[2] and orthodox Christians in particular are frequently accused of standing in the way of harmony by being intolerant. To say that one's religion is true is necessarily to say that any contradictory religion is false—hardly a form of delight in sharing. Christians are therefore said to be intolerant because they proselytize

---

1. Unesco, "Declarations," 2.
2. Which seems to be the new colloquial definition of "fundamentalist."

instead of letting people choose their own religion. Christians also talk about various moral laws in a way that implies that everyone is subject to them. Of course, those who do not live up to such standards are necessarily said to have violated that law and behaved immorally. This is another form of diversity which is difficult to appreciate. An objective moral law is therefore also considered to be intolerant. Such things are clearly contrary to the celebration of differences, and Christianity is put at odds with the culture.

TOLERANCE IN OUR CULTURE

In order to be brought back into harmony, people are instructed by television, newspapers, schools, and governments on how to be tolerant instead of intolerant. Unfortunately, such exhortations are frequently riddled with contradictions. This is the case in a casual reading of the aforementioned UNESCO document.[3] Article 1.2 gives the absolute statement that "in no circumstance can [tolerance] be used to justify infringements of . . . fundamental values" while the very next article states, "[tolerance] involves the rejection of dogmatism and absolutism." Article 1.4 suggests that "[Tolerance] also means that one's views are not to be imposed on others" while the very next article states, "Tolerance at the State level requires just and impartial legislation, law enforcement and judicial and administrative process." Such incoherencies are perhaps typical of committee documents, but they have a way of making their way into everyday thought. In *The Revenge of Conscience*, J. Budziszewski lists and explodes three contradictory approaches to tolerance that are nevertheless quite popular:

> According to the Quantitative Fallacy, tolerance means tolerating, so the more you tolerate the more tolerant you are. According to the Skeptical Fallacy, the best foundation for tolerance is to avoid having strong convictions about good and evil; therefore, the more you doubt the more tolerant you are. According to the Apologetic Fallacy, if you cannot help having strong convictions the next best foundation for tolerance is refusing to express or act upon them;

---

3. To be fair, this document does assume a large number of other UNESCO declarations as a context. There may therefore be a way to read it in light of these other declarations without contradictions. However, the declaration itself is insufficient to this task. Its most substantial failing is perhaps its extremely fuzzy distinction between fundamental and diverse values.

therefore, the more pusillanimous you are, the more tolerant you are.[4]

The Quantitative Fallacy is thematic in the aforementioned instruction to simply "welcome the differences and delight in the sharing." If one confuses tolerance with a broad command to tolerate, one would also have to tolerate intolerance. The Skeptical Fallacy can be seen bleeding into the aforementioned principle that tolerance involves rejecting absolutes. If one should not have strong convictions of good and evil, one should not be convicted that tolerance is good and intolerance evil. The Apologetic Fallacy is often seen in suggestions that one's views should not be "forced" onto others. The definition of "forced" is often expanded so far that a person cannot act as though his views are true if this action were to affect anyone else at all—even if it only caused emotional offense. This likewise cannot be coherent, because one could not act as though his convictions about tolerance are true either if such convictions affected another person—the very goal of advocacy.

The Christian reaction to these incoherencies is often disappointing. One common approach is similar to the approach taken towards the charges of misogyny considered in the previous chapter. Christians often simply claim that the Bible really does teach tolerance according to one or another of these fallacies. After all, Jesus scolded and drove off people who were stoning an adulteress, and He instructed us not to judge lest we be judged ourselves.[5] Instead of removing the conflict, it really just makes the Bible schizophrenic because Jesus also condemns adultery and instructs us to make right judgments.[6] These verses can be reconciled with each other,[7] but not by embracing contradictions from the beginning. The end result of such an approach is usually the implication that the Bible is the word of two Gods instead of one—an intolerant and touchy God of the Old Testament set against a soft-hearted Jesus of the New Testament. To make God endorse tolerance in the way it is popularly understood requires ignoring half of what He says. Furthermore, the Gospel depends

---

4. Budziszewski, *Revenge of Conscience*, 100.
5. John 8:1–11 and Matt 7:1.
6. Matt 15:19 and John 7:24.
7. Jesus is condemning hypocritical judgments in Matt 7:1 and shallow judgments in Matt 15:9; in neither case does He condemn judgment as such.

on Christ paying for humankind's failure to follow the moral law rather than on God ignoring those failures.

Of course, other Christians respond badly even when acknowledging the contradictions. Many declare tolerance to be foolishness on this basis and simply abandon it altogether. This "solution" is no better. As much as the term is misused in modern parlance, there really is a thing called bigotry, and it really is a sin. Even when one recognizes that there is something deficient about the way tolerance is being practiced today, she must also recognize that the subject ought not to be ignored. People ought to practice tolerance, but in a culture that is so muddled on the topic, they are seldom taught what tolerance really means. If there does exist a good thing called tolerance which is perverted into incoherencies on one hand and bigotry on the other, then one must look elsewhere to find out what it is.

THE PERSISTENCE OF THE FALLACIES

Appropriately unraveling these fallacies is easier when one understands why they are clung to so tenaciously. As previous chapters indicated, people do not usually embrace incoherency because they are stupid, but because they are motivated to do so. The common thread running through the three fallacies is the goal of refraining from moral judgments. When a person is told to be tolerant by indiscriminately tolerating, he is actually being told to stop thinking about right and wrong and just put up with everything. When a person is told to be tolerant by indiscriminately doubting all standards of morality, she is actually being told to ignore knowledge of right and wrong. When a person is told to indiscriminately shelve convictions about right and wrong when facing a choice, he is actually being told to separate actions from knowledge. When one hears that morality does not belong in politics or that one should not impose one's morality on others, one is really being told is that she ought to be morally neutral in any area where there are moral disagreements. Of course, as this book has already established, humans can by acts of will ignore, doubt, confuse and obfuscate even the moral laws which are really known. The consequence for sinful humanity is that every area of morality is one in which there are potential moral disagreements. And so, moral questions end up being relegated to the privacy of our homes and churches never to see the light of day. People are literally being instructed to be stupid and unthinking in their public dealings with respect to morality. Rather than the origin, moral stupidity is the end result of incoherent attempts to practice tolerance.

There could be any number of reasons that this appears desirable to so many. One possibility is that it makes things easy. A simple dogmatic rule excuses people from evaluating difficult cases. Sometimes "zero tolerance" policies are instituted for this reason—usually in schools. Although ostensibly a set of rules for students, these policies really govern officials who are relieved from judging each case and are instead required to apply an automatic punishment. The absurdity of such policies quickly becomes apparent when a child is expelled for carrying a butter knife or a bottle of aspirin in her backpack. An infinite tolerance policy, however, is no different in that respect. It still relieves administrators and bureaucrats from the burden of thought because their inaction is already determined for them.

Even laziness is an inadequate explanation, however. The hard-working can and do embrace incoherent tolerance as well. Perhaps the strongest attraction towards the removal of moral judgment is the illusion of security which it provides. When one makes moral judgments, there is always the possibility of making a mistake. When many imperfect humans are making moral judgments, there is certainty that many mistakes will be made. These mistakes often have disastrous consequences for the people involved. If one is wrongfully judged, then one can ultimately be wrongfully punished or have one's reputation ruined. The motivation to refrain from judgment is frequently a desire to avoid these situations altogether. There can be no false condemnations nor unjust punishments when there are no condemnations or punishments at all. Never again will Salem have the blood of innocent women on its hands. Never again will an adulteress be forced to wear a scarlet 'A.' No one will make mistakes when they are not allowed to act. As always, anyone who wishes to do evil does so because he is seeking after something good that has been made into an idol. It is good to avoid injustice, and so those who will not risk error teach moral neutrality in classrooms and proclaim it in print. Ironically, people are admonished to abandon our considerations of good and evil to avoid evil and secure goodness for all.

Of course, just like its expressions through a false tolerance, moral neutrality is a literal impossibility. As Budziszewski points out,

> The scandal of Neutrality is that its worshipers cannot answer the question "Why be neutral?" without committing themselves to particular goods—social peace, self-expression, self-esteem, ethnic pride, or what have you—thereby violating their own desideratum of Neutrality. Yet even this is merely a symptom of a deeper problem, that there is no such thing as Neutrality. It is not merely unachievable, like a perfect circle; it is inconceivable, like a square circle. Whether we deem it better to take a stand or be silent, we have offended this god in the very act of deeming.[8]

This contradiction at the heart of modern ideas of tolerance goes far in explaining why its practitioners are so often intolerant of those with different ideas on tolerance; their goal is a logical impossibility. One can observe people claiming that because schools need to be tolerant of many different points of view when it comes to God, they should only take the agnostic point of view. There are claims that because one ought to be tolerant of many different views when it comes to different "reproductive choices," one can only accept the pro-choice view. The pattern that emerges is that people are constantly told that because they should tolerate all points of view, they must believe only one point of view. Rather than a tool to protect diversity, an incoherent tolerance becomes a bludgeon to use against opposing points of view. Instead of avoiding wrongful judgments, attempts at moral neutrality ensure them.

WHAT THEN IS TOLERANCE?

If moral neutrality cannot save humans from intolerance, then another foundation must be laid. To recover a coherent view of tolerance, one must start with what is already clear. First, while tolerance cannot be the same as tolerating, there is certainly a connection between the two. To tolerate a thing means to put up with it despite recognizing it (either rightly or wrongly) as an evil. Second, while tolerating all things has already been shown to be incoherent, it would be abhorrent even if possible. If one were to witness a rape, for example, it would be the height of callous irresponsibility to simply tolerate it. Thirdly, tolerating some things is essential. The folly of zero-tolerance policies has already been mentioned. To act to prevent literally all evils would mean the elimination of human freedom—something God Himself tolerates. Fourthly, if it is right to tol-

---

8. Budziszewski, 40.

erate some things and wrong to tolerate others, there must be a basis for determining which is which. Martin Luther hit the nail on the head when he wrote, "One must go by the proverb, 'He cannot govern who cannot wink at faults.' Let this be his rule: Where wrong cannot be punished without greater wrong, there let him waive his rights, however just they may be."[9] One tolerates an evil in order to protect a greater good from accidental damage. Fifthly, tolerating is not binary. When confronted with the desire to restrain an evil, one does not merely have to choose between eliminating it or not. There are a range of different responses. In the case of rape, for example, one could kill the rapist on the spot, execute him after a trial, imprison him, fine him, verbally shame him, ignore him, encourage him, honor him, or reward him. Tolerating is therefore a matter of degree. This final point undercuts some of the popular canards that are thrown out against Christians. For example, "encouraging modest dress is no different than mandating the Burqa," "preaching to the unconverted is no different from executing the unconverted," or "promoting abstinence is no different than stoning fornicators." Not all acts of suppression are fundamentally the same.

If it is right to tolerate evil sometimes, wrong to tolerate it at other times, and there are different appropriate levels of tolerating in different cases, then genuine tolerance means rightly choosing appropriate responses to evil in different circumstances. As Budziszewski points out, this makes tolerance a moral virtue, a disposition towards making right choices and avoiding wrong ones. Also, as with Aristotle's conception of virtue, tolerance involves a golden mean—it is the right balance between tolerating too much and tolerating too little.[10] Despite the use of a mathematical term, the golden mean is not the average amount of toleration as though one could in each case take the most extreme reaction and the least extreme reaction and then split the difference. This would be just as much of an elimination of moral judgment as zero or infinite tolerance policies. The golden mean is instead a way of describing the right amount of toleration in order to protect greater goods and avoid greater evils.

---

9. Luther, "Temporal Authority," 124.
10. Budziszewski, 46.

TOLERANCE AND EVANGELISM

With this understanding of tolerance, it is now necessary to examine what it ought to look like in practice. Christianity is described as being intolerant on no few issues, but for the sake of brevity, this chapter will examine only one: the charge that Christian proselytizing[11] is intolerant. Using the view of tolerance given above, such a charge would mean that Christians, in attempting to suppress the alleged evils of damnation and false belief, are giving rise to greater evils. One could argue, of course, that false belief and hell are not truly at stake. However, this merely takes one back to the question of whether or not Christianity is true. Are we all sinners? Who is Jesus? What did He teach about our sin? Such questions have already been addressed in this book, and so this chapter will proceed on the basis that Christianity is true, and that sinners are therefore saved only through faith in Christ.

Life and truth are therefore two goods which are already at stake in this issue. However, the charges of intolerance frequently indicate that other goods are being put at risk by proselytizing. Peace and harmony usually top this list. Religion can become a significant source of conflict when those who embrace one religion are not satisfied that outsiders remain as outsiders. Islamic terrorism is perhaps the most timely example of this possibility becoming real, but history is peppered with such conflicts involving various religions and sects. Even when kept within the confines of verbal conflict, evangelism can create tension and discomfort among its targets, causing them to feel alienated from the greater community.[12]

The next issue to consider is the different possible levels of tolerating the evils of damnation and false belief. While addressing every potential nuance and action is not possible in this space, examining three broad approaches should be sufficient to demonstrate the point. The extreme option on one side would be to penalize non-Christians for false beliefs

---

11. Or what Christians would call evangelizing.

12. One could also make a case that cultures whose rituals and practices are intertwined with their previous religion can also be destroyed by evangelism. Much has been said on this topic—too much to evaluate in this chapter. There can be no denying that Christianity changes cultures. Some of these changes are undeniably good (many rituals and customs around the world are brutal and destructive). For those changes that are not, the question remains whether the change was a necessary part of conversion, or the side-effect of mistakes made by missionaries (for example, confusing God's moral law with the missionary's cultural ethics).

in order to encourage conversion. This could range anywhere from the execution of heretics and infidels to making non-Christians second-class citizens. On the opposite side of the range, one would find the popular suggestion of acting as though Christianity were a personal preference rather than an objectively true proposition. In the middle, one finds the option of evangelism—to proclaim the Gospel to non-Christians as God's objectively true grace to humankind. Each of these options have different levels of effectiveness in averting the evils and do different amounts of accidental damage to other goods involved.

Penalizing unbelief obviously damages peace and harmony. What is more, even if there are penalties that can be enforced without committing moral wrong,[13] it is virtually useless in averting the evils of false belief and hell. Far from protecting truth, wielding tangible penalties against sincerely held but false beliefs encourages those who do hold such beliefs to lie about them, compounding the falsehoods. It also makes any actual correction of error through communication all the more difficult because an honest conversation on the subject would be rare indeed. While relegating religion to personal preference would have less impact on peace, it is likewise counterproductive for averting false belief and its consequences. As this book has already argued, Christianity belongs in the category of truth rather than preference. Not only is pretending otherwise a falsehood in and of itself, it severely damages the ability to even speak of the issue in terms of truth. Furthermore, this approach encourages Christians to abandon the truth they already know. There cannot remain an indefinite fissure between a person's beliefs and his actions. Eventually one will conform to the other. If Christians act as though their religion is a mere preference, they will come to believe that it really is. Both of these options therefore deviate from true tolerance.

The mark of toleration is hit most accurately by evangelism. In its aversion of false belief, evangelism avoids the two extremes of driving falsehoods into hiding and embracing them as a matter of practice. Instead, the message is proclaimed as true and some believe. Falsehoods are addressed through argument and exhortation rather than through

---

13. While various encouragements and discouragements for belief are on the range of toleration, actual punishment is not. False belief is an evil, but to sincerely hold a false belief is not a moral infraction. The concept of punishment would therefore not apply. To try and apply it in an attempt to change one's belief would be to do evil so that good would result. This is not an issue of toleration at all, but simply a moral wrong.

persecution, and so the possibility of correction is maximized. But what of peace and harmony? It cannot be honestly claimed that all attempts at evangelism go smoothly. Discomfort and alienation certainly occur where the message offends rather than converts. Nevertheless, it would be difficult indeed to argue that discomfort and alienation are greater evils than remaining ignorant of a truth of this magnitude along with the reconciliation with God that goes with it. A person might feel better if her doctor tells her she does not have cancer. Nevertheless, if she really has it, a doctor should clearly tolerate the distress in order to tell the truth. Without faith in Christ, a person's sins put them in danger of far worse than cancer. Christians should be as tolerant as the doctor and forthrightly tell the truth to those in danger.

THE RISKS OF GENUINE TOLERANCE

While this argument may show that evangelism in general is the tolerant option, that still leaves the practical question of how one approaches evangelism largely unanswered. Each unique situation raises the very practical questions of how one should present the Gospel, whether the current moment is a good time, whether one is being rude and inconsiderate, and so forth. The same practical concerns arise for any other issue—for deviations from sexual morality, for theft, for hatred, or anything else. The chapter on sexuality, for example, set down an objective moral standard for chastity. It considered the rights and wrongs of sexual expression and the purpose towards which sexuality is directed. These kinds of considerations may be sufficient for informing a person on how to be chaste himself, but they are not sufficient for determining how one ought to respond to violations from others. They are necessary for discerning an appropriate response, but are not themselves a policy.

Even though the moral standard is objective, there is a role for individual cultures to play. First, the culture cannot be used as the ultimate source of right and wrong, but it may determine the consequences of suppression. As Jesus explains to the Pharisees, Moses tolerated divorce not because the moral law allowed it, but because of the hardness of hearts in the culture to which He was delivering the law.[14] The greater challenge for the ethicist may not be in determining which actions are morally wrong, but in determining how the culture will to react to various approaches

14. Matt 19:7–9.

to suppression. Should a nation outlaw sodomy because it is wrong, or would the enforcement of such laws be too great of a burden on liberty and privacy? Should a church exclude those of its members involved in premarital sex for the sake of chastity or should it keep them close and admonish them for the sake of preaching the Gospel to them? For every topic the questions multiply, and those in responsibility must be prepared to answer them. Even when objective morals have been violated, the reaction to a violation requires subjective judgment.

Second, while not every diversity among humankind is worthy of celebration, not every diversity is due to some kind of deficiency either. Just as there is not a single right way to paint a picture of a flower, there is not a single right way to pursue goods like marriage or justice. Different cultures may have different customs and rituals without one being right way and all others being wrong. At the same time, this does not preclude the possibility of judging certain practices as wrong. The diversity of ways to paint a flower hardly precludes the possibility of telling the difference between a flower and a mountain. An objective moral law across cultures has two complimentary implications. One cannot go the route of the cultural relativist and claim that there is no external standard by which a culture can be judged. Neither can one go the route of the bigot and replace the objective moral standard with his own cultural norms. While some diverse customs such as burying a living widow with her husband are simple to judge, others require a more nuanced approach. Take, for example, arranged marriages in some cultures versus the marriage-minded mutually agreeing upon spouses in our own. They may be unusual to us, but are arranged marriages truly a violation of the moral law? We often look on the practice with the romantic notion of a woman forced to leave her one true love for a horrible man her selfish and uncaring father approves of, but whom she detests. The reality, however, could be closer to the ideal that parents with the advantages of age and distance from the infatuation of youth may be able to make better choices in this area than their children can. At the same time, one can still judge as wrong those situations in which people are forced to marry against their will rather than in willing submission to their parents. One can also consider whether particular customs have outlived their usefulness or ultimately cause more problems than they solve. Considering how to tolerate the diverse customs of humankind also requires subjective judgment.

Such judgment is neither simple nor easy. Practicing tolerance must hinge on rightly understanding the relative importance of different goods, understanding how they interact with each other, understanding how these goods can be damaged, and considering how best to act consistently with all of them. No rubric can be adequate for navigating all of the implications. As Luther also points out in "Temporal Authority," good and just judgments of this nature do not spring wholly formed out of books. They are the product of a free human mind whose reasoned judgment is filled with both love and the natural law.[15] The dangers of tolerance come from the fact that free human beings can make mistakes. Therefore, even when one attempts to practice tolerance, the concerns that encourage the fallacies can remain. What is to be done about the risks of an objective moral law? What about the wrongfully condemned and those restrained by narrow-mindedness? One might be tempted to return to the fallacies, but this cannot help the victims either. As has already been demonstrated, moral neutrality is not just a bad but a contradictory idea. One cannot truly avoid the making of moral judgments; one can only pretend he makes none and then judge absentmindedly. One cannot choose to shun this responsibility without choosing to let circumstances answer in her stead. Even backing away from such decisions is making a decision. Because avoidance of judgment is impossible, the only option left is to make the best judgments one can and to practice tolerance as best as one is able. The risk of doing wrong is preferable to the certainty of doing wrong. There is nowhere else to go but forward.

CONCLUSION: RUNNING BACK TO THE GOSPEL

It is understandable that practicing tolerance as best as one can is a less than satisfying solution. One should not make the perfect the enemy of the good and thereby lose both, but neither should one pretend that the "good" is actually perfect. In the hands of sinful humanity, there can be no equivocation that people will in many cases give forth poor judgments. We will suppress things we ought to put up with and put up with things we ought to suppress. Evil will be done. At the same time sinners must practice it, for we cannot refuse to judge goodness for the sake of goodness nor can we cease to be sinners in this life. But what about the errors? What about those hurt by the errors? Practicing any virtue with a golden

15. Luther, 128.

mean will involve frequently falling off on one side or another. Knowing the moral law and understanding virtues can be extremely valuable, but these simply do not provide people with the power to actually follow the moral law and be virtuous. Our best is not good enough.

It is by God's grace that we are removed from the horns of this cruel dilemma. Not the grace of an imaginary God who makes us feel good or an unjust God who ignores wrongdoing, but the true and just God who is also merciful. The atoning death of Jesus Christ covers even those sins which are committed in the pursuit of doing good—even those wrongs which come from the best of intentions. The harm to the victims is atoned for by Christ rather than ignored, and those of us who sin are forgiven rather than punished. This same grace is no less necessary with respect to other virtues like chastity or compassion. To live well is not merely to refrain from sin but to do good. For those of us who are sinners, hitting the golden mean when practicing such virtues means taking a risk that it will be missed. While risks should never be taken lightly, they can still be taken with confidence, because justification is available apart from our own works. We can be free to practice tolerance and every other virtue when we are freed through faith in Christ from earning damnation with our every error. It is only from this foundation that we might recover a tolerance that our culture yearns for but no longer understands.

Bibliography

"1 in 5 Pregnancies Worldwide Ends in Abortion, Study Says." Fox News (12 October 2007). No pages. Online: http://www.foxnews.com/story/0,2933,301370,00.html.

Alexander, Michele G. & Fisher, Terri D. "Truth and Consequences: Using the Bogus Pipeline to Examine Sex Differences in Self-reported Sexuality." *Journal of Sex Research* 40.1 (2003): 27–35.

The American Heritage Dictionary of the English Language. Fourth ed., s.v. "feminism."

Aquinas, Thomas. *Summa Theologica*, ed. Thomas Gilby. Garden City, NY: Image Books, 1969.

Aristotle, *Metaphysics*. trans. W.D. Ross. Lawrence, KS: Digireads.com Publishing, 2006.

Barker, Kenneth, et al. *The NIV Study Bible*. Grand Rapids, MI: Zondervan, 1985.

Bauckham, Richard. *The Testimony of the Beloved Disciple*. Grand Rapids, MI: Baker Academic, 2007.

Better than Ezra. "It's Only Natural." *Before the Robots*. Artemis Records, 2005.

Brown, D. Mackenzie. *Ultimate Concern: Tillich in Dialogue*. New York: Harper & Row, 1965.

Bruce, F. F. *The Books and the Parchments*. London: Pickering & Inglis, 1950.

———. *The New Testament Documents: Are They Reliable?* Grand Rapids, MI: Eerdmans, 1960.

Budziszewski, J. *The Revenge of Conscience: Politics and the Fall of Man*. Dallas: Spence. 1999.

———. "Sex at the Edge of Night." *Office Hours*. No Pages. Online: http://www.boundless.org/2005/articles/a0001794.cfm.

———. "Theophilus Gives a Speech." *Office Hours*. No Pages. Online: http://www.boundless.org/2005/articles/a0000112.cfm.

———. *What We Can't Not Know*. Dallas: Spence Publishing Company, 2003.

Centers for Disease Control and Prevention. "HIV/AIDS and Men Who Have Sex with Men." No Pages. Online: http://www.cdc.gov/hiv/topics/msm/.

Chesterton, G.K. *The Everlasting Man*. San Francisco: Ignatius, 1993.

Chesterton, G.K. *Orthodoxy*. Annotated ed. Lenoir, NC: Reformation Press, 2002.

Clifford, Ross. *Leading Lawyers' Case for the Resurrection*. Edmonton, Alberta, Canada: Canadian Institute for Law, Theology, & Public Policy: 1996.

Cooper, John M. "The Relations between Religion and Morality in Primitive Culture." *Primitive Man*, 4. 3 (1931): 33–48.

"Declaration of Tolerance." 101 *Tools for Tolerance*. No Pages. Online: http://www.tolerance.org/101_tools/declaration.html.

Dostoevsky, Fyodor. *The Brothers Karamazov*. Translated by Constance Garnett. New York: Barnes & Noble Books, 2004.

Edwards, William D. et al. "On the Physical Death of Jesus Christ." *JAMA* 255 (1986) 1455–1463.
Geisler, Norman. *Christian Apologetics*. Grand Rapids, MI: Baker Book House, 1976.
"God Debate: Sam Harris vs. Rick Warren". *Newsweek*. No Pages. Online: http://www.msnbc.msn.com/id/17889148/site/newsweek/print/1/displaymode/1098/.
Grigg, Russel. "Trees Walking." *Creation Ex Nihilo* 21, no. 4 (1995): 54–55.
Hanegraaff, Hank. "Ask Hank." *Christian Research Journal* 29, no. 2 (2006) 54.
Hern, Warren M. "Is Pregnancy Really Normal?" (1971). No pages. Online: http://www.drhern.com/fulltext/preg/paper.htm.
Heumer, Michael. "Scary Bible Quotes." No pages. Online: http://home.earthlink.net/~owl233/biblequotes.htm.
Iowa State University Faculty. "*Statement on Intelligent Design*." No Pages. Online: http://web.archive.org/web/20071218155035/http://www.biology.iastate.edu/STATEMENT.htm.
Jastram, Nathan. "Man as Male and Female: Created in the Image of God." *Concordia Theological Quarterly*. 68:1 (January 2004) 5–95.
Josephus, Flavius. *The Antiquities of the Jews* in *Josephus' Complete Works*. Translated by William Whiston. Grand Rapids, MI: Kregel Publications, 1981.
Kierkegaard, Søren. *Concluding Unscientific Postscript to Philosophical Fragments*. Vol 1. Translated by Howard V. Hong and Edna H. Hong. Princeton, NJ: Princeton University Press, 1992.
Klamecki, Bernard J. "Medical Perspective of the Homosexual Issue." In *The Crisis of Homosexuality*, edited by J. Isamu Yamamoto, 115–130. Wheaton, IL: Victor Books, 1990.
Koehler, Edward. *A Summary of Christian Doctrine*. 2nd ed. St Louis: Concordia. 1952.
Koukl, Gregory. "Minimalist Ethic—Too Minimal." *Stand to Reason*. No Pages. Online: http://www.str.org/site/News2?page=NewsArticle&id=5448.
Kurth, Erwin. *Catechetical Helps*. St Louis: Concordia. 1961.
Kurtz, Paul and Wilson, Edwin H. "Humanist Manifesto II." No Pages. Online: http://www.americanhumanist.org/Who_We_Are/About_Humanism/Humanist_Manifesto_II.
Lake, Kirsopp. *The Historical Evidence for the Resurrection of Jesus Christ*. New York: G.P. Putnam's Sons, 1907.
Lewis, C.S. *That Hideous Strength*. 1945. New York: Scribner, 2003.
———. *Mere Christianity*. 1952. Foreword Kathleen Norris. San Francisco: HarperCollins, 2001.
———. *Miracles*. New York: Macmillan, 1960.
———. *Perelandra*. 1944. New York: Scribner, 2003.
———. *The Screwtape Letters*. 1942. San Francisco: HarperCollins, 2001.
Linton, Michael. "Friends of God." *On the Square*. (13 February 2007). No Pages. Online: http://www.firstthings.com/onthesquare/2007/02/friends-of-god.
Luther, Martin. *Luther's Small Catechism with Explanation*. Translated by Kleine Katechismus. St. Louis: Concordia Publishing House, 1991.
———. "Temporal Authority: To What Extent It Should Be Obeyed." in *The Christian in Society II*. Vol 45 of *Luther's Works*. Eds. James Atkinson, Helmut T. Lehmann. Minneapolis: Fortress Press, 1962.
McDowell, Josh. *The New Evidence that Demands a Verdict*. Nashville: Thomas Nelson Publishers, 1999.

Mohler, Albert. "The Dawkins Delusion." No Pages. Online: http://www.albertmohler.com/commentary_read.php?cdate=2006-09-26.

Montgomery, John Warwick. *History & Christianity*. Downer's Grove, IL: InterVarsity Press, 1965.

Moran, Caitlin. "Abortion: why it's the ultimate motherly act." Times of London (13 April 2007). Online: http://www.timesonline.co.uk/tol/comment/columnists/caitlin_moran/article1645946.ece.

Moreland, J.P. "A Legendary Jesus and New Testament Dating." No Pages. Online: http://web.archive.org/web/20060114031452/trueu.org/Academics/LectureHall/A000000262.cfm.

Mundy, Liza. "Too Much to Carry?" *Washington Post Magazine*, 20 May 2007, W17.

Neyman, Greg. "Creation Science Rebuttals: God's Broken Promise." No Pages. Online: http://www.answersincreation.org/broken_promise.htm.

Nietzsche, Friedrich Wilhelm. *Beyond Good and Evil*. 1913. Sioux Falls, SD: NuVision Publications. 2007.

Plato, *Symposium and Phaedrus*. ed. Appelbaum, Stanley. New York: Dover Publications, 1993.

Rose, Eugene. *Nihilism: The Root of the Revolution of the Modern Age*. Platina, CA: St. Herman Press, 1994. No Pages. Online: http://www.columbia.edu/cu/augustine/arch/nihilism.html.

Ross, Hugh. "Let Us Reason: the Waters of the Flood." No Pages. Online: http://www.reasons.org/interpreting-genesis/noahs-flood/let-us-reason-waters-flood.

Russell, Bertrand. "Is There a God?". In *The Collected Papers of Bertrand Russell*. Vol. 11, edited by John Slater & Peter Köllner, 542–548. London: Routledge, 1997.

Saletan, William. "Sex, Life, and Videotape: Ultrasound and the future of abortion." *Slate* (28 April 2007). Online: http://www.slate.com/id/2165137/.

Schaeffer, Francis A. *The God Who is There*. 30th Anniversary ed. Downers Grove, IL: InterVarsity Press, 1998.

Thomson, Judith Jarvis. "A Defense of Abortion," in *Sex, Morality, and the Law*, edited by Lori Gruen and George E. Panichas (New York: Routledge, 1997), 281–295.

Tindal, Matthew, *Christianity as Old as the Creation; or The Gospel, a Republication of the Religion of Nature*. London: n.p., 1730.

Tyler, David J. "A Review of Dr. Russ Humphreys' A Young-Earth Relativistic Cosmology." No Pages. Online: http://www.answersingenesis.org/docs/267.asp.

UNESCO. "Declaration on the Principles of Tolerance." Online: http://www.unesco.org/cpp/uk/declarations/tolerance.pdf.

University of Iowa Faculty. "Statement on Intelligent Design." No Pages. Online: http://www.biology.uiowa.edu/ID.html.

Wilcox, W. Bradford. "A Scientific Review of Abstinence and Abstinence Programs." ed. Maureen Cooney. Online: http://abstinence.pal-tech.com/assets/File/ScientificReviewTAModuleWeb_no_blankpages.pdf.

Xenosaga Episode I: Der Wille zur Macht. San Jose: Namco, 2001.

www.ingramcontent.com/pod-product-compliance
Lightning Source LLC
Chambersburg PA
CBHW062013220426
43662CB00010B/1315